A Digest of
Supreme Court Decisions Affecting Education

FOURTH EDITION

by Perry A. Zirkel
with Sharon Nalbone Richardson
and Steven S. Goldberg

Phi Delta Kappa Educational Foundation
Bloomington, Indiana U.S.A.

Cover design by
Peg Caudell

Phi Delta Kappa Educational Foundation
408 North Union Street
Post Office Box 789
Bloomington, Indiana 47402-0789
U.S.A.

Printed in the United States of America

Library of Congress Catalog Card Number 2001091824
ISBN 0-87367-835-4

To Carol Zirkel, Ray Nalbone
and Jolley Christman

Introduction

The first edition of the *Digest of Supreme Court Decisions Affecting Education*, published in 1978, was conceived by the Phi Delta Kappa Commission on the Impact of Court Decisions on Education; and supplements updating it were published in 1982, 1988, and 1994. This fourth edition updates the digest to June 2001.

This fourth edition, like the first three, is designed as a ready reference, not as an intensive or interpretive legal analysis. It provides a comprehensive, current, and concise set of individual case summaries of United States Supreme Court cases decided by the Court as of June 2001. The digest does not include cases in which the Supreme Court has denied certiorari or issued a one-judge opinion in chambers.

The digest is limited to United States Supreme Court cases because of their national impact. The Supreme Court decisions described in this digest were chosen because they directly affect students and staff in public and private schools from kindergarten through grade twelve. Older and overruled cases (for example, *Plessy* and *Gobitis*) are included for their historical importance. Although the dividing line is not a bright one, decisions involving nonschool and higher education litigants are included only if they have direct impact on students or staff.

Readers are encouraged to examine in-depth analyses and the full Supreme Court opinions of those cases that are of particular interest to them. Further, readers who wish to be informed about a particular topic should become acquainted with their respective state and lower federal court rulings, as well as with relevant state statutes and administrative regulations that apply in their jurisdiction.

Table of Contents

The Table of Contents divides the cases into seven chapters. The cases are listed chronologically within each chapter so the reader can see the progression of Supreme Court case law over time.

The Table of Contents also provides three other pieces of information, which are placed to the right of the case name. First, each case has been given a numerical code to identify the categories of litigants as follows:

1. public school litigants
2. private school litigants
3. higher education litigants
4. nonschool litigants

Second, when the Supreme Court handed down a summary affirmance of a lower court decision, rather than rendered a full opinion, the numerical designation is preceded by an asterisk (*).

Third, cases that are applicable to more than one chapter are notated at the far right as cross-references, with the case description provided in the chapter of primary relevance. For example, the actual case summary for *Patsy* v. *Board of Regents* is located in Chapter 6 (dealing with special rules for civil rights legislation). However, because *Patsy* was brought by an employee suing on the basis of discrimination, there are cross-references in the Table of Contents for Chapter 4 (dealing with employment), Chapter 5 (dealing with discrimination), and Chapter 7 (dealing with procedural issues). In Chapter 6, where the *Patsy* summary is located, the Table of Contents simply lists the title of the case without a cross-reference. In the other relevant chapters, the Table of Contents lists the designation "(Ch. 6)" to indicate that the summary is found in Chapter 6.

Format

The entry for each case summary, except summary affirmances, includes the following information: 1) the citation, 2) the facts, 3) the holding, and 4) the basis for the decision. The citations follow the style of the Harvard Law Review Association, *A Uniform System of Citation,* 15th ed. (1991). The volume number and the number of the first page of the case are given as they appear in the official reports of the Supreme Court, except where only an unofficial report of the decision ("S. Ct." for *West's Supreme Court Reporter* and "U.S.L.W." for *United States Law Week*) was available at the time of the preparation of this digest in June 2001. Except for summary affirmances, the lower court history of the decisions is not listed in the citation. For the typical case, the form of the citation is summarized below:

SPRINGFIELD v. QUICK,   63   U.S.   56   (1859)
  (appellant)   (appellee) (vol #) (U.S. Reports) (page #) (year of decision)

The facts for each decision are presented, as much as possible, in nonlegal language. For instance, even such common legal terms as "plaintiff" and "appellant" are generally not used in each summary. Because a limited amount of technical language cannot be avoided, a glossary is provided at the end of the volume. For the sake of brevity, facts not essential to the primary holding are not included in the summary.

The "holding," like the "facts," is extrapolated from the majority opinion of the Court. The one exception is for summary affirmances. Because the Supreme Court issues only a ruling agreeing with the result of the lower court's decision without an accompanying explanation, only the holding of the lower court is listed. Without the benefit of the Supreme Court's opinion or reasoning, the holding does not have the sweeping precedential effect of a full Supreme Court decision.

The vote of the Court is reported as follows: number of justices in the majority or plurality, followed by a slash (/) and the number in the concurrence, and then an "x" and the number dissenting (for example, "5/2x2"). In some cases, one or more of the members of the Court concurred with one part of the decision and dissented from another part of the decision. In such cases, numbers are arbitrarily listed as one half to indicate these split votes (for example, "5/2½ x 1½"). In any event, given the complex fragmentation in some cases, this vote count is only an approximation.

The basis for each decision is listed in terms of the constitutional precedents, statutory sections, or judicial precedents cited by the Court as its primary authority. Legal reasoning is presented only to the extent that it helps establish the authority for the decisions. Dismissals and vacated opinions, which are limited to the chapter on procedural parameters (Chapter 7), are dealt with in terms of an explanation of the Court's ruling. Finally, cross-references to earlier or subsequent cases are indicated by "supra" and "infra," respectively.

Organization of the Cases

The cases are organized in seven chapters. Chapter 1, "School District Governance and Finance," examines several aspects of the overall organization and structure of school districts. For example, school board elections may be essential to the operation of a school district; questions have arisen concerning how the Voting Rights Act affects school board elections. Similarly, finances play a major role in school operations. State systems of finance, particularly various taxing schemes, have been challenged. How a district expends federal allocations for remedial education also has been addressed. Finally, by default, general First Amendment censorship cases are included in this chapter.

Chapter 2, "Church-State Relationships in Education," concerns cases that arise primarily from the First Amendment's requirement that "Congress shall make no law respecting an establishment of religion or prohibiting the free exercise thereof." The vast majority of these religion cases fall within the "establishment clause," rather than the "free exercise clause." Examples of cases are those involving states that possibly promoted religion through Bible reading or prayer in the public schools or that used tax revenues to aid church-related institutions. Recent cases highlight the evolution of the so-called *Lemon* test and the addition of the alternative *Lee* approach. Finally, the court's 12-year *Aguilar-Agostini* reversal signals a lowering of the metaphorical "wall of separation."

Chapter 3, "Student Rights and Responsibilities," incorporates both the procedural and the substantive rights of students. Traditionally, the Supreme Court has been reluctant to interfere in school matters related to student rights. The Court's dilemma in reconciling this reluctance with its interest in ensuring individuals' constitutional guarantees is reflected in the 26-year hiatus between the flag-salute decisions and the subsequent student rights cases. A more recent example is the time span between the two major student expression decisions — the landmark *Tinker* case in 1969 and the *Fraser-Hazelwood* decisions in 1986. Recent constitutional cases seem to suggest a shifting on the balance toward institutional concerns with safety.

Chapter 4, "Employee Rights and Responsibilities," encompasses issues that confront staff members in the workplace. Several employment cases that do not involve school litigants are included because the general principle of the case directly applies to school districts as well. For example, in *Johnson* v. *Transportation Agency,* the Court held that a voluntary affirmative action plan that used sex as one factor for hiring or promoting in traditionally segregated job categories is not a violation of Title VII; this principle certainly applies to school district employment practices. Another nonschool case that is likely to have widespread implications in the education environment is *Meritor Savings Bank v. Vinson,* where the Supreme Court held that unwelcome sexual advances that create an offensive or hostile working environment violate Title VII. The absence of employee cases specific to the school context in recent years is notable.

Chapter 5, "Discrimination: Disability, National Origin, Race, and Sex," includes the increasing number of federal cases involving discrimination. An examination of these cases reveals the range of issues that has emerged over the last four decades. The initial cases focused on racial issues, such as desegregation and busing. More recent litigation has focused largely on sex discrimination and rights of individuals with disabilities. The contemporary judicial landscape is enmeshed in controversy and fluidity.

Chapter 6, "Civil Rights Cases: Special Rules," did not appear in the first edition of this book. This addition reflects the growing body of Supreme Court cases concerning the complexities of Section 1983 and other civil rights litigation. For example, the availability and calculation of attorneys' fees under Section 1988 and under other federal legislation is the subject of several Supreme Court decisions. Recent cases illustrate the Court's increasing concern with principles of federalism.

Chapter 7, "Procedural Parameters," illustrates some of the procedural prerequisites that must be met in the court context to obtain a ruling on the merits. The reader may need to refer to the Glossary to understand some of the legal terminology needed to explain issues laden with technical concepts. Such terminology could not be avoided in this chapter. Although the lay reader may not be interested in such concepts as "standing," "jurisdiction," "abstention," "pre-emption," and "mootness," these issues cannot be ignored. Without passing these procedural hurdles, the suing party cannot have the substantive claim determined. For example, the Court's ruling regarding standing in *Bender* precluded its determination of the constitutionality of school prayer groups.

This digest is designed to fill a gap in the legal literature and knowledge of educators. It is hoped that its simplicity of presentation, augmented by the prudence of its readers, will clarify Supreme Court decisions that affect education.

Perry A. Zirkel
June 2001

Table of Contents

Explanation of symbols in the Table of Contents

* summary affirmance
1 public education, grades K-12
2 private or parochial education, grades K-12
3 higher education
4 other
(Ch.) cross reference to case in indicated chapter

Chapter 4. Employee Rights and Responsibilities

Chapter 7. Procedural Parameters

CHAPTER ONE

School District Governance and Finance

Springfield v. Quick, 63 U.S. 56 (1859)

Facts: Congress reserved the sixteenth section of the public lands in each township in all new states for the support of public schools within each township. The funds were to be spent only within the township and only for educational purposes.

The State of Indiana, while maintaining the congressional reservation of each sixteenth section's funds to the educational needs of its township, provided that other sources of school revenue, for example, those arising from taxes, would be distributed to townships whose sixteenth section funds were less than a per-pupil expenditure allocated by a state program, but that such money would not be allocated to townships whose per-pupil expenditure from sixteenth section funds exceeded this amount. A township in this latter category challenged this allocation of state revenues.

Holding: [9x0] A state law that preserves the congressional allocation of sixteenth section funds to each township, but which allocates other state education revenues to townships on the basis of need, is constitutional.

Basis: The state legislature has not impinged on the federal government's reservation of sixteenth section funds and has the power to collect and disburse taxes for educational and other purposes at its discretion.

Davis v. Indiana, 94 U.S. 792 (1876)

Facts: An Act of Congress, in admitting Indiana as a state, declared that every sixteenth section of a township should be appropriated for the use of schools within the township. A state act directed that the money derived from every sixteenth section of a township should be put into a common fund along with school monies derived from general taxation and should be apportioned among the counties according to the number of pupils in each county. The state act also provided "that in no case shall the congressional township fund be diminished by such distribution, and diverted to any other township." The treasurer of the township refused to pay all the money he received into the common state fund, claiming that there was no state law that would permit this money, when paid into the county treasury, to be withdrawn or, if withdrawn, to be applied to the use of schools in the proper congressional township.

Holding: [9x0] Where the school laws of the state do not authorize each county auditor to distribute the school funds in the county treasury to the different townships but do bind him or her not to diminish the school funds, the rights of the inhabitants are sufficiently protected.

Basis: The school treasurer is the very officer who collects and pays money to the fund. The whole fund in the county treasury devoted to the use of schools was to be apportioned; and if the fund arising from the sixteenth section becomes a part of it, it also must be distributed. In addition, the statute carefully provides that in making that distribution, the appropriation of the sixteenth section to the schools of the township shall be strictly observed.

Doon v. Cummins, 142 U.S. 366 (1892)

Facts: The 1857 constitution of Iowa provided that "no county, or other political or municipal corporation shall be allowed to become indebted in any manner, or for any purpose, for an amount in the aggregate exceeding 5 percent of the value of taxable property within such county or corporation." The value of taxable property within the county was a matter of public record ascertainable from the most recent tax lists.

A school district, in order to refinance existing debts, issued bonds in excess of the constitutional limit. These bonds stated on their face that they had been issued in accordance with a state statute authorizing such refinancing. The school district made several interest payments to the buyers of the bonds and then defaulted on the bonds. In this case, one buyer claimed a right to be paid arose from his bond purchase from the school district.

Holding: [6x3] A creditor who lends to a school district an amount in excess of the constitutionally mandated limit on school district indebtedness cannot successfully sue in order to recover such funds, since the constitutional provision prevents the creation of an enforceable debt above the prescribed amount.

Basis: The original buyer of bonds from the school district was charged with the duty of noting the value of taxable property in the district. This amount is a matter of public record. Neither the recitations of legality on the face of the bonds nor the making of interest payments by the school district could create a debt in excess of that permitted in the state constitution.

Atchison Board of Education v. Dekay, 148 U.S. 591 (1893)

Facts: As permitted by state law, a school board issued bonds with interest coupons attached. The city and the school district had the same geographical boundaries. The bonds were secured by the school fund, which by law was to be raised by the city and by the school property, whose title was held by the city. The owner of certain of these bonds brought a suit against the school board for payment due him under the terms of the bonds.

The school board claimed that the bonds were invalid for the following reasons: 1) when naming the statute on whose authority they were issued, the bonds read "an act to organize cities," rather than "incorporate cities" as the act is actually titled; 2) the school board had no right to make the city liable for the bonds and could attach liability only to the school district; and 3) the city council had ratified the bonds when a majority, but not all, of the council members was present and by resolution, rather than by ordinance.

The school board also claimed that the city's growth in population since the bond issue had made the school board an improper entity to sue. The school board was a corporate entity at the time of the bond issuance, because this was the status of school boards of class two (smaller) cities under state law. The statutes were silent as to the corporate nature of the school boards of larger cities.

Holding: [9x0] 1) Bonds issued by the school board are valid despite misquotation of one word of the title of the enabling statute. 2) The city as well as the school district is properly liable since they are identical in geographic area and are closely linked; indeed, they may be one entity. 3) The bonds are valid despite the fact that only a majority of council members was present when the bonds were ratified. 4) The school board is still a corporate entity, though the school boards of class one cities, which the city has now become, are not corporate entities by statute. Therefore, the bondholder's suit can properly be brought and decided against the school board.

Basis: 1) A mere error in copying one word of an enabling statute will not invalidate an otherwise valid document. 2) Under state law at the time of the bond issuance, the school board did not have a corporate identity separate from that of the city and, under the state law, the city was liable for the properly made debts of the school board. 3) The majority of the council's acceptance by resolution of the bond issuance was sufficient; and under state law, the decision was not required to be made by an ordinance.

Indiana *ex rel.* Stanton v. Glover, 155 U.S. 513 (1895)

Facts: A creditor sought reimbursement out of a school district trustee's official bond. The trustee had executed and delivered promissory notes for school supplies without first procuring the county commissioners' approval as required by state law. State law also provided that a trustee incurring a debt in a manner contrary to state law was not only liable for his or her bond but also personally liable to the holder of any contract or other evidence of indebtedness for the amount thereof. Finally, state law provided that a trustee had no power to create a debt for school supplies unless supplies suitable and reasonably necessary had actually been delivered to and received by the township. In his lawsuit the creditor alleged violation of the trustee's obligation to comply with the terms of his employment mandated by state law, but he did not allege that necessary and suitable school supplies had actually been received by the township. In this case, he challenged the lower court's dismissal of his claim.

Holding: [9x0] Where a creditor does not allege facts creating an actual debt but only facts indicating a violation of the terms of the school district trustee's employment, he does not have a sufficient claim to reach the trustee's official employment bond.

Basis: In order for a debt to arise for school supplies, state law requires that the supplies be suitable, reasonably necessary, and actually received by the township. Since the creditor did not allege these facts, he did not successfully allege the existence of a debt that could be paid out of the official bond.

New Orleans v. Fisher, 180 U.S. 185 (1901)

Facts: A judgment creditor of the board of education brought an action against the city to recover $10,000 plus interest from the taxes levied for the purpose of paying expenses of the public schools. He alleged that these taxes constituted a trust fund, that the city negligently failed to collect the taxes punctually, and that the city also never paid the board of education any interest due on the taxes. The board of education had refused to demand an accounting from the city.

Holding: [7x0] When a city has collected school taxes and penalties thereon, and has not paid these collections over to the school board, judgment creditors of the board whose claims are payable out of these taxes are entitled to an accounting from the city if the school board refused to demand it.

Basis: The school taxes collected were held in trust by the city, and the creditors were entitled to the interposition of a court to recheck the fund.

Attorney General of Michigan *ex rel.* Kies v. Lowrey, 199 U.S. 233 (1905)

Facts: The state constitution requires the legislature to establish and provide a system of public education. In accordance with this requirement, the legislature passed laws establishing school districts. In 1881, four school districts were established in two townships. In 1901, new legislation merged parts of the four original districts to create a new district. This resulted in the old districts losing control over some of the schools they had previously administered and also altered the control of schools within the two townships. In this case, the legislature's power to alter school district boundaries was questioned.

Holding: [9x0] The state legislature has absolute power to make and change the boundaries of subordinate municipalities, including school districts. These governmental subdivisions cannot claim constitutional protection from alteration by state action.

Basis: The unsuccessful arguments are that the constitutional guarantees of republican government (Article IV) and of the unimpaired right of contract (Article I, section 10) have been violated. Under state law, the creation of school districts does not create a contract between such districts and the state. The claim that property rights protected by the

Fourteenth Amendment are infringed by the creation of a new district also is rejected.

Montana *ex rel.* Haire v. Rice, 204 U.S. 291 (1907)

Facts: An act approved in 1889 admitted several states, including Montana, to the Union. The act provided, among other things, 1) that the people of the territory about to become a state would choose delegates to a convention charged with the duty to create a state constitution and government, and 2) that certain lands be given to the State of Montana solely for the support of public schools.

The Montana State Constitution further limited the state legislature's use of such lands by requiring that all assets for the support of schools be invested and that only earned interest be used to pay school costs.

In 1905, the state legislature issued bonds. The proceeds from the sale of these bonds were to be used to subsidize an addition to the State Normal School. The bonds were to be secured by proceeds from the sale, lease, or exploitation of the lands that had been granted to Montana by the federal government for the support of the schools.

An architect who had performed services in the construction of the Normal School sought to be paid from the proceeds of the bond issue. The state treasurer refused to pay, claiming that the bond issue secured by proceeds from the sale or lease of school lands was in violation of the state constitutional requirement that only earned interest be used to support the schools.

Holding: [9x0] A state constitution may properly limit the way in which federal grants of land to the state for the purpose of support of the schools may be used; for example, it may properly require that such assets not be spent and that only earned interest be expended for the required purpose.

Basis: Where a federal act provides for the establishment of a state constitution and state legislature and also entrusts that legislature with duties and powers, the legislature must, in executing its authority, act in accordance with valid state constitutional limitations on the use of such power.

Sailors v. Board of Education, 387 U.S. 105 (1967)

Facts: In Michigan, local school boards are chosen in public elections. Then each local board, without regard to the population of its school district, has an equal voice in the appointment of a five-member county school board, which performs functions that essentially are administrative, rather than legislative. Voters challenged the constitutionality of this system whereby each local school board, regardless of its district's population, has one vote in the selection of the county board.

Holding [7/2x0] A system providing for appointment of county school board officials by elected local school board officials is constitutional.

Basis: There is no Fourteenth Amendment right to vote for administrative officials. Where there is no right to vote for an official, the "one man, one vote" requirement does not apply. The Court did not decide whether the state may provide for appointment, rather than public election, of local legislative bodies.

McInnis v. Shapiro, 293 F. Supp. 327 (N.D. Ill. 1968), *aff'd sub nom* McInnis v. Ogilvie, 394 U.S. 322 (1969)

Lower Court Holding: A state system for funding public schools that relies largely on local property taxation, sets maximum tax rates, and thus mandates wide variation in per-pupil expenditures among districts does not violate the Fourteenth Amendment's equal protection clause.

Kramer v. Union Free School District No. 15, 395 U.S. 621 (1969)

Facts: A bachelor, who neither owned nor leased taxable real property in the district, challenged a New York statute that prohibited residents, who were otherwise eligible to vote, from voting in school district elections unless they owned or leased taxable real property within the district or had children attending the local public school.

Holding: [6x3] A state statute denying residents of requisite age and citizenship the right to vote in school board elections because they do not own taxable real property in the district or have custody of public school children is unconstitutional.

Basis: The equal protection clause of the Fourteenth Amendment states that no state shall deny persons equal protection of the laws. Where the state is infringing on the right to vote, it must show that there is a compelling state interest; such state interest will be strictly scrutinized by the Court. In this case the Court held that the statute is unconstitutional because the additional voting requirements are broader than necessary in order to limit the pool of voters to those "primarily interested in educational issues." Therefore, the Court did not rule on the issue of whether or not such limitation of the pool of voters is a compelling state interest.

Turner v. Fouche, 396 U.S. 346 (1970)

Facts: Black residents of a county in Georgia previously brought an action challenging the constitutionality of the system of selection for juries and for school boards. The system in question provided that a county school board of five landowners be selected by a grand jury, which was chosen from the jury list compiled by six jury commissioners. Although the population of the county was 60% black, all the school board members were white. The trial court had ordered that a new grand jury list be compiled. In so doing, the commissioners, in accordance with their statutory powers, eliminated 178 persons (of whom 171 were black) for not being "upright" and "intelligent." Another 225 persons, many of whom were black, were eliminated because the commissioners were uninformed as to their qualifications. The resulting grand jury list was 37% black. Black residents of the county challenged the trial court's validation of this new grand jury list.

Holding: [9x0] 1) A requirement that members of county boards of education be landowners is unconstitutional. 2) Where a disproportionate number of blacks are excused from jury lists as being unfit or because those drawing up the list have insufficient information about the members of the black community, the state must prove there was no racial discrimination.

Basis: 1) The equal protection clause of the Fourteenth Amendment does not permit a state to deny the privilege of holding public office to some while extending it to others on the basis of distinctions that are not sufficiently justified. The requirement that members of the board of education be landowners violates the equal protection clause because there is no rational state interest mandating such a limitation on the privilege of holding public office. 2) While the county system for jury selection does not require racial discrimination and is not unfair as written, its operation is presumed to have been in violation of the Fourteenth Amendment since disproportionate numbers of blacks were eliminated from the jury list. The state offered no explanation to counter the resulting presumption of racial discrimination.

Hadley v. Junior College District, 397 U.S. 50 (1970)

Facts: Missouri law permitted separate school districts to unite to form a consolidated junior college district and then to elect six trustees to conduct and manage the district's affairs. The trustees were apportioned among the school districts on the basis of "school enumerations," which are defined as the number of persons from age six through twenty residing in each school district. With a particular city junior college district, a school district having between 50% and 66⅔% percent of the enumeration could elect three, or one-half, of the trustees. Similarly, a school district having between 33⅓% and 50% of the total enumeration could elect two, or one-third, of the trustees. One school district had 60% of the total college district's "enumeration" but could elect only 50% of the trustees. Residents of the school district challenged the constitutionality of the apportionment of trustees in the junior college district.

Holding: [6x3] When members of an elected body are chosen from separate school districts, the apportionment of members must ensure that equal numbers of voters in each district can vote for proportionally equal numbers of officials. A system of trustee apportionment that consistently discriminates in favor of smaller districts is unconstitutional.

Basis: Whenever a state or local government decides to select persons by popular election to perform governmental functions, the equal protection clause of the Fourteenth Amendment requires that each qualified voter have an equal opportunity to participate in that election. In establishing voting districts for such elections, the principle of "one man, one vote" must be followed as far as practicable.

Gordon v. Lance, 403 U.S. 1 (1971)

Facts: A West Virginia statute requires a 60% voter approval of measures that add to the public debt or that increase taxation more than a certain amount. A proposal calling for the issuance of general obligation bonds was submitted to the voters. By separate ballot, voters also were asked "to authorize the board of education to levy additional taxes to support current expenditures and capital improvements." The proposals were defeated because the required 60% voter approval was not attained. Certain voters in favor of the proposals sought to have the 60% rule declared unconstitutional. They claimed that the schools are in great need of improvement, that their level of quality is far below the state average, and that four similar proposals received majority votes but failed due to the 60% rule.

Holding: [6x3] A state law requiring, for bond issue approval or additional taxation, ratification by 60%, rather than a simple majority of the voters in a referendum election, is constitutional.

Basis: The laws requiring more than a simple majority for ratification of certain questions do not violate the equal protection clause of the Fourteenth Amendment unless the questions singled out for such treatment cause the laws to act unfairly toward any identifiable class of persons. Because the 60% rule in this case applies to all bond issues and taxes for whatever purpose, it does not discriminate against any identifiable class.

San Antonio Independent School District v. Rodriguez, 411 U.S. 1 (1973)

Facts: The financing of public elementary and secondary schools in Texas comes from state and local funding. Almost half of the revenues are derived from the state's Minimum Foundation Program, which is designed to provide a minimum educational offering in every school in the state. The school districts as a unit provide 20% of the funding for this program. Each district's share is apportioned under a formula designed to reflect its relative tax-paying ability, and each district raises these funds by means of a property tax. All districts raise additional monies to support their schools. This revenue source varies with the value of taxable property in the district and results in large disparities in per-pupil spending among districts. In this case, a class representing students who were poor or members of a minority group and who lived in school districts having a low tax base challenged the validity of this funding system. Such a system is used widely in the United States to fund public education.

Holding: [5x4] A funding system based on the local property tax that provides a minimum educational offering to all students is constitutional.

Basis: The equal protection clause of the Fourteenth Amendment requires that a strict test of the state law be applied when the law involved operates to the disadvantage of a suspect class of persons or interferes with the exercise of rights and liberties explicitly or implicitly protected by the Constitution. Here, there is no suspect class since students of all incomes and races suffer alike, depending on the tax base of the district in which they attend school. There is no loss of a fundamental right since education, in itself, is not constitutionally protected and since the minimum education guaranteed to every student is sufficient for the exercise of protected political (voting) and First Amendment (expression) rights. Therefore, the financing system merely must be rationally related to a legitimate state purpose to meet the requirements under the Fourteenth Amendment; local control of education fulfills this requirement. It is noted that state constitutions still may require stricter standards.

East Carroll Parish School Board v. Marshall, 424 U.S. 636 (1976)

Facts: A resident of a parish (a county) in Louisiana brought suit alleging that population disparities among the wards of the parish had unconstitutionally denied him the right to cast an effective vote in elections of the parish's governing body and the school board. After a hearing, the district court decided that the wards were unevenly apportioned and adopted a reapportionment plan calling for an at-large election of members of both the governing body and the school board. The resident appealed, contending that the multi-member, at-large reapportionment plan would tend to dilute the black vote in violation of the Fourteenth and Fifteenth Amendments and the Voting Rights Act of 1965.

Holding: [8/1x0] 1) In fashioning reapportionment plans to supplant invalid legislation, single-member districts are to be ordered, rather than multi-member districts, unless there are unusual circumstances. 2) The preclearance requirement of the Voting Rights Act does not apply to court-ordered reapportionment plans.

Basis: 1) The Court relied on a clear line of precedents in adopting and applying this rule. The Court found no special circumstances in this case to justify the use of multi-member districts. 2) The Court relied on precedent for this ruling also.

Dougherty County Board of Education v. White, 439 U.S. 32 (1978)*

Facts: Shortly after a black employee of the school district announced his candidacy for the state legislature, the school board adopted a requirement ("Rule 58") that employees must take unpaid leaves of absence while campaigning for political office. The employee sought election on three separate occasions, causing him to take leave and lose salary in three different school years. On the third time the employee was forced into this position, he filed suit, contending that Rule 58 was unenforceable because it had not been precleared under the Voting Rights Act of 1965. Under Sec. 5 of the Voting Rights Act, all states and political subdivisions must submit any proposed change affecting voting for preclearance by the Attorney General or by the district court for the District of Columbia.

Holding: [4/1x4] A school board must obtain preclearance under the Voting Rights Act for a rule requiring its employees to take unpaid leave while campaigning for political office.

Basis: The legislative history clearly indicates that Sec. 5 of the Voting Rights Act applies to all entities having power over any aspect of the electoral process. The fact that the school board was not a county or an entity that conducted voter registration was irrelevant. Based on precedents, in addition to

---

*For a subsequent ruling in this case, see White v. *Dougherty County Board of Education (infra)*.

legislative history, the Court concluded that Congress intended the Voting Rights Act to apply to any state enactment that altered the election laws in any way. An enactment that burdens an independent candidate by increasing the difficulty for him to gain a position on the general election ballot is subject to the Voting Rights Act. Thus, the rule at issue here was a "standard practice or procedure with respect to voting," which under the Voting Rights Act is subject to its preclearance requirement.

Interim Board of Trustees of Westheimer Independent School District v. Coalition to Preserve Houston, 494 F. Supp. 738 (S.D. Tex. 1980), *aff'd*, 450 U.S. 901 (1981)

Lower Court Holding: 1) Where a school board election is held in deliberate defiance of Sec. 5 of the Voting Rights Act, the election should be set aside. 2) A citizens' coalition, as the prevailing party in a Voting Rights Act case, is entitled to an award of reasonable attorneys' fees recoverable against the school district, not against the state education agency.

Bell v. New Jersey, 461 U.S. 773 (1983)*

Facts: Title I of the Elementary and Secondary Education Act (ESEA) of 1965, as amended, provided for federal grants to states to support compensatory education programs for disadvantaged children upon the states' assurances that the grants would be used only for eligible programs under Title I. Auditors determined that New Jersey and Pennsylvania had misapplied federal funds that had been granted to them under Title I. The federal Education Appeal Board assessed deficiencies against both states. The states challenged the board's right to require them to pay back the money.

Holding: [8/1x0] State recipients are liable for misused funds granted under Title I of the pre-1978 version of ESEA. The U.S. Department of Education may administratively deter-

---

*For a follow-up decision, see *Bennett v. New Jersey (infra)*.

mine the amount of the liability, and the state may seek judicial review of the agency determination.

Basis: The Court relied on the language and legislative history of the General Education Provisions Act and of the pre-1978 version of ESEA. (The 1978 amendments to ESEA made explicit the authority of the Secretary of Education to recover funds misused by a recipient.)

Lawrence County v. Lead-Deadwood School District No. 40-1, 469 U.S. 256 (1985)

Facts: The federal Payment in Lieu of Taxes Act compensates local governments for the loss of tax revenues resulting from the tax-immune status of federal lands, such as national parks, and for the cost of providing services associated with these lands. Under the Act, the Secretary of Interior makes an annual payment to each unit of local government where such lands are located, and the local government may use the payment for any governmental purpose. South Dakota enacted a statute that required local governments to distribute these federal payments in the same way they distribute general tax revenues. For example, if a county allocates 60% of its general tax revenues to its school districts, the state statute would require the county to give its schools 60% of the payments it receives from the Payment in Lieu of Taxes Act. After a county refused to distribute the funds in accordance with the state statute, a school district sued to compel the county to do so.

Holding: [7x2] A state may not regulate the distribution of funds that units of local government receive from the federal government in lieu of taxes.

Basis: The legislation adopted by South Dakota obstructs the congressional purpose of the Payment in Lieu of Taxes Act and runs afoul of the supremacy clause. The statutory language and the legislative history of the Act demonstrate Congress' intent to give local governments more discretion in spending federal aid than the state could allow them. Congress recognized that the presence of federal lands might impose a strain on a county's limited resources.

NAACP v. Hampton County Election Commission, 470 U.S. 166 (1985)

Facts: Sec. 5 of the amended Voting Rights Act of 1965 prohibits a state or political subdivision from establishing any voting qualification or procedure different from that in effect on 1 November 1964 without obtaining prior approval from the Attorney General or the federal district court for the District of Columbia. As of 1 November 1964, the public schools of Hampton County were governed by an appointed county board of education and an elected superintendent of education. In 1982, the South Carolina General Assembly enacted legislation providing that the members of this county board of education were to be elected at large, rather than appointed. This legislation was submitted to the Attorney General for preclearance under Sec. 5 of the Voting Rights Act, and approval was granted. However, in the meantime, new legislation was enacted to abolish this county board of education and to assign their duties to the two constituent local districts. The new legislation also was submitted to the Attorney General, but approval was not forthcoming by election time. Consequently, elections were held in accordance with the at-large legislation. Thereafter, the Attorney General approved the new legislation, thus rendering null and void the at-large legislation and the elections held pursuant to it. The state's election commission set a new election date. Two civil rights organizations and several county residents challenged the new election date and process as illegal under Sec. 5 of the Voting Rights Act, because a number of alleged changes in the election procedure had not been submitted to the Attorney General or to the district court for preclearance.

Holding: [7/2x0] The use of an earlier filing period and the scheduling of an election date several months later than was approved by the Attorney General are changes requiring pre-clearance under the Voting Rights Act.

Basis: The purpose of the Voting Rights Act was to eliminate state regulations that have the effect of denying citizens their right to vote because of their race. The Attorney General's interpretation of the coverage of Sec. 5, which was given considerable deference by the Court, includes any change affecting voting even though it appears to be minor or indirect, ostensibly expands voting rights, or is designed to remove the elements that caused objection by the Attorney General to a prior submitted change. The Court's inquiry is limited to whether the challenged changes have the potential for discrimination. In this case, the changes did have the potential to be discriminatory because the filing date was several months earlier and would preclude late-comers and because fewer people would vote in March than on election day in November.

Bennett v. Kentucky Department of Education, 470 U.S. 656 (1985)

Facts: Title I of the Elementary and Secondary Education Act (ESEA) of 1965, as amended, provided for federal grants to states to support compensatory education programs for disadvantaged children upon the states' assurances that the grants would be used only for eligible programs under Title I. At the time the grants were received by Kentucky, the statute and regulations required that Title I funds be used to supplement, not supplant, state and local expenditures for education. Auditors found that Kentucky had permitted school districts to use Title I funds for readiness classes offered to students in place of regular first- and second-grade classes. The Secretary of Education determined that supplanting had occurred and demanded repayment from Kentucky of the misused Title I funds.

Holding: [8x0] Neither substantial compliance nor absence of bad faith absolves a state from liability for recovery of misused Title I funds.

Basis: Citing *Bell* v. *New Jersey (supra)*, the Court clarified that recovery of misused Title I funds is a repayment of a debt, not a punishment. Thus the issue is not the fairness of imposing punitive measures. In order to receive Title I grants, the state must give certain assurances as to how the money will be used. In this case, the state did not fulfill its assurances, as properly determined by the Secretary of Education. Given the detailed provisions in the Act concerning audit determinations, the Court concluded that Congress did not intend to engraft the "substantial compliance" standard of other parts of the Act to the legal requirements affecting liability. Similarly, the Court found no indication in the Act or in *Bell* v. *New Jersey* that "misuse" of Title I funds depends on any subjective intent attributable to grant recipients. Finally, unlike *Pennhurst*,* Title I provides the requisite clarity for knowing acceptance by recipients.

Bennett v. New Jersey, 470 U.S. 632 (1985)

Facts: This case is a follow-up to *Bell* v. *New Jersey (supra)*. Between the time of the alleged misuse and the time the *Bell* case came to trial, the federal government had made amendments to ESEA that relaxed the eligibility requirements for local schools to receive Title I funds. New Jersey sought to have the new requirements apply as the standards for review in determining whether it had misused Title I funds.

Holding: [6x2] The substantive standards of the 1978 Amendments to ESEA do not apply retroactively for determining if Title I funds were misused under previously made grants.

Basis: Neither the statutory language nor the legislative history indicates that Congress intended the substantive standards of

---

Pennhurst State School and Hospital v. *Halderman*, 451 U.S. I (1981).

the 1978 Amendments to apply retroactively. Usually it is understood that statutes affecting substantive rights and responsibilities have only prospective effect. Furthermore, as a practical matter, evaluation of compliance of statutory regulations must be judged by the law in effect when the grants were made. Otherwise, grant recipients and auditors would have no method for determining whether expenditures were proper.

Kadrmas v. Dickinson Public Schools, 487 U.S. 450 (1988)

Facts: The North Dakota legislature authorized and encouraged thinly populated school districts to consolidate or "reorganize" into larger districts. Reorganization proposals were required to include provisions for transporting students to and from their homes. A school district serving a relatively populous area chose not to participate in such a reorganization for several years. The district provided free bus transportation to students in outlying areas, but the pickup points were often at a considerable distance from students' homes. After a referendum of the bus users, the district instituted a door-to-door bus service and began charging a fee. The annual fee, which was approximately $100 for one child and $150 dollars for two children, covered approximately one-tenth of the actual cost. Subsequently, the State enacted a statute authorizing school districts to charge a fee for school bus service, not to exceed the district's estimated cost of providing the service. A family who lived about 15 miles from the child's school and whose income was near the poverty level decided not to renew their bus contract when they fell behind on other bills. They arranged to transport their daughter privately, but it cost them more than the fee. The parents filed suit to enjoin the district from collecting a bus service fee.

Holding: [5x4] The equal protection clause does not forbid a state from allowing some local school boards, but not others, from assessing a fee for transporting children between their homes and the public schools.

Basis: The Court rejected the claim that poverty is a suspect class and that education is a fundamental right; each of these claims would have required a heightened level of equal protection scrutiny. Applying the traditional, relaxed test for equal protection, the Court concluded that encouraging school bus service was a legitimate state objective and that it was "rational" for the state to refrain from undermining this objective by requiring that the service, if offered, be free.

McIntyre v. Ohio Elections Commission, 514 U.S. 334 (1995)

Facts: An individual distributed leaflets purporting to express the views of "Concerned Parents and Taxpayers" opposing a school tax levy. As a result, the state elections commission fined her for violating a state statute that prohibited the distribution of campaign literature that does not contain the name and address of the person or campaign official issuing the literature. She appealed her conviction.

Holding: [6/1x2] A governmental prohibition of the distribution of anonymous campaign literature violates First Amendment freedom of speech.

Basis: Citing its precedents, the Court concluded that the prohibition here is a content regulation of core political speech, thus meriting strict scrutiny, rather than a reasonableness test. The state's asserted interests in preventing fraudulent and libelous statements and in providing the electorate with relevant information is plainly insufficient to support the disclosure requirement because the speaker's identity is no different from other contents of the document and the identifying information adds little evaluative information where the author is a private citizen unknown to the reader. Moreover, the extremely broad prohibition is not the narrowly tailored, least restrictive alternative.

United States v. Lopez, 514 U.S. 549 (1995)

Facts: A high school senior was caught carrying a concealed handgun into his high school. The police charged him with violating the Gun-Free School Zones Act of 1990, which forbids "any individual knowingly to posses a firearm at a place that [he] know . . . is a school zone." The Act defines "school zone" as "in, or on the grounds of . . . or within a distance of 1,000 feet from . . . a public, parochial or private school." He moved to dismiss the indictment, claiming that this prohibition is beyond Congress' constitutional authority.

Holding: [5x4] The Gun-Free School Zones Act exceeds Congress's commerce clause authority and, thus, is invalid.

Basis: The Court reasoned that although it had previously upheld a wide variety of federal statutes regulating intrastate economic activity that substantially affected interstate commerce, the possession of a gun in a school zone is, in no sense, such an activity. It is a criminal statute that has nothing to do with an economic enterprise and does not, when viewed in the aggregate, substantially affect interstate commerce. To uphold the government's contention to the contrary would require the Court to pile inference upon inference in a manner that would convert congressional commerce clause authority to a general police power of the sort held only by the states. Thus, principles of federalism guided the majority's decision.

Denver Area Educational Telecommunications Consortium, Inc. v. Federal Communications Commission, 518 U.S. 727 (1996)

Facts: The federal Cable Television Consumer Protection and Competition Act of 1992, as implemented by FCC regulations, applies to "leased access channels," which are reserved for commercial lease by parties unaffiliated with the cable television system operator, and "public access channels," which are required by local governments for public, governmental, and educational programming. The Act leaves to the discretion of the operator of both types of channels to allow or prohibit programming that "it reasonably believes . . . depicts sexual . . . activities or organs in a patently offensive manner." The Act requires operators of leased access channels to segregate patently offensive programming on a single channel, to block that channel from viewer access, and to unblock (or later reblock) it within 30 days of a subscriber's written request. Previously, federal law prohibited operators from exercising any editorial control over the program contents on either type of access channel. Various channel operators, including an educational telecommunications consortium, filed suit, claiming that these provisions violated their First Amendment freedom of expression and the Fifth Amendment* void-for-vagueness doctrine.

Holding: [4½/2½x3] 1) The general censoring authorization of the federal cable television law concerning leased access channels violates neither First Amendment expression nor Fifth Amendment vagueness. 2) Its censoring provision concerning public access channels violates First Amendment expression. 3) Its "segregate and block" requirements, which apply to leased access channels, also violates the First Amendment.

Basis: In a multiply fractured opinion, 1) a plurality of the Court concluded that the general censoring provision for leased access channels is a sufficiently tailored response to an extraordinarily important child-protection problem involving a complex balance of interests and that its definition of the regulated materials is not, in light of the Court's obscenity rulings, vague or overbroad; 2) a plurality concluded that

---

*The Fifth Amendment, which is applicable to the federal government, has a due process clause parallel to the one in the Fourteenth Amendment, which is applicable to the states. Although public schools fit under the Fourteenth Amendment, the target of this case was a federal law, thus implicating the Fifth Amendment.

the same censoring provision for public access channels was based on one or more distinctions between these two types of channels; and 3) a majority concluded that the "segregate and block" requirements specific to leased access channels is not appropriately tailored to achieve its basic, legitimate objective of protecting children from exposure to patently offensive materials; the "V-chip" and "lockbox" provisions of other federal cable channel statutes suggest that this means is overly restrictive while its benefits are speculative.

Reno v. American Civil Liberties Union, 521 U.S. 844 (1997)*

Facts: A pair of provisions of the Communications Decency Act of 1996 sought to protect minors from harmful material on the Internet. One provision criminalized the "knowing" transmission of "obscene or indecent" messages to any recipient under 18 years of age. The other provision prohibited the "knowing" sending or displaying to a person under 18 of any message "that, in context, depicts or describes, in terms patently offensive as measured by community standards, sexual or excretory activities or organs." The Act also provided affirmative defenses to those who take "good faith, . . . effective. . . actions" to restrict access by minors to the prohibited communications and those who restrict such access by requiring certain designated forms of age proof, such as a verified credit card. Various affected individuals filed suit, challenging the constitutionality of these two provisions.

Holding: [7/1x1] The Communications Decency Act's "indecent transmission" — except for its restriction of "obscene" material — and "patently offensive display" provisions abridge First Amendment freedom of speech.

---

*For other recent but less directly relevant First Amendment speech rulings, see *Greater New Orleans Broadcasting Association, Inc.* v. *United States*, 527 U.S. 173 (1999), and *Arkansas Educational Television Commission* v. *Forbes*, 523 U.S. 666 (1998).

Basis: Contrary to the government's arguments, the Court initially observed that its child-pornography precedents raise,
rather than relieve, doubts about the constitutionality of the
disputed provisions. The Court then identified the following
infirmities in these provisions: the failure to define key terms,
such as "indecent," in a criminalizing context; the lack —
compared to the Court's three-pronged definition of obscenity — of sufficient limitations; the unprecedented overlap
with adult speech, particularly in light of less restrictive and
at least equally effective alternatives; their content-based,
rather than "time, place, and manner," regulation; the "heck-
ler's veto" potency in light of the broad-based nature of the
Internet; and the illusory affirmative defenses. On the other
hand, given that obscene speech may be totally banned and
the Act allows severability, the Court severed and preserved
the constitutionality of the "obscene" restriction.

National Endowment for the Arts v. Finley, 524 U.S. 569 (1998)

Facts: The National Foundation on the Arts and Humanities Act
vests the National Endowment for the Arts with substantial
discretion to award financial grants to support the arts. The
Act identifies only broad funding priorities, including "artis-
tic and cultural significant, giving emphasis to. . . creativity
and cultural diversity" and the encouragement of "public. . .
education. . . and appreciation of the arts." In 1989, controversial photographs that appeared in two exhibits funded by
the endowment prompted public outcry over the agency's
grant-making procedures. Congress reacted by enacting a
1990 amendment that directs the endowment to take into
consideration "general standards of decency and respect for
the diverse beliefs and values of the American public" in its
grant awards. Individual performance artists who had
applied for funding before the amendment took effect but
whose applications were denied after it took effect filed suit

on the grounds of First Amendment freedom of expression and Fifth Amendment vagueness.*

Holding: [5/3x1] The amendment that requires consideration of general standards of decency and respect violates neither First Amendment speech nor Fifth Amendment vagueness.

Basis: 1) Given that the First Amendment challenge was to the constitutionality of the amendment on its face, not just as applied to the particular grant applicant, the Court concluded that they had failed to sustain their substantial burden of demonstrating that the amendment would likely lead to suppression of free expression. The Court pointed out that the amendment only added "considerations" to the grant-making process, neither precluding awards to projects that might be deemed indecent or disrespectful nor placing conditions on grants, and that the amendment was a bipartisan effort to counterweigh competing proposals to eliminate or substantially constrain the agency's grant-making authority. Citing its previous First Amendment decisions, including *Board of Education v. Pico (infra)*, the Court also concluded that both the "decency" and "respect" prongs of the amendment were permissible factors, much like educational suitability. 2) Although admitting that the amendment's terms were "undeniably opaque," the government has much more latitude when acting as patron rather than sovereign. Unlike such terms in a criminal statute or regulatory scheme, these considerations are within the acceptable range of such typical grant-making subjective criteria as "excellence."

---

*For the parallelism of the Fifth and Fourteenth Amendments for the purposes of the due process basis for the void for vagueness doctrine, see the footnote under *Denver Area Educational Telecommunications Consortium (supra)*.

CHAPTER TWO

Church-State Relationships in Education

Pierce v. Society of Sisters, 268 U.S. 510 (1925)

Facts: An Oregon law, which was to take effect in 1926, required all normal children between the ages of eight and sixteen to attend public schools until the completion of the eighth grade. Even before becoming enforceable, the law seriously impaired the operation of sectarian and secular private schools within the state. Its enforcement would perhaps result in the destruction of well-established, private elementary school corporations and would greatly diminish the value of property long held for that purpose. In this case, private school corporations sought a court order restraining enforcement of this law.

Holding: [9x0] The state may reasonably regulate all schools and may require that all children attend some school, but the state may not deny children the right to attend adequate private schools and force them to attend only public schools.

Basis: The Fourteenth Amendment protects persons from arbitrary state action impairing life, liberty, or property interests. 1) The act requiring children to attend only public primary schools is not reasonably related to a legitimate state purpose because children could be adequately educated in private, as well as in public, schools. 2) The act unreasonably interferes with the liberty of parents to direct the education of their children. 3) The property interests of the private school corporations are severely threatened by the act's impairment of the liberty of their students and patrons.

Cochran v. Louisiana State Board of Education, 281 U.S. 370 (1930)

Facts: A state law required that tax money be spent to supply textbooks to all school children at no charge. Public and private school students, including students of private, sectarian schools, were benefited by the program. Suit was brought by a group of taxpayers in Louisiana to restrain the state board of education from expending funds to purchase schoolbooks and to supply them free of charge to the school children of the state, on the ground that it violated the Constitution.

Holding: [9x0] A state statute providing secular textbooks to school children attending private sectarian schools as well as to those attending public schools is constitutional.

Basis: The Fourteenth Amendment forbids the states from depriving a person of life, liberty, or property without due process of law. However, the provision of secular texts to all school children serves a public interest and does not benefit the private interest of church schools or of parents of parochial school students in such a way as to violate the due process clause.

Everson v. Board of Education, 330 U.S. 1 (1947)

Facts: A New Jersey statute authorized local school districts to make rules and contracts for the transportation of children to and from schools. Acting in accordance with this statute, a local board of education reimbursed parents of school children for the bus fares of students to and from school. While the statute excluded students of private schools operated for profit, it included children who attended private, sectarian schools. In this case, a taxpayer challenged the constitutionality of such payments made to the parents of children attending these private, sectarian schools.

Holding: [5x4] A law authorizing reimbursement of the parents of school children for the bus fares of their children to and from private, sectarian schools, when included in a general program of reimbursement for the bus fares of public school children, is constitutional.

Basis: 1) The due process clause of the Fourteenth Amendment forbids state action that deprives persons of life, liberty, or property without due process of law. However, the claim that reimbursement for bus fares taxes the public in order to serve the private desires of those sending their children to private, sectarian schools, and therefore is prohibited by the Fourteenth Amendment, is without merit. The state can properly decide that the safe transportation of all school children is in the public interest. 2) The establishment clause of the First Amendment, made applicable to the states by the Fourteenth Amendment, prohibits state establishment of religion. However, the provision of such governmental services as police and fire protection, sewage lines and sidewalks, or general reimbursement for school bus fares, without which the church schools would be severely hampered, is viewed by the Court as neutrality toward religion, rather than as support of it.

Illinois *ex rel.* McCollum v. Board of Education, 333 U.S. 203 (1948)

Facts: An Illinois school board permitted representatives of several religions to teach religion classes to those students in grades four through nine whose parents signed cards indicating that they wanted them to attend. The classes were held during school hours and inside the school building. Students who attended the classes were excused from their secular schedule for that period of time. Other students remained in their regular classes. In this case, a taxpayer challenged the constitutionality of the program.

Holding: [3/5x1] A program permitting religious instruction within public schools during school hours and excusing students attending such a class from a part of the secular schedule is unconstitutional.

Basis: The First Amendment prohibits state establishment of religion and requires the separation of church and state. The Court finds the program allowing the use of state buildings for religious instruction and providing state support of religious class attendance, through application of the compulsory attendance law, to be unconstitutional because it fails to maintain the required separation of church and state.

Zorach v. Clauson, 343 U.S. 306 (1952)

Facts: A school district had a program of "released time" religious instruction under which public school students were permitted, with their parents' written request, to leave the building during school hours in order to go to religious centers for instruction or prayer. The students who were not released for religious purposes were required to stay in school. The religious organizations paid all costs and provided all facilities for the program. Public funds were not expended for the program and religious classes were not held in the public school buildings. Taxpayers, who were residents of the school district and whose children attended its public schools, challenged the policy, contending that, in essence, it is not different from the one involved in *McCollum (supra).*

Holding: [6x3] A law that allows public schools to adjust their schedules in order to release children for religious instruction outside the schools' facilities and that requires no state financial support of such instruction is constitutional.

Basis: By releasing children from school for religious instruction, the state has not acted counter to the First Amendment, which prohibits laws creating a state establishment of religion and laws denying the free exercise of religion.

Engel v. Vitale, 370 U.S. 421 (1962)

Facts: A local board of education, acting under authority of a New York State law, ordered a brief nondenominational prayer to be said aloud by each class, in the presence of a teacher, at the beginning of each school day. The prayer had been composed by the state board of regents, which also had established the procedure for its recitation. Those children not wishing to pray were to be excused from the exercise.

Parents brought action to challenge the constitutionality of both the state law that authorized the school district to mandate the use of prayer in public schools and the school district's action of ordering recitation of this particular prayer.

Holding: [5/1x1] State encouragement of the regular recitation of prayer in the public school system is unconstitutional.

Basis: The statute authorizing prayer recitation in the public schools is in direct violation of the First Amendment prohibition of a state establishment of religion.

Abington School District v. Schempp; Murray v. Curlett, 374 U.S. 203 (1963)

Facts: A Pennsylvania law required that 10 Bible verses be read with no comment at the beginning of the school day. The Bible readings were to be followed by the recitation of the Lord's Prayer, held in the school building, and conducted by public school personnel. On written parental request, a child could be excused from the exercise. Baltimore adopted a similar rule for its school system. Two separate families challenged the constitutionality of the practice required by state statute and local regulations, respectively.

Holding: [5/3x1] It is unconstitutional for a state law to promote the reading of verses from the Bible and the recitation of prayer on school grounds under the supervision of school personnel during school hours, even when attendance is not compulsory.

Basis: The establishment clause of the First Amendment, made applicable to the states by the Fourteenth Amendment, requires the states to be neutral toward religion and forbids state establishment of religion. A law requiring a prayer at the beginning of the school day is an impermissible establishment of religion, whether or not students are required to participate.

Chamberlin v. Dade County Board of Public Instruction, 377 U.S. 402 (1964)

Facts: A Florida statute required devotional Bible reading and the recitation of prayers in the Florida public schools.

Holding: [6/3x0] A state statute may not authorize the reading of Bible verses and the recitation of prayer on school grounds, during school hours, and under the supervision of school personnel.

Basis: The Court followed *Abington School District* v. *Schempp (supra)*, in which it held that school prayer laws are a state establishment of religion and therefore are in violation of the First and Fourteenth Amendments.

Board of Education v. Allen, 392 U.S. 236 (1968)

Facts: A New York law required local public school authorities to lend textbooks free of charge to both public and private school students in grades seven through twelve. In this case, a local school board, desiring to block the allocation of state funds for students of private, religious schools, challenged the constitutionality of the statute.

Holding: [5/1x3] A law which provides for the state-subsidized loan of secular textbooks to private, as well as to public, school students is constitutional.

Basis: Since the books loaned are part of a general program to further the secular education of all students and are not, in fact, used to teach religion, the program is not an establishment of religion. The Court also noted that the state aid goes to parents and students, rather than to the religious schools directly, and therefore would not be a state establishment of religion.

Walz v. Tax Commission, 397 U.S. 664 (1970)

Facts: A city law provided property tax exemptions for nonprofit religious, educational, or charitable enterprises. A real estate owner argued that the exemption indirectly requires him to make a contribution to religious institutions and therefore is unconstitutional.

Holding: [6/2x1] A law permitting a tax exemption for nonprofit religious, educational, or charitable enterprises is constitutional.

Basis: The First Amendment prohibits the state establishment of religion and the excessive entanglement of the church and the state. Tax exemptions for religious institutions are historically sanctioned as being neutral toward, rather than supportive of, religion. The Court found that such exemptions lessen, rather than increase, church-state entanglement.

Lemon v. Kurtzman; Earley v. Dicenso, 403 U.S. 602 (1971) ("Lemon I")*

Facts: This case raised questions about Pennsylvania and Rhode Island statutes that provided for state aid to church-related elementary and secondary schools. Both statutes were enacted with the objective of aiding the quality of secular education in the nonpublic schools. The constitutionality of both statutes was challenged.

    The Rhode Island statute supplemented the salaries of teachers of secular subjects in nonpublic elementary schools so that these schools could attract competent teachers. The supplement could not exceed 15% of the teacher's annual

---

*For cases permitting state aid (construction funds for building to be used for secular purposes) to church-affiliated institutions of higher education, see *Tilton* v. *Richardson*, 403 U.S. 672 (1971); *Hunt* v. *McNair*, 413 U.S. 734 (1973); and *Roemer* v. *Board of Public Works*, 426 U.S. 736 (1976). These cases include in their reasoning a distinction between higher education and elementary-secondary education in terms of the pervasiveness of the religious influence.

salary; and the salary itself, when supplemented, could not exceed the maximum paid to public school teachers. The teacher had to be certified, be employed at a nonpublic school at which the average per-pupil expenditure on secular education was less than the average in the public schools, teach only courses offered in the public schools, and use only instructional materials used in the public schools. Teachers also had to agree in writing not to teach a course in religion. In Rhode Island the nonpublic elementary schools serve about 25% of the student population, and about 95% of these schools are affiliated with the Roman Catholic Church.

The Pennsylvania statute authorized the state to reimburse nonpublic schools solely for their actual expenditures for teachers' salaries, textbooks, and instructional materials that were used for secular courses. The subsidized course also had to be offered by the public schools. The nonpublic schools had to maintain prescribed accounting procedures and had to have texts and instructional materials approved by the state. The statute benefited schools that served a substantial number of students in the state. More than 96% of these students attended church-related schools, most of which were affiliated with the Roman Catholic Church.

Holding: [5/3x1] 1) A law providing a state subsidy for nonpublic school teachers' salaries is unconstitutional, even where the funds are paid only to teachers of secular subjects. 2) A law providing for state reimbursement to nonpublic schools for expenses incurred in the teaching of secular subjects also is unconstitutional.

Basis: Both statutes are unconstitutional under the establishment clause of the First Amendment insofar as they create an excessive entanglement between government and religion. The tripartite test is that a statute or other governmental policy 1) must have a secular legislative purpose, 2) must have a principal effect that neither advances nor inhibits religion, and 3) must not foster "an excessive government entanglement with religion." As to the Rhode Island program, state-subsidized teachers would have to be monitored extensively by the state to ensure that they did not teach religion. This would involve an excessive entanglement between church and state. As to the Pennsylvania program, the aid would be given directly to the nonpublic schools. This, combined with the surveillance and accounting procedures that would be required, would create excessive church-state entanglement.

Johnson v. Sanders, 319 F. Supp. 421 (D. Conn. 1970), *aff'd*, 403 U.S. 955 (1971)

Lower Court Holding: A state law reimbursing religious schools for the teaching of secular courses, resulting in state support of education in a setting surrounded by sectarian observances, and offered to a student body largely restricted to a religious group, is unconstitutional.

Wisconsin v. Yoder, 406 U.S. 205 (1972)

Facts: Members of the Old Order Amish religious community, a Christian sect that has been a distinct and identifiable group for three centuries, were convicted of violating Wisconsin's compulsory school attendance law. The law required parents to send their children to school until age 16. The Amish refused to send their children to any formal school, public or private, beyond the eighth grade because they believed that further formal education would seriously impede their children's preparation for adult life and for religious practice within the Amish communities. The Amish did provide their teenagers with substantial practical training at home for Amish adulthood. Further, it was shown that the children would most likely be self-sufficient citizens. The Amish challenged the constitutionality of the school attendance law as it applied to them.

Holding: [5½/3x½] Where compulsory school attendance beyond the eighth grade will have a detrimental effect on the way of life of an established religious community in which religious belief and practice are inseparable from daily work, the compulsory attendance law must yield to the parents' desires as to the form of their children's education.

Basis: The Court ruled on the free exercise clause of the First Amendment. Since the religious belief and practice of the Amish is inseparable from their daily way of life, a law that interferes with Amish life also infringes on the free exercise of their religion. The state may infringe on this right only for a compelling reason. Since the Amish way of life is not analogous to a health or safety hazard to the children and does not tend to create adults incapable of responsible citizenship or self-sufficiency, the state cannot successfully argue that it is empowered as *parens patriae* to override the parents' interest for the benefit of their children. The Court limited the exemption to grades 9 to 12 and noted that the State could constitutionally regulate the alternate agrarian education.

Lemon v. Kurtzman, 411 U.S. 192 (1973) ("Lemon II")

Facts: A Pennsylvania law had provided for state reimbursement of sectarian schools for secular education functions that they performed. The state was to monitor the programs to ensure that state funds were spent on only secular courses of instruction. No attempts were made to enjoin the operation of the program, although a lawsuit challenging the law's validity was begun soon after the law was passed. Relying on the statute, sectarian schools entered into contracts with the state for performance of and compensation for services. The Court later invalidated the statute in *Lemon I (supra)*. The federal district court then enjoined the state for reimbursement for services performed after the law was invalidated but permitted payments for services performed prior to that date, including services performed during the 1970-71 school year. In this case, the propriety of state payments to religious schools for services performed in 1970-71 was challenged.

Holding: [4/1x3] Religious schools that contract for reimbursement under a state law reasonably presumed to be valid and that are to be compensated for only secular services performed prior to judicial invalidation of the relevant state law may be allowed to receive the compensation for which they contracted.

Basis: 1) The district court is permitted broad discretion in fashioning a remedy. Here, it reasonably permitted payment for services rendered in reliance on the law's validity. 2) There is no violation of the First Amendment establishment clause with regard to excessive entanglement between church and state because the program cannot continue beyond these final payments, and because the services that already had been performed by the religious schools were monitored in order to ensure that they were secular in nature.

Levitt v. Committee for Public Education and Religious Liberty, 413 U.S. 472 (1973)

Facts: A New York statute enabled the legislature to appropriate funds to reimburse nonpublic schools for the performance of various services required by the state. Of these services, the most expensive was the administration, grading, compiling, and reporting of test results. There were two types of tests administered in the schools: the state-prepared tests, such as Regents exams and student aptitude tests, and the traditional, in-school, teacher-prepared tests. The latter constituted the overwhelming majority of the tests. A lump sum per pupil was allotted annually under the statute, and the beneficiary nonpublic schools were not required to account for the money received or to specify how it was spent. In this case, a group of New York taxpayers challenged the validity of the statute.

Holding: [8x1] A statute that authorizes the state to reimburse nonpublic schools for state-required student services (for example, testing) and that does not limit such reimbursement to the secular functions of such schools is unconstitutional.

Basis: The First Amendment proscribes laws creating a state establishment of religion. Here, the Court's inquiry is whether the statute's primary purpose was to advance religion and whether the statute would lead to excessive government entanglement. Where the state allocates funds directly to religious schools, and especially where the use of such funds is not limited to secular functions, there is impermissible state support of religion. The legislature, not the courts, should reduce the allotments to an amount corresponding with the actual costs incurred in performing reimbursable secular functions.

Committee for Public Education and Religious Liberty v. Nyquist, 413 U.S. 756 (1973)

Facts: The State of New York established three financial aid programs for nonpublic elementary and secondary schools. One program was to supply funds to qualifying nonpublic schools for repair and maintenance of equipment and facilities. Another provided for a tuition reimbursement to low-income parents with children enrolled in elementary or secondary nonpublic schools. The third program provided for a state income-tax credit to middle-income parents with children enrolled in nonpublic schools. Most of the schools that were to benefit from these programs were sectarian schools. A group of taxpayers challenged the validity of the laws authorizing the expenditure of state funds for the benefit of such institutions.

Holding: [6/1x2] 1) A law providing for direct payments to sectarian schools for repair and maintenance of equipment and facilities is unconstitutional, even when limited to 50% of comparable state aid to public schools. 2) Tuition reimbursements and income-tax credits for parents of nonpublic school children are unconstitutional, even if the dollar amount of the reimbursements is a statistically small portion of the total tuitions paid.

Basis: The Court found violations of prongs 2 and 3 of the tripartite test enumerated in *Lemon I (supra)*. The repair and maintenance provisions directly support the religious, as well as the secular, functions of the beneficiary schools and therefore unconstitutionally advance religion; the tax provisions directly support the enrollment of children in religious schools and therefore unconstitutionally advance religion; and the potential for continuing political strife over further appropriations to aid religion creates an excessive state entanglement with religion.

Sloan v. Lemon, 413 U.S. 825 (1973)

Facts: In an earlier case, *Lemon I (supra)*, the Court ruled that a law aiding nonpublic elementary and secondary education was unconstitutional. The law in that case provided for reimbursement of sectarian schools for expenses incurred in the teaching of nonsectarian courses. The Court ruled that the state supervision necessary to guarantee that the aid would benefit only secular activities would foster "excessive entanglement" between church and state. In an attempt to avoid the entanglement problem, the Pennsylvania legislature enacted a law under which the state could reimburse parents with children in nonpublic schools for a portion of their tuition expenses. This new law specifically precluded state regulation of the schools and imposed no restrictions on the uses to which allotments could be put by beneficiary parents. In this case, the validity of the new law was challenged.

Holding: [7x2] A law providing for state reimbursement of parents with children enrolled in sectarian schools for tuition paid to such schools is unconstitutional.

Basis: The First Amendment proscribes laws creating a state establishment of religion. State payment to parents of children in sectarian schools encourages enrollment in such schools and therefore has the impermissible effect of advancing religion with state funds.

Wheeler v. Barrera, 417 U.S. 402 (1974)

Facts: Title I, which provided funding for remedial programs for educationally deprived children in areas with a high concentration of children from low-income families, was the first federal aid-to-education program authorizing assistance for private, as well as public, school children. The primary responsibility for designing and effectuating a Title I program rested with the "local educational agency" (for example, the local school board). The plan then had to be approved by the state education agency and by the U.S. Commissioner of Education. In order to be approved at the state level, the plan had to provide eligible private school students with services that are "comparable in quality, scope, and opportunity for participation to those provided for public school children with needs of equally high priority." The law did not require that identical services be provided, nor did it intend that state constitutional spending proscriptions (for example, those against the use of public funds to employ private school teachers) be pre-empted as a condition for accepting federal funds.

Although most of Missouri's Title I money was spent to employ remedial teachers, state officials had refused to appropriate any money to pay nonpublic school teachers working during regular school hours. However, some Title I funds were allocated to nonpublic schools. In this case, parents of nonpublic school students argued that state school officials were illegally approving Title I programs that did not offer comparable services to their children.

Holding: [5/3x1] Title I's requirement that comparable services be provided to private school children does not require a state to administer a program calling for the use of Title I teachers in nonpublic schools during regular school hours. Where such a program would be contrary to state law, officials may formulate alternative plans.

Basis: The decision is based on Title I's requirement that comparable, although not identical, services be provided for eligible private school students. The issue of whether or not the First Amendment would permit Title I subsidy of teachers working within nonpublic schools is not decided in this case.

Public Funds for Public Schools of New Jersey v. Marburger, 358 F. Supp. 29 (D. N.J. 1973), *aff'd*, 417 U.S. 961 (1974)

Lower Court Holding: State legislation that provides state aid to the parents of nonpublic school students as reimbursement for secular, nonideological textbooks, materials, and supplies and that provides that the amount left from the total will be assigned to nonpublic schools violates the First Amendment's establishment clause.

Meek v. Pittenger, 421 U.S. 349 (1975)

Facts: In order to ensure that nonpublic school children would receive auxiliary services, textbooks, and instructional materials that were provided free to public school children, the Pennsylvania General Assembly passed two acts in 1972. One act authorized state provision of auxiliary services, including counseling, testing, and remedial education for the educationally disadvantaged. These services were to be provided within the nonpublic schools but staffed by employees of the public school system. The other act authorized the lending of secular textbooks, either directly or through an intermediary, to nonpublic school children. It also authorized the lending of other instructional materials and equipment directly to the nonpublic schools. The great majority of schools that were to benefit from the laws were sectarian schools. In this case, the validity of the two acts was challenged.

Holding: [3/3x3] 1) An act authorizing the state-subsidized loan of secular texts to nonpublic school students as well as to public school students is constitutional. 2) An act authorizing the provision of personnel or instructional materials that could be used for religious, as well as secular, education is unconstitutional.

Basis: The establishment clause of the First Amendment, made applicable to the states by the Fourteenth Amendment, prohibits state support of religious institutions. While the Court has allowed the state loan of secular texts to nonpublic school children as well as to public school children, it found that the provision of millions of dollars of additional aid to sectarian schools is too direct and substantial an aid to the total educational function of such schools to be constitutional. The provision of staff or materials, susceptible to use in religious instruction as well as secular instruction, is unconstitutional because it would require excessive state entanglement with religious institutions in order to ensure that state aid is not used to support the religious function of such institutions. The Court also noted the probability of political entanglement as the result of legal suits over future appropriations of funds largely for the benefit of sectarian schools.

Wolman v. Walter, 433 U.S. 229 (1977)

Facts: An Ohio law providing state aid to nonpublic elementary and secondary schools was challenged by a group of citizens and taxpayers. Most of the schools standing to benefit from the program were sectarian institutions.

    The statute authorized the provision of the following: 1) secular texts, 2) standardized testing and diagnostic services, 3) therapeutic and remedial services administered by public school personnel at religiously neutral locations, 4) instructional materials and equipment comparable to those supplied to public schools, and 5) transportation and other services for field trips.

Holding: [6½ x 2½] A state may constitutionally supply sectarian private schools with the following: 1) secular texts that are approved by public school authorities and that are loaned to private school students or their parents; 2) standardized tests and scoring services such as are used in the public schools, provided that nonpublic school personnel are not involved in test drafting or scoring and nonpublic schools are not reimbursed for costs of test administration; 3) diagnostic speech, hearing, and psychological services performed in the nonpublic schools by public school personnel; and 4) therapeutic guidance and remedial services staffed by public school personnel and performed in religiously neutral territory (that is, not on private school grounds). A state may not constitutionally provide nonpublic schools with instructional equipment and materials or with transportation and services for field trips.

Basis: Under the tripartite test, the state provision of secular texts, standardized tests, and diagnostic and therapeutic or remedial services as described above is constitutional. The loan of instructional materials to the private schools, rather than to individual students, is excessive state aid to the advancement of religion and is unconstitutional. The state support of nonpublic school field trips is a benefit to sectarian education, rather than to individual students, and is therefore unconstitutional state aid to sectarian education. Also, the state surveillance of field trips that would be required to ensure their secular nature would result in unconstitutional church-state entanglement.

New York v. Cathedral Academy, 434 U.S. 125 (1977)*

Facts: In response to *Levitt (supra),* which declared New York's Mandated Services Act unconstitutional, the state legislature authorized what the Court's injunction had prohibited: reimbursement to sectarian schools for expenses incurred in performing state-mandated services for the academic year that largely predated the Court's decision. A parochial school brought this action for reimbursement under the new Act.

---

*For a Supreme Court ruling on another statute related to the same situation, see *Committee for Public Education and Religious Liberty v. Regan (infra).*

Holding: [6x3] Once a state statute has been held to be unconstitutional, another state statute authorizing payments for services provided under that unconstitutional statute is also unconstitutional if constitutional and equitable considerations
weigh against its effectuation.

Basis: New York's special reimbursement act is unconstitutional
because it has the primary effect of aiding religion. Even if
the reimbursement act contemplates an audit mechanism to
resolve the establishment of religion problem, this type of
detailed inquiry violates the excessive entanglement test.

National Labor Relations Board v. Catholic Bishop of Chicago, 440 U.S. 490 (1979)

Facts: The National Labor Relations Board (NLRB) began to
assert jurisdiction over private schools and universities in
the 1970s. For parochial schools that meet the NLRB's jurisdictional standards with respect to interstate commerce, its
policy had been to decline jurisdiction only when the
schools were "completely religious," not just "religious associated." In line with this policy, the NLRB certified unions
as bargaining agents for lay teachers at two groups of
Catholic high schools. The schools refused to bargain with
the unions, challenging the NLRB's exercise of jurisdiction
on both statutory and constitutional grounds. NLRB considered the schools' refusal to bargain an unfair labor practice and sought enforcement of its bargaining order.

Holding: [5x4] Schools operated by a church to teach both religious
and secular subjects are not under the jurisdiction granted by
the National Labor Relations Act, and the NLRB is therefore
without authority to issue orders against such schools.

Basis: Citing its previous church-state cases (for example, *Lemon
II, supra*), the Court pointed to the pervasiveness of religious
authority in church-operated schools and concluded that the
NLRB's exercise of jurisdiction would give rise to various
constitutional questions. In such cases, the affirmative inten-

tion of Congress needs to be clearly expressed. The Court found no intention in the legislative history of the National Labor Relations Act and thus declined to decide whether such an exercise of the NLRB's jurisdiction violates the guarantees of the free exercise clause of the First Amendment.

Beggans v. Public Funds for Public Schools of New Jersey, 590 F.2d S14 (3d Cir. 1979), *aff'd,* 442 U.S. 907 (1979)

Lower Court Holding: A state statute that provides a tax exemption for children attending nonpublic elementary or secondary schools is unconstitutional.

Committee for Public Education and Religious Liberty v. Regan, 444 U.S. 646 (1980)*

Facts: After a state statute that appropriated public funding to reimburse both parochial and secular nonpublic schools for performing various mandated services, including the administration, grading, and reporting of the results of tests, was held to be unconstitutional in *Levitt (supra),* the state legislature enacted a new statute providing reimbursement to such schools for performing various testing and reporting services mandated by state law. Unlike the earlier statute, the new version 1) did not include reimbursement for teacher-made tests, and 2) provided an auditing mechanism to ensure that only the actual costs incurred in providing the covered secular services would be reimbursed.

Holding: [5x4] A state statute that provides for payment to nonpublic schools for the actual costs of administering and grading required state-prepared tests is constitutional.

---

*This decision should not be confused with *New York* v. *Cathedral Academy (supra),* which dealt with a statute designed to provide retrospective relief to schools that had relied on the statute held unconstitutional in *Levitt.* This decision relates to a statute that attempts to revise prospectively the statute held unconstitutional in *Levitt.*

Basis: Wolman v. *Walter (supra)* controls this case. Although the Ohio statute at issue in *Wolman* is not identical to the New York statute at issue here, the differences are not significant. The state-prepared tests and record-keeping/reporting functions meet the secular purpose and primary effect test (see *Lemon I, supra)*; and the statute's fiscal arrangements avoid the excessive entanglement standard.

Stone v. Graham, 449 U.S. 39 (1980)

Facts: A state statute required the posting of a copy of the Ten Commandments, procured with private contributions, on the wall of each public school classroom. The statute further provided that each of the 16x20-inch posters of the Commandments bear a notation in small print stating that the "secular" application of the Ten Commandments is clearly seen as the basis of the fundamental legal code of Western civilization and of the common law of the United States.

Holding: [5x4] A state statute that required the posting of the Ten Commandments in every public school classroom is unconstitutional, notwithstanding that the posted copies are privately contributed and labeled as secular material.

Basis: Alluding to the tripartite test that it has developed for determining whether a state statute is permissible under the First Amendment's establishment clause, the Court found the statute not to have a secular purpose and therefore to be unconstitutional. As in *Abington (supra)*, the Court concluded that "the recitation of a supposed secular purpose cannot blind us to the undeniably religious nature of such material." It is not significant that the Bible verses in this case were merely posted on the wall, rather than read aloud as in *Abington (supra)*.

St. Martin Evangelical Lutheran Church v. South Dakota, 451 U.S. 772 (1981)

Facts: A church-sponsored elementary Christian day school and a secondary school controlled and supported by the Lutheran Synod both claimed to be exempt from paying their school employees' unemployment compensation taxes. The Federal Unemployment Tax Act* provided an exemption for "service performed — 1) in the employment of (A) a church or convention or association of churches, or (B) an organization . . . which is operated, supervised, controlled, or principally supported by a church or a convention or association of churches."

Holding: [8/1x0] Elementary and secondary schools that have no separate legal existence from a church or from a convention or association of churches are exempt from federal unemployment compensation taxes.

Basis: The language of the legislation and its history support an interpretation distinguishing between church schools integrated into a church's structure and those separately incorporated. The matter thus being statutorily settled, the Court did not consider the First Amendment issues raised by the Christian day school.

Mueller v. Allen, 463 U.S. 388 (1983)

Facts: Minnesota enacted a statute allowing taxpayers, in computing their state income tax, to deduct certain expenses incurred in educating their children. The deduction was limited to expenses incurred for tuition, textbooks, and transportation of students attending elementary or secondary schools. A group of taxpayers challenged the tax deduction claiming that the Minnesota statute violated the establishment clause of the First Amendment by providing financial assistance to sectarian institutions.

Holding: [5x4] A state statute that allows state taxpayers, in computing their state income tax, to deduct expenses incurred in providing tuition, textbooks, and transportation for their

---

*For a subsequent decision concerning another part of this statute, see *California* v. *Grace Brethren Church (infra)*.

children attending an elementary or secondary school does not violate the establishment clause.

Basis: The Court applied the tripartite test from previous precedents (for example, *Lemon I, supra*). The statute's presumed secular purpose was to facilitate the education of the state's citizenry. The statute's effect was found to be facially neutral in three important respects: 1) its deduction for educational expenses was among several other deductions, 2) it was available to both public and nonpublic school parents, and 3) it provided assistance directly to the parents, rather than to the schools. The statute's effect also was found to be neutral in application; the Court was loath to consider statistics regarding usage, especially given the public benefits of private schools. Finally, the fact that state officials had to determine whether particular textbooks qualify for the tax deduction was not deemed to be a source of comprehensive, discriminating, and continuing state surveillance and therefore did not constitute excessive entanglement.

Wallace v. Jaffree, 705 F.2d 1526 (5th Cir. 1985), *aff'd,* 466 U.S. 924 (1985)

Lower Court Holding: A state statute authorizing oral organized school prayer violates the First Amendment's establishment clause.

Wallace v. Jaffree, 472 U.S. 38 (1985)

Facts: The Alabama Legislature passed a statute authorizing a daily one-minute period of silence in public schools "for meditation or voluntary prayer." An Alabama resident filed a complaint on behalf of his three minor children, alleging that the statute violated the establishment clause of the First Amendment.

Holding: [4/2x3] A silent meditation statute that does not have a clearly secular purpose violates the establishment clause of the First Amendment.

Basis: The Court ruled that the statute failed the first prong of the tripartite test, finding it to have no secular purpose at all. This finding was based on unrebutted evidence of legislative intent and the inclusion of the words, "or voluntary prayer," in the legislation.

Grand Rapids School District v. Ball, 473 U.S. 373 (1985)*

Facts: A school district adopted two programs, "shared time" and "community education," that provided classes to nonpublic school students at public expense in classrooms located in and leased from the nonpublic schools. The shared time program offered supplementary courses during the school day, while the community education program offered courses at the end of the regular school day. The shared time teachers were full-time employees of the public schools, but a significant portion of them formerly taught in nonpublic schools. The community education teachers were part-time public school employees who were usually otherwise employed full-time by the same nonpublic school in which their community education classes were held. Of the 41 nonpublic schools served by those programs, 40 were parochial. Taxpayers brought suit alleging that these two programs violated the establishment clause.

Holding: [5/1x3] Programs for children enrolled in nonpublic, predominantly parochial schools in which classes are financed by the public school system, taught by teachers hired by the public school system, and conducted in "leased" classrooms in the nonpublic schools are unconstitutional.

Basis: The Court ruled that the programs passed the first prong but violated the second prong of the tripartite test. The programs had the effect of promoting religion in three ways:

---

*Reversed, as to "shared time" program by *Agostini* v. *Felton (infra).*

1) the state-paid instructors, influenced by the pervasively sectarian nature of the religious schools in which they worked, may subtly or overtly indoctrinate the students in particular religious tenets at public expense; 2) the symbolic union of church and state inherent in the provision of secular, state-provided instruction in the religious school buildings threatened to convey a message of state support for religion to students and to the general public; and 3) the programs in effect subsidized the religious functions of the parochial schools by taking over a substantial portion of their responsibility for teaching secular subjects.

Aguilar v. Felton, 473 U.S. 402 (1985)*

Facts: New York City used federal funds received under the Title I program of the Elementary and Secondary Education Act to pay the salaries of public school employees who taught deprived children from low-income families in public and parochial schools. Taxpayers challenged the city's use of federal funds to finance programs that involved sending public school teachers and other professionals into religious schools to provide remedial instruction, as well as clinical and guidance services, alleging a violation of the establishment clause.

Holding: [6x3] A publicly funded educational program for parochial school students that involves pervasive monitoring and administration by public school authorities is unconstitutional.

Basis: The Court ruled that the program failed the third prong of the tripartite test. 1) The aid was provided in a pervasively sectarian environment. 2) Because assistance was provided in the form of teachers, ongoing inspection was required to ensure the absence of a religious message. 3) Administrative personnel from the public and parochial school systems had to work together, and the program necessitated frequent

---

*Reversed by *Agostini* v. *Felton (infra).*

contacts between the regular parochial school teachers and the remedial teachers.

Edwards v. Aguillard, 482 U.S. 578 (1987)

Facts: Louisiana's legislature passed the "Balanced Treatment for Creation-Science and Evolution-Science in Public School Instruction Act." The Act did not require the teaching of either theory unless the other was taught. It also provided special protections for the teaching of creation-science. A group of parents, teachers, and religious leaders challenged the constitutionality of the Act on its face. School authorities charged with implementing the Act defended it on the ground that its stated purpose was to protect a legitimate secular interest: academic freedom.

Holding: [5/2x2] A prohibition of the teaching of the theory of evolution in public schools unless accompanied by instruction in creation-science violates the establishment clause.

Basis: The Court found that the Act lacked a clear secular purpose, thus violating the first prong of the tripartite test. Making an analogy to *Wallace* v. *Jaffree (supra)*, the Court did not regard the Act as furthering its stated purpose, even if "academic freedom" were read broadly to mean teaching all of the relevant evidence, because the Act did not grant additional teacher flexibility and because its provisions evidenced a discriminatory preference for the teaching of creation-science and against the teaching of evolution. Citing *Stone (supra)*, *Abington (supra)*, and *Epperson (infra)*, the Court also regarded as being relevant the fluctuating religious climate in society. Finally, the Court relied on legislative history, particularly statements made by the Act's sponsor during pre-enactment hearings, rather than the post-enactment testimony of outside experts.

Bowen v. Kendrick, 487 U.S. 589 (1988)

Facts: Taxpayers, clergymen, and a religious organization challenged the constitutionality of the Adolescent Family Life

Act (AFLA) under the religion clauses of the First Amendment. The AFLA authorizes federal grants to public or private nonprofit organizations that provide services and research in the area of premarital adolescent sexual relations and pregnancy. It also provides that: 1) a grantee must furnish certain services, including counseling and education relating to family life and adolescent premarital sexual relations; 2) the complexity of the problem requires the involvement of religious and charitable organizations in the private sector; and 3) grantees may not use funds for certain purposes, including family planning and the promotion of abortion. The recipients include religious denominations.

Holding: [5/2x4] The AFLA does not violate the establishment clause.

Basis: Under the first prong of the three-part *Lemon* test, AFLA has a valid secular purpose. On its face, the Act was motivated primarily, if not entirely, by the legitimate goal of eliminating social and economic problems caused by teenage sexuality, pregnancy, and parenthood. Although the Act increased the role of religious organizations, the challenged provisions were motivated by other, secular concerns, such as enlisting private-sector groups to enhance community participation. As for the second prong, the Act does not have the primary effect of advancing religion. It authorizes grants to institutions that are capable of providing services. The Act does not require grantees to be affiliated with any religion, and the services provided are not religious. The third prong was not at issue.

County of Allegheny v. American Civil Liberties Union, 492 U.S. 573 (1989)

Facts: A city presents two holiday displays each year on public property. The first is a crêche depicting the Christian nativity scene, which was placed on the county court house grounds. Its manger included an angel holding a banner proclaiming,

"Glory to God in the Highest." A sign near the crèche clarified that a Catholic organization donated it. The second display was an 18-foot Chanukah menorah provided by a Jewish organization and placed outside the city-county building next to a 45-foot Christmas tree. At the foot of the tree was a sign that bore the mayor's name and proclaimed the city's "Salute to Liberty." The menorah, while owned by a Jewish group, is stored, erected, and removed every year by the city. A civil liberties organization sought an injunction against the governmental agencies, asserting that the displays violated the establishment clause of the First Amendment.

Holding: [5x4] A municipality's menorah and crèche displays are permissible under the establishment clause.

Basis: The test set forth in *Lemon* prohibits the primary effect of a governmental practice from either enhancing or inhibiting religion. The test supports the conclusion that both displays are permissible in the context of the holiday season. The requirement of neutrality toward religion does not require ending all contact between government and religion.

Board of Education v. Mergens, 496 U.S. 226 (1990)

Facts: On a voluntary basis, several clubs and groups met after school hours at a public high school. School officials denied the request of a group of students to have a Christian club meet on the same basis as other clubs, except that it would have no faculty sponsor. The students sued, alleging that the refusal to allow their club to meet violated the Equal Access Act, which prohibits public secondary schools that receive federal financial assistance from discriminating against students who wish to meet within a "limited open forum," which is defined as offering an opportunity for one or more "noncurriculum related" groups to meet on the school's premises during noninstructional hours.

Holding: [7/2x0] 1) The Equal Access Act does not violate the establishment clause. 2) "Noncurriculum related" under the

Act means that the subject matter of the group is not actually taught or will not soon be taught in a regularly offered course, the subject matter of the group does not concern the body of courses as a whole, participation in the group is not required for a particular course, and participation in the group does not result in academic credit.

Basis: 1) The Court concluded that the logic of *Widmar* v. *Vincent* (454 U.S. 263, 1983) effectively applies to the Equal Access Act. The first and third prongs of the tripartite test were easily met by the terms of the Act. The second, or primary effect, prong was met based on the maturity of high school students, the lack of official coercion during noninstructional hours, and the broad spectrum of student clubs. 2) The Court relied on the language of the Act and its legislative history to arrive at its statutory interpretation of "noncurriculum related." Applying this interpretation, the Court concluded that the school's scuba club, chess club, and special educator service group each created the requisite limited open forum.

Lee v. Weisman, 505 U.S. 577 (1992)

Facts: The school district permitted middle school and high school principals, at their discretion, to invite clergymen to offer invocations and benedictions at graduation ceremonies. A middle school principal invited a rabbi to offer prayers at the graduation ceremonies at his school. The principal gave the rabbi a pamphlet that provided guidelines for the composition of public prayers at the ceremonies and advised him that the prayers should be "non-sectarian." One of the graduating students sued the school district, claiming a violation of the establishment clause and seeking an injunction.

Holding: [5/2x4] Invocations or benedictions led by clergy at an official public school graduation ceremony violate the establishment clause of the First Amendment.

Basis: Avoiding the *Lemon* test, the Court relied on the factors of control, or direction, and coercion. The first factor was met by school officials' choices about a religious ceremony and the selection of the clergy; the pamphlet that included guidelines and the principal's advice shows that the ceremony and the content of the prayers were controlled by the state. The second factor was met by psychological and social pressure. Prayer exercises in public schools carry a special risk of coercion. Although attendance is technically voluntary, secondary school graduations in our society are, in a real sense, coercive.

Lamb's Chapel v. Center Moriches Union Free School District, 508 U.S. 384 (1993)

Facts: Under New York law, school boards may have regulations permitting school property to be used after hours for certain purposes, but not including religious meetings. The school district issued regulations allowing social, civic, and recreational uses of its schools, but specifically prohibited the use of property for religious purposes. An evangelical church and its pastor sought to use a school for a religious-oriented film about family values and child-rearing. The district rejected their request on the ground that the film was religious in nature. The church sued, claiming a violation of First Amendment freedom of expression.

Holding: [6/2x0] Refusing to allow a church access to school property to exhibit a religiously oriented film, when the school district allows other organizations access for similar purposes, violates the free speech clause of the First Amendment.

Basis: The government violates the First Amendment when it denies access to a speaker based on the views he espouses, when the subject matter is otherwise includable. Permitting an organization to show the film on district property would not have been an establishment of religion under the *Lemon* test, since the film would not have been shown during school hours, would not have been sponsored by the school district, and would have been open to the public. There would be no realistic chance that the public would perceive that the district was endorsing religion.

Zobrest v. Catalina Foothills School District, 509 U.S. 1 (1993)

Facts: The parents of a hearing-impaired child transferred him from a public school to a parochial school. They requested the school district to provide him with a sign-language interpreter for his classes in the parochial school, claiming that this related service should continue at the new location under the Individuals with Disabilities Education Act (IDEA). The school district was willing to provide the service, regardless of whether it was required under IDEA, but declined to do so on the ground that it would violate the establishment clause.

Holding: [5x4] The establishment clause does not bar a school district from providing a sign-language interpreter to a hearing-impaired student on the premises of a parochial school.

Basis: Avoiding the tripartite test, the Court used the neutrality principle to reach a relatively narrow result. More specifically, government programs that neutrally provide benefits to a broad class of citizens are not readily subject to an establishment clause challenge just because users of sectarian institutions also may receive some "attenuated" financial benefit. Here, the service provided is part of a general program that distributes benefits neutrally to those children defined as disabled under federal law, without regard to the public/nonpublic or sectarian/nonsectarian nature of the school that the child attends. By allowing parents to choose a school of their choice, the government ensures that a paid sign-language interpreter will be provided only as a consequence of the parents' individual decisions. Because the IDEA creates no financial incentive for parents to choose a private school, an interpreter's presence cannot be attributed to state decision making. Unlike the programs disallowed in *Meek (supra)*, here the state does not give direct aid to private schools.

Board of Education v. Grumet, 512 U.S. 687 (1994)

Facts: A village in New York State that is an enclave of the Satmar sect of Hasidim, a strict form of Judaism, had been part of a public school district. However, special state legislation carved out a separate district that followed village lines. Although the statute gave authority over primary and secondary schools, the locally elected board operated only a special education program. The other village children attend parochial schools that do not offer special education programs. The head of the state school boards association and others brought a lawsuit, claiming that the new district violated the establishment clause of the First Amendment.

Holding: [5/1x3] Special state legislation creating a school district, even if for the purpose of providing only special education, for a religiously separatist or homogeneous community is unconstitutional.

Basis: Although the Constitution allows the state to accommodate religions by accommodating special burdens, the statute crosses the line of permissible accommodation resulting in establishment. The result of the law is that the legislature has delegated its civic authority on the basis of religious belief, rather than on neutral principles. The special statute brings about an impermissible "fusion" of government and religion functions.

Agostini v. Felton, 521 U.S. 203 (1997)

Facts: Approximately 10 years after the trial court issued an injunction under *Aguilar* v. *Felton (supra)*, the defendant New York City school officials filed motions to seek relief from the costs of providing Title I services while also complying with the Court's strictures against providing these services on the premises of parochial schools. They cited the assertions of five Justices in *Board of Education* v. *Grumet (supra)* that *Aguilar* should be reconsidered in light of intervening precedents.

Holding: [5x4] A publicly funded program providing supplemental, remedial instruction to economically disadvantaged students on the premises of parochial schools, with proper safeguards for neutrality, is constitutional. Thus, *Aguilar* and the "shared time" ruling of *Grand Rapids School District* v. *Ball (supra)* are reversed.

Basis: The majority concluded that the Court's more recent establishment clause decisions — in particular *Zobrest (supra)* — removed the assumptions of *Aguilar* and *Grand Rapids* that all government aid that directly affects the educational function of religious schools is invalid and that any public employee working on a religious school's premises is inevitably inculcating religion. Similarly, administrative cooperation between government and parochial schools is not necessarily excessive entanglement. Moreover, the third source of the previously supposed excessive entanglement, pervasive monitoring, is no longer required in light of *Zobrest.*

City of Boerne v. Flores, 521 U.S. 507 (1997)

Facts: The Catholic Archbishop of San Antonio applied for a building permit to enlarge a church. Local zoning authorities denied the permit, relying on a historic preservation ordinance. The Archbishop filed suit, relying primarily on the Religious Freedom Restoration Act of 1993. Congress had enacted this statute in direct response to a Supreme Court decision that declined to apply the multi-step balancing test under the First Amendment free exercise clause to a state law of general applicability that incidentally burdened religious adherents.* The Act prohibited government from substantially burdening a person's free exercise of religion,

---

*See *Employment Division* v. *Smith*, 494 U.S. 872 (1990) (upheld constitutionality of a state law prohibiting sacramental use of peyote, which was used to deny unemployment benefits to Native American Church members who lost their jobs based on such use).

even from a rule of general applicability, except for a compelling interest and the least restrictive means of furthering it.

Holding: [5½/1½x3] The Religious Freedom Restoration Act exceeds Congress' power under the Fourteenth Amendment and, thus, is unconstitutional.*

Basis: The Court concluded that, based on its precedents, Congress may enact legislation enforcing the constitutional right to free exercise of religion, but its enforcement power is only preventive or remedial. In contrast, it may not enforce a constitutional right by changing the substance of what the right, as construed by the Court, is. Although Congress is entitled to deference, it may not — based on the constitutionally mandated separation of powers — infringe on the judiciary's interpretive power. For example, the Court questioned the applicability of the least restrictive means requirement. Using the widespread and persistent violations that led to the Voting Rights Act cases as an instructive comparison, the Court concluded that the Religious Freedom Restoration Act contradicted vital principles necessary to maintain separation of powers and the federal-state balance.

Santa Fe Independent School District v. Doe, 530 U.S. 290 (2000)

Facts: Prior to 1995, a student elected as the high school's student council chaplain delivered a prayer over the public address system before each home varsity football game. Individual Mormon and Catholic students filed suit, challenging the constitutionality of the practice. While the suit was pending, the school district revised its policy to authorize two student elections, one to determine whether invocations should be delivered at the games and the second to select the student to deliver them.

*See the Appendix for Sec. 5 of the Fourteenth Amendment.

Holding: [6x3] 1) A school district policy permitting student-led, student-initiated prayer at football games violates the establishment clause. 2) The case is not moot even though the revised policy has not been implemented yet.

Basis: 1) The Court found that the policy in its revised (and implicitly in its original) form violate the *Lee* v. *Weisman* *(supra)* and *Lemon* criteria. The policy controls the framework for authorizing the invocation, and the majoritarian process effectively negates the role of the reasonable dissenter. Although attendance is voluntary, some students, such as cheerleaders, band members, and the football players, are required to be there; and for the others there is undeniably high social pressure. Similarly, the purpose of the policy was to encourage and preserve the selection of a religious message, and its primary effect was the actual or perceived endorsement of this message. Finding that the pregame ceremony was not a public forum, the Court distinguished its recent ruling in a higher education case.* The Court also rejected the characterization of the ceremony as private speech. 2) Mere passage of a policy that has the purpose and perception of government establishment of religion is sufficient to defeat a mootness defense.

Mitchell v. Helms, 530 U.S. 793 (2000)

Facts: Chapter 2 of the Education Consolidation and Improvement Act of 1981 channels federal funds through state education agencies to local education agencies. Under the Act, the local education agencies, in turn, lend educational mate-

---

Rosenberger v. *Rector and Visitors of University of Virginia*, 505 U.S. 819 (1995), which held that a public university's refusal to authorize payments from its student activities fund for a student religious publication, while allowing such payments for a wide variety of other student organizations, is a violation of First Amendment speech. For a partially related decision in higher education, see *Board of Regents* v. *Southworth*, 529 U.S. 217 (2000), which held that a state university's student activities fee does not violate the First Amendment where viewpoint neutrality is maintained.

rials and equipment, such as library and media materials and computer software and hardware, not only to public schools but also to private, including parochial, elementary and secondary schools to implement "secular, neutral, and nonideological" programs. On average, approximately 30% of Chapter 2 funds spent in Jefferson Parish, Louisiana, were allocated for private schools, most of which were Catholic or otherwise religiously affiliated. Individual taxpayers filed suit, claiming that Chapter 2, as applied in this district, violated the First Amendment's establishment clause.

Holding: [4/2x3] Chapter 2's loan of educational materials and equipment to parochial schools, as part of a neutral, secular program for all k-12 schools, does not violate the establishment clause.

Basis: Citing its recent decisions in *Zobrest* and *Agostini (supra)*, the Court concluded that the Chapter 2 program met the evolved criteria of the *Lemon* test.

Good News Club v. Milford Central School, 121 S. Ct. 2093 (2001)

Facts: Under New York law, a school district adopted a policy authorizing residents to use the district's one building after school for, among other things, 1) instruction in education, learning, or the arts and 2) social, civic, recreational, and entertainment uses pertaining to the community welfare. The policy prohibits use of the school building "by any individual or organization for religious purposes." A married couple, who are residents and sponsors of the Good News Club, a private Christian organization for children ages 6 to 12, submitted a request to hold the Club's weekly after-school meetings in the building. The superintendent denied the request on the ground that the proposed use — to sing Christian songs, hear Bible lessons, memorize scripture, and pray — fit within the religious-use exclusion. The club representatives filed suit, claiming that the denial violated their rights under First Amendment freedom of expression, Fourteenth Amendment equal protection, and the Religious Freedom Restoration Act.

Holding: [5/1x3] A school district may not deny access to its facilities, if 1) its policies or practices have established its facilities to be at least a limited public forum and 2) the basis of the denial is the religious viewpoint of the otherwise eligible organization or individual.

Basis: Citing various precedents under First Amendment expression, particularly *Lamb's Chapel* (*supra*), the majority observed that the government's restriction of speech in a limited public forum must not be discrimination on the basis of viewpoint and must be reasonable in light of the forum's purposes. Because it was undisputed that the district's policy established the building as a limited public forum, the majority concluded that its denial constituted viewpoint discrimination and, thus, did not proceed to determine whether it met the second, reasonableness criterion. The majority found the only apparent difference between the club and the *Lamb's Chapel* group — that the Club teaches moral lessons from a Christian perspective through live storytelling and prayer, rather than through films — to be inconsequential. The majority also disagreed with the Second Circuit's view in this case, which was that something that is quintessentially or decidedly religious in nature cannot also be characterized properly as the teaching of morals and character development from a particular viewpoint. Rather, the majority concluded, there is no logical difference in kind between the club's invocation of Christianity and the other organizations' invocation of teamwork, loyalty, or patriotism to provide a foundation for their lessons. Also tracking *Lamb's Chapel*, the majority rejected the district's establishment clause defense, because the meetings were to be held after school hours, not sponsored by the school, and open to any student who obtained parental consent, not just to club members.

Reciting various reasons, the majority found unpersuasive the purported distinction that the students in this case were elementary school age. For example, the Court rejected possible coercion or perceived endorsement in the light of these factual limitations: the meetings were after the school day had ended, the instructors were not school teachers, and the meetings were in a secondary school classroom.

CHAPTER THREE

Student Rights and Responsibilities

Jacobson v. Massachusetts, 197 U.S. 11 (1905)

Facts: State law empowered the board of health of a city or town to require the vaccination of all its inhabitants and to provide free vaccinations if such action was necessary for public health or safety. Children who should not be vaccinated for medical reasons were excused from compliance with the order. Noting an increase in the incidence of smallpox within the city, local health officials instituted a program of mandatory vaccination. In this case, an adult resident of the city sought to have the program declared unconstitutional.

Holding: [7x2] A law that mandates compulsory vaccination in order to protect the public health and that does not require that one whose health does not permit vaccination to participate in the program is constitutional.

Basis: The Fourteenth Amendment protects persons from arbitrary state action infringing on life, liberty, or property interests. However, state laws that infringe on personal liberty but are reasonable measures taken by the legislature to protect public health and safety are constitutional. The states have a "police power" to protect public health, safety, and welfare.

Zucht v. King, 260 U.S. 174 (1922)

Facts: City ordinances provided that no child or other person shall attend a public school or other place of education without first having presented a certificate of vaccination. In accord with this law, public officials excluded a student from both public and private schools because she was not vaccinated and refused to be vaccinated. The student argued that there was, at the time, no medical situation requiring vaccination and that the law is overbroad in that 1) it makes vaccination mandatory, and 2) it leaves enforcement to the board of health without limiting the board's discretion.

Holding: [9x0] A vaccination law conditioning public and private school attendance on compulsory vaccination and leaving the operation of the vaccination program to the board of health is constitutional.

Basis: The police power of the states enables them to mandate compulsory vaccination in order to safeguard public health, safety, and welfare. The fact that the board of health is given broad discretion in the implementation of the program does not invalidate the statute.

Minersville School District v. Gobitis, 310 U.S. 586 (1940)*

Facts: The local school board required all public school students and teachers to salute the American flag as part of a daily school exercise. Two children who refused to salute the flag because of religious convictions were denied education in the public schools. They challenged the validity of the compulsory flag-salute regulations.

Holding: [7/1x1] A school board regulation requiring students and teachers to salute the American flag, even if to do so is contrary to their religious belief, is constitutional.

Basis: The First Amendment guarantees of personal freedom of speech and belief are balanced against the right of the state to legislate measures reasonably likely to promote the survival

---

*Reversed by *West Virginia State Board of Education* v. *Barnette (infra).*

of the government and good citizenship. The flag-salute ceremony is reasonably likely to support these goals; and it is reasonable for the legislature to conclude that excusing some children from the exercise would diminish its unifying, patriotic effect. In addition, the impairment of First Amendment freedoms is ameliorated by the retention of the personal right to work in an orderly and legal way for a change in the policy and to teach one's children at home or in religious school the premises and priorities of one's religious belief. For these reasons, the mandatory flag-salute law is constitutional.

Taylor v. Mississippi, 319 U.S. 583 (1943)

Facts: Under a state statute, teaching or encouraging others not to "salute, honor or respect" the national or state flags was a criminal offense. Several members of the Jehovah's Witnesses, who were convicted for expressing their religious belief that flag saluting and nationalism are unchristian, challenged the constitutionality of the statute. The literature that they distributed specifically criticized the practice of opening flag-salute exercises in public schools.

Holding: [9x0] The state may not punish those who, for religious reasons, urge and advise that people cease saluting the national and state flags.

Basis: The First Amendment, which is made applicable to the states by the Fourteenth Amendment, protects the rights of freedom of expression and of belief from arbitrary governmental intrusion. Unless accompanied by subversive intent or the creation of a clear and present danger to the government, the expression of opinion cannot constitutionally be burdened with criminal sanctions.

West Virginia State Board of Education v. Barnette, 319 U.S. 624 (1943)

Facts: Public school pupils were expelled for their failure to participate in a compulsory flag-salute program. As a result, students became liable to prosecution as delinquents and their parents became liable for noncompliance with the compulsory education law. The students challenged the constitutionality of the school board's action of conditioning public school attendance on compliance with a mandatory flag-salute program.

Holding: [3/3x3] Public school officials may not require students to salute and pledge allegiance to the flag at the risk of punishment and expulsion from school. *Gobitis (supra)* is thus explicitly overruled.

Basis: The First Amendment protects expressions of political opinion and symbolic speech. The refusal to salute the flag is an expression of opinion within the meaning of this Amendment. The Fourteenth Amendment prohibits state impairment of First Amendment rights absent a present and substantial danger to interests that the state may lawfully protect. The mere passive refusal to salute the flag does not create a danger to the state such that the First Amendment rights to belief and expression may be impaired.

Tinker v. Des Moines Independent Community School District, 393 U.S. 503 (1969)*

Facts: Three public school pupils who wore black armbands to class in order to protest the government's policy in Vietnam were suspended from school. It was not shown that substantial interference with school work or school discipline had resulted or could reasonably have been predicted to result from the students' conduct. School authorities did not prohibit the wearing of other symbols with political or controversial significance; they were interested in suppressing students' expressions of opinion about a specific subject, the Vietnam

---

*For a subsequent higher education decision that extended *Tinker* to the associational right of student organizations, see *Healy* v. *James*, 408 U.S. 169 (1972).

War. The students sought a court order restraining the officials from disciplining them and declaring the suspensions unconstitutional.

Holding: [5/2x2] It is unconstitutional to discipline students for the peaceful wearing of armbands or for other symbolic expressions of opinion unless it can be shown that material interference with, or substantial disruption of, the school's routine did or would occur.

Basis: The peaceful wearing of armbands is an expression of opinion entitled to protection under the First Amendment, which is made applicable to the states by the Fourteenth Amendment. Since students are "persons" under the Constitution, school officials may constitutionally infringe on students' First Amendment rights only when the particular expression of opinion proscribed would materially and substantially interfere with the operation of the school and the rights of other students to learn. Mere apprehension of disturbance is not a sufficient basis for such action on the part of school authorities.

Police Department v. Mosley, 408 U.S. 92 (1972)

Facts: A lone, peaceful picketer habitually demonstrated at a high school against alleged racial discrimination at the school. An ordinance that was about to become effective provided as follows:

> A person commits disorderly conduct when he knowingly: (i) pickets or demonstrates on a public way within 150 feet of any primary or secondary school building while the school is in session and one-half hour before the school is in session and one-half hour after the school session has been concluded, *provided that this subsection does not prohibit the peaceful picketing of any school involved in a labor dispute.* (emphasis added)

Since the picketer's demonstration was not related to a labor dispute, his conduct would be prohibited by the ordinance. In this case, the picketer sought to have the ordinance declared unconstitutional and to enjoin the police department from enforcing it.

Holding: [7/1x2] An ordinance prohibiting all non-labor picketing near the schools while they are in session is unconstitutionally overbroad.

Basis: Since picketing involves expressive conduct within the protection of the First Amendment, limitations on picketing are carefully scrutinized by the Court. They must be narrowly tailored to serve a substantial, legitimate governmental interest to be valid under the Fourteenth Amendment. Disruption must be imminent to validate an official ban on picketing, and the judgment as to the likelihood of disorder must be made on an individualized basis and not by means of broad classifications, especially not by means of classifications based on subject matter. Thus the Court concluded that this discrimination violated the equal protection requirement of the Fourteenth Amendment.

Grayned v. Rockford, 408 U.S. 104 (1972)

Facts: A student was arrested for participating in a demonstration in front of a high school. He was tried and convicted of violating two city ordinances. He challenged their constitutionality, claiming that they were invalid on their face. The statutes in question are as follows:

1. Anti-picketing ordinance:

A person commits disorderly conduct when he knowingly: (i) pickets or demonstrates on a public way within 150 feet of any primary or secondary school building while the school is in session and one-half hour before the school is in session and one-half hour after the school session has been concluded, *provided that this subsection does not prohibit the peaceful picketing of any school involved in a labor dispute* . . . (emphasis added)

2. Anti-noise ordinance:

[N]o person, while on the public or private grounds adjacent to any building in which a school or any class thereof is in session, shall willfully make or assist in the making of any noise or diversion which disturbs or tends to disturb the peace or good order of such school session or class thereof . . .

Holding: [8½ x ½] 1) An ordinance prohibiting all non-labor picketing near the schools while they are in session is unconstitutionally overbroad. 2) An ordinance prohibiting the willful making of noise incompatible with normal school activity and limited as to time (when school is in session) and place (adjacent to the school) is constitutional.

Basis: 1) Since picketing involves expressive conduct within the protection of the First Amendment, limitations on picketing are carefully scrutinized by the Court. They must be narrowly tailored to serve a substantial legitimate governmental interest to be valid under the Fourteenth Amendment. Substantial disruption must be imminent to validate an official ban on picketing; and the judgment as to the likelihood of disorder must be made on an individualized basis and not by means of broad classifications, especially not by means of classifications based on subject matter. This same ordinance was invalidated in *Police Department* v. *Mosley (supra).* 2) The anti-noise ordinance is not so vague as to be an unconstitutional denial of due process under the Fourteenth Amendment. It is properly limited as to time, place, and scope. It does not prohibit conduct protected by the First and Fourteenth Amendments because it punishes only conduct that actually disrupts or is about to disrupt normal school activities. Under the ordinance, the decision is to be made, as is proper, on an individualized basis.

Goss v. Lopez, 419 U.S. 565 (1975)*

Facts: Ohio law empowered principals to suspend students for up to 10 days without giving them notice of the reasons for such action or a hearing that would afford them an opportunity to explain their view of the incident in question. Several high school students, who were suspended for 10 days without a hearing of any kind, challenged the constitutionality of the statutes. They sought court orders restraining the school officials from issuing future suspensions and requiring the school officials to remove references to the past suspensions from their school records.

Holding: [5x4] Students who are suspended for up to 10 days must be accorded the following: 1) oral or written notice of the charges, 2) an explanation of the evidence if the student denies the charges, and 3) an opportunity for the student to present his view of the incident. Unless a student's continued presence in the school poses a threat to persons, property, or the academic program, the required procedures shall precede suspension. If it is necessary that the student be removed immediately, the notice and hearing must follow within a reasonable time.

Basis: The procedures applicable to short-term suspensions are required by the Fourteenth Amendment, which prohibits the states from impairing a person's life, liberty, or property interest without due process of law. 1) The students have a "property" interest in public education. Although there is no constitutional provision guaranteeing free public education, the state's compulsory education statute creates a constitutionally protected property interest. 2) The students have a

---

*For a predecessor decision, which defined due process rights in juvenile court, see *In re Gault*, 387 U.S. I (1967).

"liberty" interest in their reputation. Due process is required "where a person's good name is at stake. . . because of what the government is doing to him." The Court found that suspension could damage a student's reputation with teachers and other students and interfere with future education and employment opportunities. The temporary nature of the impairment will determine "what process is due," but will not obviate the need for some procedural protection unless the impairment of rights is negligible. Balancing the individual's limited loss of property and liberty against the government's interest in order and discipline, the Court concluded that an informal notice and hearing satisfied the requirements of due process. The Court noted that suspensions for longer periods of time may require more formal procedures, which could include legal counsel and the right to present and confront witnesses.

Baker v. Owen, 395 F. Supp. 294 (M.D.N.C.), *aff'd*, 423 U.S. 907 (1975)

Lower Court Holding: A statute allowing reasonable corporal punishment for the purpose of maintaining order in the schools is constitutional if it is administered in accordance with the following procedural protections: 1) except for acts of misconduct that are so antisocial or disruptive as to shock the conscience, corporal punishment may not be used unless the student has first been warned that the conduct for which he is being punished will occasion its use and unless other means have first been used to modify the student's behavior; 2) a second teacher or other school official must be present at the time the punishment is inflicted and must be informed, prior to its infliction and in the student's presence, of the reason for punishment; and 3) the school official who administered the punishment must provide, on parental request, a written explanation of the reasons for punishment and the name of the second official who was present.

Ingraham v. Wright, 430 U.S. 651 (1977)

Facts: A Florida statute permitted limited corporal punishment but required prior consultation between the punishing teacher and the school principal and specified that the punishment not be "degrading or unduly severe." In this case, punishment consisted of paddling two students with a flat wooden paddle. Evidence suggested that the paddling was exceptionally harsh; one student required medical attention and missed 11 days of school, while the other reported loss of the full use of an arm for a week. The students argued that the severe paddling they received constituted cruel and unusual punishment in violation of the Eighth Amendment and deprived them of a liberty interest without a hearing as required by the Fourteenth Amendment.

Holding: [5x4] Corporal punishment does not violate the cruel and unusual clause of the Eighth Amendment or the due process clause of the Fourteenth Amendment.

Basis: 1) The cruel and unusual punishment clause of the Eighth Amendment does not apply to questions of discipline in public schools but is limited to protecting those convicted of a crime. 2) While corporal punishment in the public schools does involve a student's liberty interest, the Court ruled that traditional common law remedies were sufficient to afford due process. The threat of civil suit and possible criminal action against school officials is sufficient to protect the student's procedural due process rights in corporal punishment cases.

Idaho Department of Employment v. Smith, 434 U.S. 100 (1977)

Facts: A state statute stated that "no person shall be deemed to be unemployed while he is attending a regular established school, excluding night school." A student became ineligible for state unemployment benefits when she enrolled in summer school, attending classes from 7 a.m. to 9 a.m. Her attendance did not interfere with her availability for future employment in her usual occupation as a retail clerk.

Holding: [5/1 x3] A state statute that denies unemployment benefits to otherwise eligible persons who attend school during the day, but not to otherwise eligible persons who attend night school, is not a violation of the equal protection clause of the Fourteenth Amendment.

Basis: It is rational for the state legislature to conclude that because daytime employment is far more plentiful than night-time work, attending school during daytime hours imposes a greater restriction on obtaining full-time employment than does attending school at night. Moreover, the statutory classification served as a predictable and economical means for determining eligibility for benefits.

Board of Curators v. Horowitz, 435 U.S. 78 (1978)*

Facts: A student on probation in her final year of medical school was informed of the faculty's dissatisfaction with her clinical performance and of their recommendation that she be dropped from the school unless she showed a dramatic improvement in her clinical competence, peer and patient relations, personal hygiene, and ability to accept criticism. As an "appeal" to their decision not to permit her to graduate on schedule, she was permitted to take a set of oral and practical examinations. The exams were evaluated as mostly unfavorable by several practicing physicians. Upon receiving reports of her remaining work for the year, the student-faculty council recommended that she be dropped from the school. The faculty coordinating committee and the dean approved the recommendation and notified the student. She appealed in writing to the university's provost, who sustained the school's decision after reviewing the record. The

---

*For a subsequent elaboration of this decision, see *Regents of the University of Michigan* v. *Ewing*, 474 U.S. 214 (1985).

student was not allowed a hearing before the council or the committee.

Holding: [5½/2 x 1½] The dismissal of a student from school for academic reasons does not require a hearing.

Basis: Even assuming the student was deprived of a liberty or property interest, she was accorded at least as much due process as the Fourteenth Amendment requires. A long line of court decisions concur that academic evaluations of a student are not amenable to the fact-finding process of judicial and administrative decision making.

Plyler v. Doe, 457 U.S. 202 (1982)*

Facts: In 1975, the Texas legislature revised its education laws to withhold from local school districts any state funds for the education of children who were illegal aliens. The statute further authorized local school districts to deny enrollment to these children. A class action suit was filed on behalf of certain school-age children of Mexican descent.

Holding: [5x4] A state statute that denies illegal aliens the free public education that is provided to other children violates the equal protection clause of the Fourteenth Amendment.

Basis: The equal protection clause, which provides that no state shall "deny to any person within its jurisdiction the equal protection of the laws," applies to all persons regardless of citizenship. The legislative history of and precedents relating to the Fourteenth Amendment confirm this conclusion. The mandate of equal protection requires a state to demonstrate a compelling justification to treat differentially a suspect class or a fundamental right. While undocumented aliens are not a suspect class and while education is not a fun-

---

*For a residency case involving nonimmigrant aliens in the higher education context, see *Toll* v. *Moreno*, 458 U.S. 1 (1982). For a residency case involving nonaliens in the higher education context, see *Vlandis* v. *Kline*, 412 U.S. 441 (1973).

damental right, the combination requires the government to justify a denial by showing some substantial state interest. Neither the undocumented status of these children nor the preservation of limited state resources establishes this requisite level of governmental interest.

Board of Education, Island Trees Union Free School District No. 26 v. Pico, 457 U.S. 853 (1982)

Facts: A local school board directed the removal of certain books from the high school and junior high school libraries at least in part because they regarded them as "anti-American, anti-Christian, anti-Semitic, and just plain filthy." The board then appointed a committee to review the books and make recommendations; however, the board largely rejected the committee's recommendations and determined that all the books under review should remain excluded. Several students filed suit against the school board, alleging that this action denied them their rights under the First Amendment.

Holding: [3½/1½x4] Local school boards may not remove books from school libraries simply because they dislike the ideas contained in those books and seek by their removal to prescribe what shall be acceptable beliefs.

Basis: A plurality regarded school boards as having significant discretion to determine the content of their school libraries, but in light of the First Amendment rights of students, this discretion may not be exercised in a narrowly partisan or political manner that protects official orthodoxy. In contrast, if the board's motivation was to remove pervasively vulgar or educationally unsuitable books, its action would not constitute official suppression of ideas. The plurality found sufficient evidence of improper motive to remand the case for a trial based on the board's statements and their avoidance of established, regular, and facially unbiased procedures for the review of controversial materials. The single swing vote, cast by Justice White, was narrowly based on the unresolved factual issue meriting a trial so that a proper record of factual findings may be made.

Martinez v. Bynum, 461 U.S. 321 (1983)*

Facts: Texas Education Code permits a school district to deny tuition-free admission to its public schools for a minor who lives apart from a "parent, guardian, or other person having lawful control of him if his presence in the district is for the primary purpose of attending the public free schools." A minor boy went to live with his sister for the sole purpose of attending public school in Texas. His parents are Mexican citizens who reside in Mexico and who have retained their guardianship rights. The school district denied this child tuition-free education because he did not meet the state residency requirement. The family challenged the constitutionality of the state residency requirement.

Holding: [7/1x1] A state residency requirement that conditions admission to tuition-free public schools on a primary intention other than merely attending these schools does not violate the equal protection clause or the constitutional right to interstate travel.

Basis: The Court accepted two defenses for maintaining bona fide residency requirements: 1) these requirements, when appropriately defined and uniformly applied, further the substantial state interest in ensuring that services provided for its residents are enjoyed only by residents; and 2) these requirements are important for proper planning and operations in the local control of public education. Thus the Constitution permits states to restrict eligibility for public school attendance to its bona fide residents. In previous cases, the Court has recognized a two-part definition of residence as a minimum standard to constitute bona fide residency: 1) when a person

---

*For a decision concerning another aspect of the same statute, see *Plyler* v. *Doe (supra)*.

voluntarily takes up his abode in a given place with intention to remain permanently or for an indefinite period of time, and 2) when a person takes up his abode in a given place without any present intention to remove therefrom. The Court ruled that Texas' residency requirement was more generous than this minimum standard and therefore met the criteria for being a bona fide residency requirement.

New Jersey v. T.L.O., 469 U.S. 325 (1985)

Facts: A teacher, on discovering a 14-year-old student smoking cigarettes in a school lavatory in violation of a school rule, took her to the principal's office. When the girl denied that she had been smoking and claimed that she never smoked, the assistant vice principal demanded to search her purse. After finding a pack of cigarettes, he noticed a package of rolling papers commonly associated with marijuana. His further search uncovered some marijuana, a pipe, plastic bags, a fairly large amount of money, and writings implicating her in drug dealing. Thereafter, the state brought delinquency charges against the student. The student moved to suppress the evidence and her subsequent confession, which, she argued, was tainted by an unlawful search.

Holding: [5/2½ x 1½] The Fourth Amendment does not require school officials to obtain a warrant or show probable cause before searching a student who is under their authority; rather, the constitutionality of the search depends on its reasonableness in two steps: 1) under ordinary circumstances, the search of a student at its inception requires reasonable grounds for suspecting the search will turn up evidence that the student has violated either the law or the rules of the school; 2) the scope of the search must be reasonably related to the objectives of the search, the age and sex of the student, and the nature of the infraction.

Basis: Since the basic purpose of the Fourth Amendment is to safeguard the privacy and security of individuals against arbitrary invasions by governmental officials, the Fourth Amendment's prohibition on unreasonable searches and seizures applies to the activities of civil, as well as criminal, authorities. In carrying out searches and other disciplinary functions in furtherance of publicly mandated educational and disciplinary policies, school officials act as governmental representatives of the state. However, the level of justification under the Fourth Amendment depends on the context in which the search takes place. The school setting requires some easing of the restrictions to which ordinary searches by public authorities are performed. The warrant requirement and the probable cause standard are unsuited to the school environment; requiring these standards before searching a child would unduly interfere with the swift and informal disciplinary procedures needed in schools. The school setting also requires some modification of the level of suspicion of illicit activity needed to justify a search.

The Court determined the appropriate level based on balancing the student's interest in privacy and school authorities' interest in discipline. Since a teacher had reported that the student was smoking in the lavatory, the assistant vice principal's suspicion that cigarettes might be found in her purse was a commonsense conclusion on which practical people are entitled to rely. Similarly, the discovery of rolling papers gave rise to a reasonable suspicion that the student was carrying marijuana as well as cigarettes in her purse, justifying further exploration of her purse.

Bethel School District v. Fraser, 478 U.S. 675 (1986)

Facts: A student delivered a lewd speech at a high school assembly, nominating a friend for a student office. His nominating speech was filled with sexual metaphor and innuendo, although it contained no explicit foul language. In response, some of the students hooted and yelled, and a few seemed embarrassed. The next morning the student was informed that his speech had violated a school rule concerning obscene or profane language. The student was suspended for three days and informed that his name would be removed from a list of candidates for graduation speaker. The student's father filed a civil rights action alleging that his son's First Amendment right to freedom of speech had been violated.

Holding: [5/2x2] The First Amendment does not preclude school officials from disciplining students for offensively lewd or indecent speech.

Basis: The Court balanced the student's freedom to advocate unpopular and controversial views against society's interest in teaching students the boundaries of socially appropriate behavior. A basic purpose of the American public school system is to inculcate the fundamental values of the community. The speech in question was plainly offensive to both teachers and students. The Court relied on precedent that recognized the interest in protecting minors from exposure to vulgar and offensive language.

Hazelwood School District v. Kuhlmeier, 484 U.S. 260 (1988)

Facts: Students in a high school journalism course wrote and edited the school newspaper. The principal reviewed the material prior to publication and deleted two pages containing articles on divorce and teenage pregnancy.

Holding: [5x3] Public school authorities do not offend the First Amendment by exercising editorial control over the content of student speech in school-sponsored expressive activities as long as their actions are reasonably related to valid educational purposes.

Basis: Citing the line of precedents including *Tinker* and *Fraser (supra)*, the Court reasoned that the public school setting is a special context for the First Amendment, and that a school need not tolerate student speech that is inconsistent with its basic educational mission if the speech is sponsored by the school or is part of the school curriculum. The Court distinguished this case from those requiring a wider latitude for "public forums," which are defined as facilities or media that school officials by policy or practice have clearly opened for indiscriminate use by the general public or some segment of the public, such as student organizations.

Vernonia School District 47J v. Acton, 515 U.S. 646 (1995)

Facts: Motivated by the discovery that athletes were leaders in the student drug culture and concerned with the increased risk of sports-related injuries, the school district in this case adopted a policy that authorized random urinalysis drug testing of students who participated in its athletic programs. A student who refused the testing and was thereby denied participation in his school's football team filed suit, claiming that the policy violated the privacy protections in the · federal and Oregon constitutions.*

Holding: [6x3] A school district's random urinalysis drug testing of student athletes does not violate the Fourth Amendment.

Basis: Based on its precedents, the Court treated the drug testing as a search and applied the Fourth Amendment balancing test to determine its reasonableness. On the one side is the individual's interest in privacy, which the Court viewed as limited based on 1) the individuals being public school students, not adults; 2) their lower privacy expectations in light of medical examinations and vaccinations; 3) the even lesser privacy expectations of student athletes in light of communal undress, preseason physicals, and intrusive rules; and 4) the prudent procedures for collection, analysis, and reporting. On the other side is the government's interest in

---

*On remand, the Ninth Circuit Court of Appeals subsequently ruled that the policy did not violate the parallel provision in this state's constitution. *Acton v. Vernonia School District*, 66 F.3d 217 (9th Cir. 1995).

safe and adequate education, which the Court viewed as countervailing here based on the importance of deterring children's drug use, particularly in the safety-related activity of athletics. The immediacy of the concern was self-evident, and the alternative of using individualized reasonable suspicion was problematic and not necessary.

CHAPTER FOUR

Employee Rights and Responsibilities

Meyer v. Nebraska, 262 U.S. 390 (1923)

Facts: A state law prohibited the in-school teaching of any subject in a foreign language or of any modern foreign language to children who had not yet completed the eighth grade. The law extended to both public and private school teachers. A private school teacher was convicted for teaching German to a child who had not yet completed the eighth grade. He challenged the constitutionality of the law.

Holding: [7/2x0] A state law that prohibits the teaching of modern foreign languages to children in kindergarten through eighth grade is unconstitutional.

Basis: The Fourteenth Amendment protects individuals from arbitrary or unreasonable state action impairing life, liberty, or property interests. The right to practice the profession of teacher is a right protected by the Fourteenth Amendment. The stated purpose of the restriction on the right to teach was that children who know only English through grade eight will be better citizens. However, because there is no clear danger to the state that stems from younger children studying foreign languages, the reason given is unreasonable and arbitrary and therefore insufficient to support the limitation on the right to teach.

Bartels v. Iowa, 262 U.S. 404 (1923)

Facts: This case consolidated the appeals of parochial school teachers in Iowa and Ohio who were convicted of the violation of state statutes prohibiting the teaching of foreign languages to students who had not yet completed the eighth grade. The case also included a request to enjoin enforcement of a Nebraska statute penalizing the teaching of foreign languages to young children in schools.

Holding: [7x2] A state law forbidding, under penalty, the teaching in any private, parochial, or public school of any foreign language to any child who has not passed the eighth grade is unconstitutional.

Basis: 1) The laws limiting the teaching of modern foreign languages improperly invade the Fourteenth Amendment liberty interests of teachers, parents, and students. 2) This decision is based on *Meyer* v. *Nebraska (supra).*

Phelps v. Board of Education, 300 U.S. 319 (1937)

Facts: A New Jersey law provided that teachers who had served for at least three years could not be dismissed or be subjected to a salary reduction except for cause and after a hearing on the merits of the case. In 1933, the law was amended enabling local boards to reduce the salaries of such tenured teachers. The new law prohibited discrimination in payment between individuals in the same class of service and set a minimum beyond which boards could not go in reducing salary. Pursuant to this law, a school board set up classifications and lowered salaries by varying percentages according to classification. Those in the higher pay brackets suffered a larger percentage reduction in pay than those in lower brackets. Consequently, the lowest paid individuals in the higher pay brackets received less pay than the highest paid individuals in the lower bracket. In this case, teachers challenged the validity of school board action taken pursuant to the New Jersey law.

Holding: [9x0] It is constitutional for a state tenure law to be amended to permit reduction of teacher salaries and for school boards to take action under such an amendment as long as they do not discriminate unfairly against individuals in any classification of school employees.

Basis: 1) Article I, Sec. 10, of the U.S. Constitution prohibits laws that impair contract rights. However, the Court viewed the tenure laws as a statement of legislative policy, and thus subject to modification, rather than as a contract. 2) The Fourteenth Amendment prohibits state action denying persons the equal protection of the laws. However, the Court takes as reasonable the division of personnel into classes for the application of a percentage reduction in pay. The Court, noting that all individuals in a given class are treated alike, found that the incidental inequalities resulting from the plan's operation were not sufficient to invalidate the plan under the Fourteenth Amendment.

Dodge v. Board of Education, 302 U.S. 74 (1937)

Facts: A state statute provided a $1,500 annual annuity to teachers who reached the compulsory retirement age and an annual annuity ranging from $1,000 to $1,500 to teachers who took voluntary early retirement after 25 years of service. In 1935 the statute was amended to reduce the annuity of all currently and prospectively retired teachers. In this case, teachers challenged the right of the state to reduce the annuities.

Holding: [9x0] A statute fixing terms of retirement and the amount of the annual annuity to be paid to teachers does not create a right to continuation of its terms for either currently or prospectively retired teachers and may be altered by further legislation.

Basis: Article I, Sec. 10, of the U.S. Constitution forbids laws impairing contracts, and the due process clause of the Fourteenth Amendment prohibits state impairment of an individual's vested rights without due process of law. The Court found that the statute providing for annuities was not a contract with the teachers but a policy of the state, which the state could modify by further legislation. Since the payments were gratuities involving no agreement of the parties, no vested rights accrued.

Indiana *ex rel.* Anderson v. Brand, 303 U.S. 95 (1938)

Facts: A state law required that all contracts between teachers and school corporations be written, signed by the parties, and made a matter of public record. Each such contract was to specify the starting date, duration of employment, and the salary to be paid. A subsequently enacted teacher tenure act provided that teachers who had served for five or more successive years would have tenure and could be dismissed only for cause. This statute was amended to exclude teachers in township schools from its coverage. A teacher in a township school challenged her loss of tenure caused by the amendment of the tenure act.

Holding: [7x1] A teacher tenure act creates in teachers, qualifying under its terms, contractual rights that cannot be altered by the state without good reason. The state's modification of those terms for township teachers was improper.

Basis: Article I, Sec. 10, of the U.S. Constitution prohibits laws impairing contract rights. The Court viewed the teacher tenure act as a law creating contract rights in teachers. The state can modify such rights, as an exercise of its police power, only if such modification is for the public good. The teacher tenure act is reasonable in that it protects teachers from arbitrary school board action. Because the amendment to exclude township teachers was not beneficial to the public, it was not a valid exercise of the police power.

Garner v. Board of Public Works, 341 U.S. 716 (1951)

Facts: A 1941 amendment to the Los Angeles city charter enabled the city to deny public employment to anybody who, within the five years prior to the effective date of the amendment, had advised, advocated, or taught the overthrow of the government by force or who belonged to organizations that so advocated. An ordinance passed in 1948 required city employees to swear that for the preceding five years they had not advocated or taught violent revolution, that they currently did not and would not advocate or teach violent revolution, and that they have neither belonged to nor presently belong to such an organization. Employees who refused to take the oath were discharged. They challenged the constitutionality of the ordinance.

Holding: [4/1½x3½] It is constitutional for an ordinance to require that city employees swear they have not been, are not, and will not be advocates of violent overthrow of the government or members of organizations that so advocate, provided that the penalty of discharge from employment is utilized only when membership in such an organization is knowing, rather than innocent.

Basis: 1) A law is unconstitutional if it is ex post facto, that is, if it punishes conduct that was lawful at the time it was done. The Court found that since the 1941 amendment to the city charter barred from employment those who committed the acts proscribed by the 1948 oath, the oath could not successfully be challenged as ex post facto. 2) Bills of attainder are laws that act to punish a certain group without the benefit of a judicial trial. The Court found no punishment involved in this case. Rather, the Court found that the city's standards were reasonable and that its inquiry as to matters that may be relevant to employee fitness did not offend due process of law. Since the oath was held to be constitutional, all who refused to take it and were discharged should be given the opportunity to take the oath and resume employment.

Adler v. Board of Education, 342 U.S. 485 (1952)

Facts: A New York City civil service statute made ineligible for employment in the public schools any member of any organization that advocates the overthrow of the government by force or illegal means. A list of proscribed organizations was drawn up and membership in any organization on the list was, on its face, evidence of disqualification for employment in the public schools. However, no organization could be placed on the list without a hearing. Similarly, no person could be fired or denied employment on the basis of membership in an organization without a hearing. The decision reached at the hearing was then subject to review in the courts. If the employee could show that, despite membership in a proscribed organization, he was fit to be a teacher, the sanction would not be applied. The New York courts interpreted the law to require that membership in a proscribed organization be knowing (that is, that the member knew the subversive nature of the organization he or she joined) before sanctions may be applied.

Holding: [7x3] A law disqualifying knowing members of proscribed organizations from employment in the public schools is constitutional where the presumption of unfitness to teach may be rebutted at a required hearing.

Basis: The Court found the law to be sufficiently narrow for the void-for-vagueness doctrine of the Fourteenth Amendment's due process clause because it penalized only knowing membership and provided for a hearing. The Court found no infringement of First Amendment freedom of speech and assembly since it found that employment in the public schools is not a right but a privilege that may be conditioned on reasonable state requirements.

Wieman v. Updegraff, 344 U.S. 183 (1952)

Facts: An Oklahoma statute required each state employee, as a condition of employment, to take a "loyalty oath" stating that the employee currently was not and for the preceding five years had not been a member of any organization listed by the United States Attorney General as "communist front" or "subversive." Several employees of an Oklahoma state college failed to take the oath. Although the state supreme court interpreted the statute as limited to the list of prohibited organizations in existence at the time of the statute's enactment, it denied the employees' request that they be permitted to take the oath as so interpreted. The employees sought a declaration that the statute was unconstitutional and sought an order to require state officers to pay them regardless of their failure to take the oath.

Holding: [5x3] It is unconstitutional for a statute to condition public employment on the taking of a loyalty oath based on innocent, as well as knowing, membership in a subversive organization.

Basis: 1) The decision is based on the due process clause of the Fourteenth Amendment. To be valid under this clause, a statute must require that those to be penalized have actual knowledge of which organizations are banned and of the actual proscribed purposes of any organization to which they may belong. The Court stated: "Indiscriminate classification of innocent with knowing activity must fall as an assertion of arbitrary power." The Court assumed that the oath penalized innocent as well as knowing membership, since the employees' request to take the oath as limited by the state court's interpretation was refused by that court. 2) The Court also found the statute to be an impermissible interference with the First Amendment freedom of association. To require such an oath, on pain of a teacher's loss of his or her position in case of refusal to take the oath, penalizes a teacher for exercising the guaranteed right of association.

Slochower v. Board of Higher Education, 350 U.S. 551 (1956)

Facts: Sec. 903 of the New York City Charter provided that city employees who take the Fifth Amendment before a legislative committee to avoid answering a question relating to their official conduct can be discharged from their job. A teacher in a city-operated college was discharged without notice or a hearing because he refused to answer a federal legislative committee's questions concerning his communist activities on the ground that his answer might tend to incriminate him. The local board already possessed the information requested by the legislative committee. Under New York City law, the teacher had tenure and could be discharged only for cause and only after having notice of the reasons, a hearing, and an opportunity for appeal. The teacher challenged the constitutionality of the termination of his employment under Sec. 903.

Holding: [3/2x4] A board's action pursuant to a statute dismissing a teacher due to the teacher's refusal to answer questions irrelevant to an inquiry as to that teacher's fitness to teach and without a hearing is unconstitutional.

Basis: 1) The due process clause of the Fourteenth Amendment protects the people from arbitrary state action. Since no inference of guilt can constitutionally be drawn from the taking of the Fifth Amendment and since the inquiry in question was unrelated to the board's search for information as to the employee's fitness to teach, the dismissal of the teacher was arbitrary and unconstitutional. 2) The Supreme Court did not find a constitutional right to public employment but followed *Wieman (supra)* in extending constitutional protection to a "public servant whose exclusion from such employment pursuant to a statute is patently arbitrary or discriminatory."

Beilan v. Board of Public Education, 357 U.S. 399 (1958)

Facts: A public school teacher refused to answer his superintendent's questions about his communist activities and affiliations. The teacher refused to answer even after the superintendent stressed that the purpose of the inquiry was to determine his fitness to teach and warned that his refusal to answer could result in dismissal. After a hearing, at which the teacher's loyalty, political beliefs, and associations were not at issue, the board of education found that the teacher's refusal to answer the superintendent's questions constituted "incompetency," which is ground for discharge under state law, and discharged him. The teacher claimed that the board's action was unconstitutional.

Holding: [4/1x4] A board of education's discharge of a teacher for failure to respond to a superintendent's inquiry concerning his fitness to teach is in accord with the Constitution.

Basis: The school board may constitutionally inquire into an employee's fitness to teach, and such inquiry need not be limited to the employee's in-school activity. Such inquiry is not an infringement on the employee's First Amendment rights of freedom of speech, belief, or association.

Lerner v. Casey, 357 U.S. 468 (1958)

Facts: A city employee was summoned to the office of the city's investigation unit and asked whether he was then a member of the Communist Party. He refused to answer and claimed his privilege against self-incrimination under the Fifth Amendment. Based on his refusal, the city found that his employment would endanger national and state security and suspended him. The employee was later discharged after he failed to avail himself of an opportunity to submit statements showing why he should be reinstated. The employee sued for reinstatement, alleging a violation of his constitutional right of due process.

Holding: [5/2x2] The discharge, pursuant to a state security law, of a public employee who refuses to answer questions relevant to his or her employment is constitutional.

Basis: The employee's discharge was not based on an inference of Communist Party membership drawn from the exercise of his Fifth Amendment privilege against self-incrimination, but rather on a finding of "doubtful trust and reliability" resulting from his refusal to answer questions asked by his employer and relevant to his employment.

Shelton v. Tucker, 364 U.S. 479 (1960)

Facts: An Arkansas statute required every teacher, as a condition of employment in a state-supported school or college, to file an annual affidavit listing all organizations to which he or she belonged or regularly contributed within the preceding five years. Teachers in the state school system had no tenure and were not covered by a civil service system. The statute thus required them to disclose the information to those who could fire them at will, without notice of the reasons or an opportunity for a hearing, at the end of any school year. In addition, the statute did not require that the information gathered be kept confidential. Teachers claimed that the statute unconstitutionally interfered with their personal, associational, and academic freedoms.

Holding: [5x4] It is unconstitutional for a statute to require teachers in public schools and colleges, as a condition of employment, to list all organizations to which they have belonged or contributed in the past five years.

Basis: The state has a right to investigate the fitness and competence of teachers, but the broad sweep of this statute interferes with associations that have no bearing on teacher fitness, goes far beyond what might be a legitimate inquiry, and thereby unconstitutionally impairs the teachers' right of freedom of association. This First Amendment right of freedom of association is protected from unnecessary or overbroad state interference by the due process clause of the Fourteenth Amendment. Limitation of the power of the states to interfere with personal freedoms of speech, inquiry, and association is especially important when those faced with impairment of rights are members of the academic community.

Cramp v. Board of Public Instruction, 368 U.S. 278 (1961)

Facts: A Florida statute required all employees of the state and its subdivisions to swear in writing that they had never lent "aid, support, advice, counsel or influence to the Communist Party." It required the immediate discharge of any employee failing to take the oath. A teacher refused to subscribe to the oath and challenged the statute, claiming that its meaning was so vague as to deprive him of liberty. State courts interpreted the statute to apply only to acts done knowingly.

Holding: [7x2] A statute requiring state employees to swear that they never "knowingly lent their aid, support, advice, counsel or influence to the Communist Party" at the risk of prosecution for perjury or discharge from employment is unconstitutional.

Basis: The law is so vague that it is difficult to determine what conduct is covered and what conduct is not. This vagueness violates the Fourteenth Amendment guarantee of due process of law. A statute is particularly scrutinized for vagueness when it operates, as it does here, to inhibit the exercise of freedoms affirmatively protected by the Constitution.

Baggett v. Bullitt, 377 U.S. 360 (1964)

Facts: Members of the faculty, staff, and student body of a public university challenged the validity of state statutes, passed in 1931 and 1955, that required the execution of two oaths as a condition of employment. The 1931 legislation, applicable only to teachers applying for a license to teach or renewing an existing contract, required such individuals to swear to "by precept and example . . . promote respect for the flag and the institutions of the United States . . . and the state of Washington, reverence for law and order, and undivided allegiance to the government of the United States." The 1955 legislation, applicable to all state employees, required each such individual to swear that he or she was not a "subversive person" and to disclaim membership in the Communist Party or any other subversive organization. The employee must, in taking this oath, affirm that he or she would not "commit, advise, teach, abet, or advocate another to commit or aid in the commission of any act intended to overthrow or alter, or assist in the overthrow or alteration, of the constitutional form of government by revolution, force, or violence."

Holding: [7x2] Loyalty oath statutes that are written so vaguely that they could reasonably lead to prosecution for legally or constitutionally protected behavior are unconstitutional.

Basis: While the power of a state to take proper steps to safeguard the public service from disloyal conduct is not denied, statutes that define disloyalty must not be vague in their terms and must allow public employees to know what is and what is not disloyal. In contrast, the 1931 and 1955 statutes and the required oaths based on them were unduly vague, uncertain, and broad. Therefore, they were invalid under the due process clause of the Fourteenth Amendment. Vague language is especially susceptible to constitutional attack when it threatens to impair the exercise of First Amendment rights of freedom of speech and of association.

Elfbrandt v. Russell, 384 U.S. 11 (1966)

Facts: An Arizona act that required an oath from state employees was challenged by a teacher. She based her refusal on good conscience, claiming that the meaning of the oath was unclear and that she could not obtain a hearing in order to have the meaning determined. The oath read:

> I do solemnly swear . . . that I will support the Constitution of the United States and . . . of the State of Arizona; that I will bear true faith and allegiance to the same, and defend them against all enemies, foreign and domestic, and that I will faithfully and impartially discharge the duties of the Office of (name of office).

Anyone taking the oath was subject to prosecution for perjury and to discharge from office if he or she knowingly and willfully became or remained a member of the Communist Party or any other organization that advocated the overthrow of the government.

Holding: [5x4] A loyalty oath statute that attaches sanctions to membership without requiring the "specific intent" to further the illegal aims of the organization is unconstitutional.

Basis: The due process clause of the Fourteenth Amendment requires that a statute infringing on protected constitutional rights, in this case freedom of political association, be narrowly drawn to define and punish specific conduct constituting a clear and present danger to a substantial interest of the state. Those who join an organization without sharing in its unlawful purpose pose no threat to constitutional government.

Keyishian v. Board of Regents, 385 U.S. 589 (1967)

Facts: New York had a complicated network of laws providing for the discharge of employees of the state education system who utter "treasonable" or "seditious" words, do "treasonable" or "seditious" acts, advocate or distribute written material in support of violent revolution, or belong to "subversive" organizations. Faculty and staff members of the State University of New York refused to certify that they were not and had not been members of "subversive" organizations and therefore were faced with discharge from their jobs. They sought to have the New York teacher loyalty laws and regulations declared unconstitutional .

Holding: [5x4] Loyalty oath statutes that make membership in an organization, as such, sufficient for termination of employment are unconstitutionally overbroad. To be valid, a loyalty law must be limited to knowing, active members who help to pursue the illegal goals of the subversive organization.

Basis: The opinion is based on the First Amendment freedoms of speech and association. The Court gives these safeguards particular importance when the issue involved is academic freedom.

Whitehill v. Elkins, 389 U.S. 54 (1967)

Facts: A teacher who was offered a position at the University of Maryland refused to take an oath certifying that he was not "engaged in one way or another in the attempt to overthrow the Government . . . by force or violence." The oath was part of a statutorily mandated procedure for determining whether a prospective employee was a "subversive." The term "subversive" was defined by Maryland statutes to include one who is a member of an organization that would alter, overthrow, or destroy the government by revolution, force, or violence. The teacher challenged the validity of the oath.

Holding: [6x3] A statutorily prescribed loyalty oath conditioning public employment on mere membership in a subversive organization is unconstitutional.

Basis: First Amendment freedoms of speech and association are infringed by the oath's lack of clarity since it may be read to proscribe mere passive, as well as knowing, membership in an organization and support of peaceful, as well as violent, revolution. The due process clause of the Fourteenth Amendment prohibits such infringement. In addition, due process of law does not allow prosecution for perjury to rest on a vague oath.

Pickering v. Board of Education, 391 U.S. 563 (1968)

Facts: The board of education dismissed a teacher for writing and sending to a newspaper for publication a letter criticizing the board's allocation of school funds between educational and athletic programs and the board's way of informing, or not informing, the public of the "real" reasons why additional tax revenues were being sought for schools. The dismissal resulted from a determination by the board, after a full hearing, that the publication of the letter was "detrimental to the efficient operation and administration of the schools of the district" and that, under the relevant Illinois statute, the "interest of the school required" the teacher's dismissal.

Some of the statements in the teacher's letter were substantially true. Others were false but seemed to be the product of faulty research, rather than being knowingly, maliciously, or recklessly false. The teacher challenged the constitutionality of this dismissal.

Holding: [7/2x0] Absent proof of false statements knowingly or recklessly made, a teacher's exercise of his or her right to speak on issues of public importance (for example, on the raising and disbursement of funds for education) may not be the basis for dismissal from public employment.

Basis: The teacher's First Amendment right to freedom of expression is balanced against the state interest in efficient public schools. Where a teacher's comments deal with a matter of public interest and do not impair the day-to-day operation of the schools or the performance of duties, dismissal based on such comments violates the teacher's First Amendment rights, since the teacher is entitled to the same protection under that Amendment that any other member of the general public would have. The Court did not decide whether a statement that was knowingly or recklessly false would, if not proven to have harmful effects, still be protected by the First Amendment.

Maryland v. Wirtz, 392 U.S. 183 (1968)*

Facts: The Fair Labor Standards Act of 1938 required every employer to pay each of his employees "engaged in commerce or in the production of goods for commerce" certain minimum wages and overtime pay. The original Act's definition of "employer" excluded the federal and state governments. In 1961, the Act's coverage was extended beyond employees directly connected with interstate commerce to include all employees of enterprises engaged in commerce or in production for commerce. In 1966, the Act's definition of

---

*Reversed by *National League of Cities v. Usery (infra)*, which in turn was overruled by *Garcia (infra)*.

"employer" was modified to remove the exemption for states and their subdivisions with respect to employees of hospitals, institutions, and schools. In this case, 28 states and a school district challenged the validity of these amendments.

Holding: [7x2] The amendments to the Fair Labor Standards Act, which extend the Act's application to school employees, are constitutional.

Basis: The Court found the Act and its "enterprise" concept to be clearly within the power of Congress under the commerce clause. It is a rational regulation of activities that have a substantial effect on interstate commerce and on national labor conditions. The amount of congressional interference is minimal, extending only to wages and hours. The argument that the Tenth Amendment prohibits such interference with the states was rejected by the majority.

Epperson v. Arkansas, 393 U.S. 97 (1968)

Facts: An Arkansas statute prohibited teachers in any state-supported school from teaching the Darwinian theory of the evolution of man. Violators faced dismissal from their jobs. A school district's biology text contained a chapter on the proscribed theory. A teacher at the high school sought to have the statute invalidated so that she could include the chapter on evolution in her program of instruction.

Holding: [6/3x0] A law forbidding the teaching of the Darwinian theory of the evolution of man is unconstitutional.

Basis: The statute violates the First Amendment's prohibition of state establishment of religion as incorporated through the Fourteenth Amendment. The purpose of the statute was not to excise all discussion of evolution from the curriculum but to proscribe a discussion of the subject that was considered by a religious group to be in conflict with the Bible. Such state action is not within the bounds of neutrality toward religion required by the First Amendment.

Connell v. Higginbotham, 403 U.S. 207 (1971)

Facts: A teacher was dismissed for her failure to sign a loyalty oath that stated that the signer would solemnly swear "that I will support the Constitution of the United States and of the State of Florida" and "that I do not believe in the overthrow of the Government of the United States or of the State of Florida by force or violence." She challenged the constitutionality of the two clauses.

Holding: [5/3½ x 1½] 1) A loyalty oath provision conditioning public employment on the employee's required affirmation that he or she will support the federal and state constitutions is valid. 2) A provision requiring a public employee to swear that he or she does not believe in the violent overthrow of the federal or state government is invalid where it provides for dismissal without a hearing.

Basis: 1) Oaths that are prospectively promissory, and which do not require specific future acts, are not unconstitutional infringements on First Amendment rights of freedom of speech and association. 2) The majority found that mere refusal to take the oath is not irrebuttable proof of unfitness to teach. Thus the statute's provision for dismissal without a hearing offends the due process clause of the Fourteenth Amendment.

Cole v. Richardson, 405 U.S. 676 (1972)

Facts: In Massachusetts a public employee was discharged because she refused to subscribe to the following loyalty oath:

> I do solemnly swear . . . that I will uphold and defend the Constitution of the United States . . . and the Constitution of the Commonwealth of Massachusetts and that I *will* oppose the overthrow of the government of the United States or this Commonwealth by force, violence or by any illegal or unconstitutional method. (emphasis added)

The employee claimed that the oath is unconstitutional and sought to have its application enjoined.

Holding: [2/2x3] 1) A loyalty oath required for public employment that is addressed to future rather than to past conduct and that speaks in general rather than in specific terms is constitutional. 2) An employee refusing to take a constitutional oath has no right to a hearing prior to discharge from employment.

Basis: 1) The First Amendment freedoms of speech and association are not impaired by the oath since it does not bar past, present, or future membership in any organization or past expressions of opinion or belief. The Court found the oath to not require that specific action be taken in an actual or hypothetical future situation but rather to be "simply an acknowledgement of a willingness to abide by constitutional processes of government." 2) Fourteenth Amendment due process protection of a hearing prior to discharge from employment is not required, since there is no constitutionally protected right to overthrow the government by unconstitutional means and the oath is merely an expression of a commitment to live by the constitutional processes of our system of government.

Board of Regents v. Roth, 408 U.S. 564 (1972)

Facts: A teacher was hired by a state university for a fixed term of one academic year and was later notified that he would not be rehired for the following year. State law, university regulations, and the teacher's contract did not provide for a pretermination hearing or require that reasons for dismissal be given to a nontenured teacher whose employment was not renewed at the end of an academic year. In this case, the teacher challenged the constitutionality of the state university's action in dismissing him without notice of the reasons for its decision and without a hearing.

Holding: [5x3] The state or locality constitutionally may choose not to renew a nontenured teacher at the end of a contractually fixed period of employment without providing the employee with the reasons for the decision or with a pretermination hearing if he has not been deprived of liberty or property.

Basis: The Fourteenth Amendment mandates that state action impairing a person's life, liberty, or property interest meet the requirement of due process of law. If, as in this case, no life, liberty, or property interest is impaired, no due process of law is required by the Fourteenth Amendment. The Court ruled that a nontenured teacher who is not rehired at the end of an academic year is, absent any employer's statement that would damage his reputation, free to seek other employment. A person is not deprived of "liberty" protected by the Fourteenth Amendment when he or she simply is not rehired in one job and remains as free as before to seek another.* The Court found that no state law, university policy, or term of the employment contract contained language creating an entitlement or expectation of continued employment. A teacher has no constitutionally protected "property" interest in continued employment, absent any statutory or administrative standards granting eligibility for re-employment. The Court did not decide whether the teacher had been fired for speech protected by the First Amendment.

Perry v. Sindermann, 408 U.S. 593 (1972)

Facts: A teacher in the state college system, who had been employed for 10 years under a series of one-year contracts and who was without formal tenure rights, was fired after he had publicly criticized the policies of the board of regents. The regents issued a press release stating that insubordination was the reason for dismissal but provided the teacher with no official statement of reasons. There was no pretermination hearing. The teacher challenged the validity of the regents' termination of his employment, claiming that their decision was unconstitutionally based on his expressions of

---

*For subsequent Supreme Court cases that delineate the "liberty" interest, see *Bishop v. Wood (infra)* and *Paul v. Davis*, 424 U.S. 693 (1976).

opinion on matters of public concern and also was invalid for failing to accord him the right to a pretermination hearing. Although he had no formal tenured or contractual interest in being rehired, he relied on *de facto* tenure based on language in the college's official faculty guide and in the guidelines promulgated for the state college and university system. The guidelines provided that a teacher with seven years of employment in the system is tenured and can be dismissed only for cause.

Holding: [6½x1½] 1) Teachers' public criticism of their superiors on matters of public concern is constitutionally protected and may not be the basis for termination of employment regardless of tenure status. 2) A teacher's subjective expectation of tenure will not require the administration to provide reasons and a pretermination hearing at which the sufficiency of those reasons may be challenged. However, an objective expectation of re-employment (for example, arising from rules and understandings officially fostered and promulgated by the public employer) will require that such procedural safeguards precede termination of employment.

Basis: 1) The First Amendment, made applicable to the states through the Fourteenth Amendment, prohibits state action that impairs freedom of speech and expression. A person may not be denied a governmental benefit because of the exercise of constitutionally protected rights. 2) An objective expectation of tenure creates a "property" interest in continued employment, which is protected by the due process clause of the Fourteenth Amendment. The state may not impair a life, liberty, or property interest without affording the injured party appropriate procedural protections.

McCarthy v. Philadelphia Civil Service Commission, 424 U.S. 645 (1976)

Facts: After several years of service, a public employee was discharged because he moved his permanent residence from inside to outside the city boundaries. A municipal ordinance required employees of the city to reside in the city. The employee challenged the constitutionality of the ordinance under which he was discharged.

Holding: [6/3x0] An ordinance may properly require city employees to reside in the city at the time of their application for employment and as a condition of continued employment.

Basis: There is a federally protected right to interstate travel, but this right is not infringed by laws requiring prior residency of a certain duration as a condition of eligibility and is not infringed by laws containing present and continuing residency requirements. Such rules have a rational purpose. The status of city employees who resided outside of the city at the time of the ordinance's effective date was not at issue in this case.

Bishop v. Wood, 426 U.S. 341 (1976)

Facts: A permanently employed policeman was discharged without a hearing. He was told that the dismissal was based on his failure to perform his duties adequately and on conduct unsuited to an officer. A city ordinance provided that permanent employees be given notice if their work is deficient so that they have an opportunity to bring their performance up to a satisfactory level. It also provided for dismissal for cause. There was no statutory or contractual provision for a pretermination hearing but, upon request, a terminated permanent employee was entitled to notice of the reasons for discharge. The policeman claimed a constitutional right to a pretermination hearing.

Holding: [5x4] Where, according to state court decisions, there is no statutory or contractual entitlement to continued employment and where the reasons for discharge, although damaging to the employee's reputation, are not made public, there is no constitutional right to a pretermination hearing.

Basis: In order to be protected by the due process clause of the Fourteenth Amendment, an employee facing discharge must also face impairment of a liberty or property interest by the state's termination of his employment. 1) Where the state court and local federal court decisions indicate that there is no entitlement to or expectation of continued employment such as is protected by the Fourteenth Amendment, the Court will not find a constitutionally protected property interest requiring a pretermination hearing. 2) Where the reasons for discharge, although damaging to the employee, are not made public, there is no harm done to the employee's reputation and his or her ability to find other employment is unimpaired. The employee's liberty interest under the Fourteenth Amendment is not infringed.

Hortonville Joint School District No. 1 v. Hortonville Education Association, 426 U.S. 482 (1976)

Facts: Prolonged negotiations between teachers and a Wisconsin school board failed to produce a contract, and the teachers went on strike. Under state law the board had the power to negotiate terms of employment with teachers and was the only body vested by statute with the power to employ and dismiss teachers. There was no statute providing for review of board decisions on such matters. However, there was a statutory prohibition against teacher strikes. The teachers refused repeated board urgings that they return to work. The board then held a hearing for the striking teachers and voted to terminate their employment. The teachers contended that they had been denied due process of law required by the Fourteenth Amendment because they were discharged by the school board, a decision-making body that they claimed was not impartial.

Holding: [6x3] Absent a showing of bias or malice, a local school board can validly conduct a hearing to terminate illegally striking teachers even though the board was negotiating labor questions with the teachers.

Basis: Using a balancing approach, the Court deferred to the state's interest in maintaining the allocation of responsibility for school matters that is established by statute. Where there is no showing of personal, financial, or anti-union bias, the presumption stands that the school board will fulfill the Fourteenth Amendment due process requirement of impartiality.

National League of Cities v. Usery, 426 U.S. 833 (1976)*

Facts: The original Fair Labor Standards Act of 1938 specifically excluded the states from its coverage. In 1966 the definition of "employer" under the Act was extended to include the state governments with respect to employees of state hospitals, institutions, and schools. This extension was upheld by the Supreme Court in *Maryland* v. *Wirtz (supra)*. In 1974 the Act was amended to extend its minimum wage and maximum hours to almost all employees of the states and their political subdivisions. In this case, a number of cities and states challenged the validity of these amendments.

Holding: [4/1x4] The 1966 and 1974 amendments to the Fair Labor Standards Act are unconstitutional. *Maryland* v. *Wirtz (supra)* is overruled.

Basis: In the absence of a national emergency, the Tenth Amendment forbids Congress to exercise power in a fashion that impairs the integrity of the states as governmental units or that impairs their ability to function in a federal system. The Fair Labor Standards Act, as amended in 1966 and 1974, infringes on the states' sovereignty by attempting to prescribe minimum wages and maximum salaries for state employees performing traditional governmental functions.

---

*This decision was overruled in *Garcia (infra)*.

Massachusetts Board of Retirement v. Murgia, 427 U.S. 307 (1976)*

Facts: A state statute required uniformed state police officers to retire when they reached age 50. In accord with this statute, a 50-year-old officer was retired although he was still physically capable of doing his job and did not wish to retire. He challenged the constitutionality of the statute.

Holding: [7x1] A law requiring state police officers to retire at age 50 is constitutional.

Basis: The policeman claimed that the law denied him equal protection of the laws guaranteed by the Fourteenth Amendment. To be constitutional, the state's forced retirement of 50-year-old policemen need only be rationally related to a legitimate state purpose. A standard more protective of the employees' rights would be used by the courts if employment as an officer were a fundamental right or if classifications based on age 50 were discriminatory against a minority group historically mistreated and therefore in need of extra protection. Age groups are not considered such a class. (In contrast, racial and national origin minority groups are afforded extra protection.) Since police work is physically demanding and since physical prowess diminishes with advancing age, the state regulation is rational. The state's decision not to do more individualized assessments of physical ability may not be wise, but it is not unconstitutional.

Madison v. Wisconsin Employment Relations Commission, 429 U.S. 167 (1976)

Facts: The board of education and the teachers' union, the exclusive bargaining agent, were negotiating a collective bargaining agreement. One issue under discussion was the union's demand for a "fair share" (agency shop) clause requiring all

---

*For a related case based on statutory construction, see *United Airlines* v. *McMann*, 430 U.S. 963 (1977).

teachers within the bargaining unit to pay union dues, whether or not they were union members. Wisconsin had a law prohibiting school boards from negotiating with individual teachers once an exclusive bargaining agent had been elected.

During an open public meeting held by the school board, a teacher who was not a representative of the union spoke briefly, urging that a decision on the "fair share" clause be delayed until the matter was studied by an impartial committee and until the teachers and the public were properly informed about the issue. The state employment relations commission found the board guilty of the prohibited practice of negotiating with a party other than the exclusive bargaining agent and ordered that the board cease to permit any employees other than union officials to speak at board meetings on matters subject to collective bargaining. The school board challenged this ruling.

Holding: [6/3x0] An order prohibiting teachers who are not union representatives from speaking during public meetings, if the matter they wish to discuss is subject to collective bargaining, is unconstitutional.

Basis: 1) The teachers have a First Amendment right to communicate with the board. When the board holds a public meeting in order to hear the views of the people, it may not be required to infringe on the First Amendment rights of some part of the public on the basis of employment or the content of speech. 2) The non-union teacher's brief statement was a concerned citizen's expression of public opinion and not an attempt to negotiate with the board. The union remained the sole and unchallenged collective bargaining agent. The teacher's First Amendment freedom of speech could not reasonably be curtailed as a danger to labor-management relations.

Mount Healthy City School District v. Doyle, 429 U.S. 274 (1977)

Facts: A nontenured teacher, who previously had been involved in several altercations with other teachers, employees, and stu-

dents, including an incident in which he made obscene gestures to female students, phoned in to a radio station the
substance of the school principal's memorandum to faculty
concerning a teacher dress code. The radio station announced
the adoption of the dress code as a news item. Thereafter, the
school board, on the recommendation of the superintendent,
told the teacher he would not be rehired. The board cited the
teacher's lack of tact in handling professional matters and
mentioned specifically the obscene gesture and radio station
incidents. The teacher challenged the validity of the termination of his employment based on the above-mentioned
grounds.

Holding: [9x0] In order to prevail in a First Amendment case, a
school employee must show that his expression is protected
and that it was a substantial or motivating factor in the
board's adverse action, and the board must fail to show that
it would have taken the adverse action in the absence of the
employee's protected conduct.

Basis: The First Amendment, made applicable to the states by the
Fourteenth Amendment, protects the teacher's right to freedom of speech. Since the teacher's conduct did not disrupt the
orderly operation of the school, it was constitutionally protected and could not serve as the basis for the termination of
his employment. However, by engaging in "constitutionally
protected conduct," a teacher should not be able to prevent an
employer from assessing his or her entire performance record
and from reaching a decision not to rehire on the basis of that
record.

Codd v. Velger, 429 U.S. 624 (1977)

Facts: A police officer was dismissed from employment during
his probationary training period because he put a revolver to
his head in an apparent suicide attempt. This information
was placed in a file that a later employer examined with his
permission. The employee was dismissed from his second

job and was refused several others as well. He was not afforded a hearing prior to his dismissals. He claimed that the city's failure to provide him with a hearing entitled him to reinstatement and to money damages. He did not claim that the statement in the file was untrue.

Holding: [4/1x4] A dismissed nontenured employee claiming that his or her reputation and chances for future employment have been impaired by information placed in a file and seeking reinstatement and damages because the employee was not afforded a pretermination hearing must allege that the prejudicial information contained in the file is false. In the absence of such an assertion, the employee's claim fails.

Basis: The due process clause of the Fourteenth Amendment protects a person's liberty interest in his or her good name and continued prospects for employment. Therefore, even a nontenured employee is entitled to a hearing prior to termination if the employer creates and disseminates a false and defamatory impression about the employee and the reasons for dismissal. If a nontenured employee does not assert that the information disseminated is false, then the employee cannot assert a claim for damages arising from the lack of a hearing. A hearing would be of no use to the employee in an attempt to clear his or her name, as the employee would be unable to refute the information in the file.

Abood v. Detroit Board of Education, 471 U.S. 209 (1977)

Facts: Michigan legislation authorized a union and a local government employer to agree on an "agency shop" arrangement by which each employee represented by the union must pay the union dues or, if the employee is not a union member, an equivalent amount. An employee who failed to comply faced discharge from employment. The authorized teachers' union entered into an agency shop agreement with the school board. Teachers opposed to collective bargaining for public employees challenged the constitutionality of the agreement, which forced them to support the union's collective activities. They also challenged the allocation of part of their money to the support of a variety of union activities that are economic, political, professional, or religious in nature and not directly related to the union's collective bargaining function.

Holding: [6/3x0] 1) Local governmental employment may constitutionally be conditioned on an employee's payment of union dues or their equivalent, when such funds are used by the union for collective bargaining, contract administration, and grievance adjustment purposes. 2) However, the Constitution requires that funds paid by employees as a condition of continued government employment not be used by the union for ideological, political purposes that are not directly related to its collective bargaining function.

Basis: The First Amendment guarantees of speech and belief, made applicable to the states by the Fourteenth Amendment, forbid that public employment be conditioned on the payment of union dues that are used to force ideological conformity or support of a political position.

Givhan v. Western Line Consolidated School District, 439 U.S. 410 (1979)

Facts: A black teacher was employed in a school district under a desegregation order. At the end of the 1970-71 school year, her contract was not renewed based on several reasons, including manifestations of an antagonistic attitude. She filed a complaint intervening in a desegregation suit and sought reinstatement on First Amendment grounds. In an effort to show that its decision was justified, the school district introduced evidence of, among other things, a series of private encounters between the teacher and the principal, in which she allegedly made petty and unreasonable demands in a manner described by the principal as "insulting," "loud," and "arrogant."

Holding: [9x0] The *Mount Healthy* First Amendment test is applicable to private expression. Thus, if a teacher is dismissed primarily based on her private expression of criticism to her principal of school board policies and practices, she is entitled to reinstatement if she would have been rehired but for her criticism.

Basis: The Court's decisions in *Pickering*, *Perry*, and *Mount Healthy* (all *supra*) do not support the conclusion that a public employee forfeits her protection against governmental abridgment of freedom of expression if she decides to express her views privately rather than publicly. While these cases each arose in the context of a public employee's public expression, the rule to be derived from them is not dependent on that largely coincidental fact. Nor is the "captive audience" rationale applicable; having opened his office door to the teacher, the principal was hardly in a position to argue that he was the unwilling recipient of her views. *Mount Healthy* held that if a teacher can show her First Amendment rights were violated by a school board's dismissal of her, the school board can, nevertheless, justify its dismissal if it can show it would have dismissed her anyway for independent reasons. Thus she must show she would still be employed but for First Amendment violations.

Harrah Independent School District v. Martin, 440 U.S. 194 (1979)

Facts: One of the regulations in a tenured teacher's contract required teachers holding only a bachelor's degree to earn five semester hours of college credit every three years. Under the terms of this continuing education regulation, noncompliance was sanctioned by withholding salary raises. The teacher persistently refused to comply with such regulations, resulting in the forfeiture of salary increases in the 1972-74 school years. After her contract had been renewed for 1973-74, the legislature enacted a law mandating certain salary raises for teachers regardless of their compliance with continuing education requirements. The school board, thus deprived of its previous method of sanction, notified the teacher that it would not renew her contract for the 1974-75 school year unless she completed five semester hours by 10 April 1974. She refused to comply; and after notice and a hearing, the board voted at the April 1974 meeting not to renew her contract for the following year based on the statutorily specified grounds of "willful neglect of duty."

Holding: [8/1x0] A school board's rule establishing contract non-renewal as the sanction for not complying with a continuing education requirement is constitutional.

Basis: A claim of a denial of substantive due process under these circumstances is wholly untenable because: 1) the teacher's interest is not anything like the personal matters of procreation, marriage, and family life involved in prior due process cases affirmatively decided by the Court; and 2) the board's rule was reasonably established and effectuated.

A reliance on the equal protection clause is likewise not valid because: 1) the teacher has not asserted a suspect classification or fundamental right, and 2) the board's continuing education rule is rationally related to the legitimate concern about the educational qualifications of its teachers.

Ambach v. Norwick, 441 U.S. 68 (1979)

Facts: Two unsuccessful applicants for teaching certification in New York State sued to enjoin enforcement of a New York statute that forbids aliens from obtaining public school teacher certification. Both teachers were married to U.S. citizens, had been in this country for more than 10 years, and had earned admirable academic records at U.S. colleges. The New York statute contained exceptions, including an exception where the Commissioner of Education determines a special need for the person's skills or competencies.

Holding: [5x4] A statute that generally prohibits, with some exceptions, aliens from obtaining teacher certification is constitutional.

Basis: The Court's general limitation of statutory exclusions of aliens is less strict in the area of public employment, specifically for functions that go to the heart of representative government. Thus, rather than the strict scrutiny with which the government generally views classifications based on alienage, such public interest exclusions are accorded a relaxed standard, wherein the employer need show only a rational relationship to a legitimate governmental interest, rather than a compelling justification. The role of public education, and the degree of responsibility and discretion teachers possess in fulfilling that role, supports the conclusion that public school teachers come well within the "governmental function" principle recognized in previous Supreme Court decisions. The citizenship requirement for a teaching certificate bears a rational relationship to the legitimate state interest in public education because the people of New York, acting through their legislature, have made a judgment that persons who are citizens generally are better qualified than those who have rejected the open invitation to commit their primary duty and loyalty to this country.

Perry Education Association v. Perry Local Educators' Association, 460 U.S. 37 (1983)*

Facts: A union was elected exclusive bargaining representative for the teachers in the school district. The collective bargaining agreement with the board of education provided that this union, but no other union, would have access to the interschool mail system and teacher mailboxes. A rival union brought a civil rights action against the union and the school board, alleging that the preferential access to the district's internal mail system violated the First Amendment and the equal protection clause of the Fourteenth Amendment.

---

*For a more recent ruling, where the Court refused to apply the heightened scrutiny of *Perry Education Association* to a content-neutral injunction creating a buffer zone around an abortion clinic, see *Madsden v. Women's Health Center*, 512 U.S. 753 (1994).

Holding: [5x4] A school district's preferential access system whereby the exclusive bargaining agent, but no rival union, is allowed access to interschool mail systems and teacher mailboxes does not violate the First Amendment or the equal protection clause of the Fourteenth Amendment.

Basis: The Court classified governmental forums for expression into three categories for First Amendment purposes. For "general public forums," such as parks and streets, the rights of the government to limit expressive activity are strictly circumscribed, requiring a compelling justification and a narrowly drawn, content-based regulation. For "limited public forums," such as school board meetings and state university meeting facilities, the same protection applies, but only to activities of entities of similar character to the one for which the forum was opened. For forums that have not been opened by tradition or designation for either general or limited purposes, the government need only show that its content-based regulation is reasonable and not aimed at suppressing an opposing viewpoint. The district's interschool mail system was found to be in this third category in relation to labor, as compared to civic, organizations. The exclusion of minority unions was reasonably justified by the statutory recognition of exclusive representation and by the substantial alternative channels available to the rival union. The same reasonable justification applied to and defeated the equal protection claim.

Connick v. Myers, 461 U.S. 138 (1983)*

Facts: An employee served on an "at will" basis as an assistant district attorney for approximately five years. During her tenure, she performed her responsibilities competently. After being involuntarily transferred, despite her strenuous objections, she developed and disseminated a questionnaire

---

*For a subsequent Supreme Court decision applying this analysis, see *Rankin v. McPherson*, 483 U.S. 378 (1987).

soliciting the views of her fellow staff members concerning office transfer policy, office morale, the need for a grievance committee, the level of confidence in supervisors, and whether employees felt pressured to work in political campaigns. Shortly thereafter she was terminated because of her refusal to accept the transfer and because the distribution of the questionnaire was considered an act of insubordination. Myers filed a civil rights suit, contending that her employment was wrongfully terminated because she had exercised her constitutionally protected right of free speech.

Holding: [5x4] When a public employee speaks not as a citizen on matters of public concern, but instead as an employee on matters of only personal interest, absent the most unusual circumstances, the First Amendment does not offer sufficient protection to challenge the wisdom of a personnel decision taken by a public agency allegedly in reaction to the employee's expression. Where an employee does express a matter of public concern, the public employer's adverse action will nevertheless withstand a First Amendment challenge if the public value of the statement is outweighed by the government's interest in efficiency.

Basis: Reviewing *Pickering (supra)*, its antecedents, and its progeny, the Court found full protection limited to public employee expression relating to political, social, or other speech of legitimate concern to the community. Whether a public employee's speech addresses a matter of public concern must be determined by the content, form, manner, and context of the statement as revealed by the whole record. Using this test, the Court found that the questionnaire items concerning office transfer policy, office morale, the need for a grievance committee, and the lack of confidence in supervisors were not, in this case, matters of public concern. The items dealing with pressure to work on political campaigns were a matter of legitimate interest to the community. Applying the *Pickering* balancing test, the Court found the interest of the employee in this item to be outweighed by the government's interest in efficiency, in that the questionnaire undermined close working relationships in the immediate office.

Board of Education v. Vail, 706 F.2d 1435 (7th Cir. 1983), *aff'd by an equally divided court,* 466 U.S. 377 (1984)*

Lower Court Holding: A nontenured school district employee who has an implied employment contract enforceable under state laws or who legitimately and reasonably relies on an employment promise has a property interest protected by the Fourteenth Amendment's due process clause.

Garcia v. San Antonio Metropolitan Transit Authority, 469 U.S. 528 (1985)

Facts: San Antonio Metropolitan Transit Authority (SAMTA) is a public mass-transit authority that has received substantial federal financial assistance. Because SAMTA had been viewed as performing a "traditional governmental function," it had been exempt during the past decade from the minimum-wage and overtime requirements of the Fair Labor Standards Act (FLSA). This exemption was based on a previous Supreme Court decision, *National League of Cities* v. *Usery (supra)*, which held that the commerce clause of the Constitution does not empower Congress to enforce such requirements against the states in areas of traditional governmental functions. In 1979, the Wage and Hour Administration of the Department of Labor issued an opinion that SAMTA's operations were not immune from the requirements of the FLSA. SAMTA filed an action in federal court, seeking declaratory relief.

Holding: [5x4] The commerce clause does not preclude application of the minimum-wage and overtime requirements of the

---

*This decision has negligible, if any, value as a precedent.

Fair Labor Standards Act to the areas of traditional functions of state and local government. *National League of Cities* v. *Usery* is overruled.

Basis: The Court focused on the third of four prerequisites for governmental immunity enumerated in its precedents; that is, for a state to successfully claim immunity from a federal statute, the challenged federal statute must directly impair the state's ability to structure integral operations in areas of traditional governmental functions. However, after examining how this "traditional governmental functions" criterion had been applied by both the lower courts and the Supreme Court, the Court concluded that it was difficult, if not impossible, to detect an organizing principle. Similarly, the Court concluded that any attempt to identify constitutional limitations on the scope of Congress' powers under the Constitution's commerce clause merely by relying on *a priori* definitions of state sovereignty is unworkable in practice and unsound in policy. Rather, the Court decided that the constitutional scheme of federalism provided a procedural limit to the commerce clause in relation to state sovereignty. In these cases, the internal safeguards of the political process had performed as intended by the Constitution.

Cleveland Board of Education v. Loudermill, 470 U.S. 532 (1985)

Facts: Two school district employees, a security guard and a bus mechanic, were terminated without prior notice or a hearing. Each was given a post-termination notice and hearing as required by state law, which conditions dismissal for their category of public employment on a showing of cause. Both filed suit, alleging a deprivation of their procedural due process rights under the Fourteenth Amendment.

Holding: [6/1½x1½] A public employee who can be discharged only for cause is constitutionally entitled to oral or written notice of the charges against him, an explanation of the employer's evidence against him, and an opportunity to present his side of the story prior to termination. Where coupled with post-termination procedures of a formal evidentiary hearing, the pretermination "hearing" need not be elaborate.

Basis: For the terminated employees to have a Fourteenth Amendment due process claim, they must have had a property (or liberty) right in continued employment. Under Ohio law, the individuals had a property interest in continued employment. Next, as precedent also has made clear, the amount of process that is due depends on a balancing of the competing interests at stake: 1) the private interests in retaining employment, 2) the governmental interest in the expeditious removal of unsatisfactory employees, and 3) the mutual interest in minimizing the risk of erroneous termination. The Court assessed the second factor as not outweighing the first and third, thus concluding that some form of pretermination hearing was warranted.

White v. Dougherty County Board of Education, 579 F. Supp. 1480 (M.D. Ga. 1984), *aff'd,* 470 U.S. 1067 (1985)

Lower Court Holding: A school board's policy requiring employees holding elective office to abide by the same leave policies that are applicable to all employees does not violate the Voting Rights Act of 1964.

Chicago Teachers Union, Local No. 1 v. Hudson, 475 U.S. 292 (1986)

Facts: For several years the union had acted as the exclusive collective bargaining unit for school employees. Approximately 95% of the employees were members of the union. The nonmembers had received the benefits of the union's representation without making any financial contribution to its cost. In an attempt to solve this "free rider" problem, the union and the school board negotiated an agency shop provision in the labor contract, whereby the board would be required to deduct "proportionate share payments" from the pay checks of nonmembers. The union determined that the proportionate share was 95% of union dues, and it established a three-step procedure for considering nonmember objections to the scope of the deduction. The three steps were review by the union's executive committee within 30 days; review by its executive board when appealed within another 30 days; and, if the objector continued to protest, the union president would select and provide an arbitrator. If an objection was sustained at the arbitration stage, the remedy would be a reduction in future deductions and a rebate of a portion of the past deductions found to be impermissible. Nonunion employees challenged the constitutionality of this procedure.

Holding: [7/2x0] Under an agency shop agreement, a nonmember is constitutionally entitled to have his objections to the amount of the agency fee addressed in an expeditious, fair, and objective manner. The procedure must 1) minimize the risk that nonunion employees' contributions might be temporarily used for purposes not permitted by the First Amendment, 2) supply nonunion employees with adequate information about the base for calculating the agency fee, and 3) provide for a reasonably prompt decision by an impartial decision maker. An escrow arrangement provides the first, but not second and third of these requirements.

Basis: Citing *Abood*, the Court identified the nonmembers' interest, under the First Amendment, as not being forced to subsidize ideological activity that they oppose, and the union's interest, under the applicable collective bargaining statute, as requiring all employees to provide their fair share of the cost of collective-bargaining activities. Citing its post-*Abood*, private sector decision,* the Court emphasized that a pure rebate procedure is not narrowly tailored enough to

---

Ellis v. *Railway Clerks*, 466 U.S. 435 (1984).

minimize infringement of the objecting nonmembers' interest. Similarly, the advance reduction of dues procedure was flawed because it did not provide nonmembers with adequate information to fairly address their burden of raising an objection. Finally, the three-step review procedure, as contrasted with traditional expedited arbitration, was entirely controlled from start to belated end by the union. The subsequently added escrow arrangement addressed only the first defect, for which a 100% escrow was not considered to be constitutionally required.

Garland Independent School District v. Texas State Teachers Association, 777 F.2d 1046 (5th Cir. 1985), aff'd, 479 U.S. 801 (1986)

Lower Court Holding: A school district rule that forbids teachers from discussing during school hours any teacher organization or related activity and that prohibits teachers from using school communication facilities to distribute union-related information, where collective bargaining is not authorized by state statute, violates the First Amendment.

Ansonia Board of Education v. Philbrook, 479 U.S. 60 (1986)*

Facts: A teacher was absent approximately six school days per year because his religion, the Worldwide Church of God, required him to refrain from secular employment during designated holidays. Under the collective bargaining agreement between the school board and the teachers union, teachers were permitted to use three days leave each year for observance of religious holidays; but they were not permitted to use any accumulated sick leave or personal leave for religious holidays. The teacher repeatedly requested the

---

*For a case based on the free exercise clause rather than Title VII and targeted at the unemployment board rather than the employer, see *Hobbie* v. *Unemployment Appeals Comm'n of Florida*, 480 U.S. 136 (1987).

school board to either adopt a policy allowing the use of three personal leave days for religious observance or to allow the teacher to pay the cost of a substitute and receive his full pay for the holidays he was absent. The board consistently rejected both proposals. The teacher filed suit, alleging that the board had violated Title VII's prohibition against religious discrimination.

Holding: [8x1] Under Title VII, a school board must provide a reasonable accommodation of an employee's religious beliefs if it does not cause undue hardship to the school district. But where there is more than one reasonable accommodation possible, the board does not have to provide the employee's preferred alternative. The alternative of unpaid leave is a reasonable accommodation if personal or other paid leave is accorded without discrimination against religious purposes.

Basis: The Court found no basis in either Title VII or its legislative history for requiring an employer to choose any particular reasonable accommodation. Thus, where an employer has already reasonably accommodated an employee's religious needs, the statutory inquiry is over. The employer is not required to show that each of the employee's alternative accommodations would result in undue hardship. Unpaid leave merely represents a loss of income for the period the employee is not at work, and thus has no direct effect on employment status or opportunities. However, it is not a reasonable accommodation if it is provided for all purposes except religious ones.

O'Connor v. Ortega, 480 U.S. 209 (1987)

Facts: A psychiatrist who directed the professional education program at a state hospital was suspected of management improprieties. The improprieties concerned acquisition of equipment, sexual harassment, and disciplinary actions. He was placed on administrative leave pending investigation.

During the administrative leave, the investigating team entered and thoroughly searched his office, seizing several personal items from his desk and file cabinet. Some of these items were used as evidence against him in a subsequent administrative hearing that resulted in his termination. He filed suit under Sec. 1983, alleging that the search of his office violated the Fourth Amendment.

Holding: [4/1x4] Public employer intrusions of the constitutionally protected privacy interests of their employees' offices, desks, or file cabinets for noninvestigative work-related purposes and for investigation of work-related misconduct do not require a warrant or probable cause.

Basis: The view of a majority (plurality plus a concurrence) of the Court was that public employees' generally have a reasonable expectation of privacy in the workplace, including office, desks, and file cabinets, against intrusions by not only law enforcement officials but also supervisors. However, "operational realities" (for example, policies or regulations) may reduce or remove this expectation in certain situations. The plurality balanced this employee's reasonable expectation against the government's need for supervision, control, and the efficient operation of the workplace, concluding that the standard for a public employer's legitimate work-related noninvestigatory search or investigatory searches of work-related misconduct was reasonable under the circumstances. Justice Scalia, in his swing vote, disagreed with this standard, viewing government searches to retrieve work-related materials or to investigate violations of workplace rules as not violating the Fourth Amendment whether conducted by law enforcement officials or supervisors.

Regents of the University of California v. Public Employment Relations Board, 485 U.S. 589 (1988)

Facts: The federal Private Express Statutes generally prohibit the private carriage of letters over postal routes without the payment of postage to the U.S. Postal Service. On the basis of those statutes, a public university refused the request of the union to carry unstamped letters from the union to certain of the employees, whom the union was attempting to organize. The union filed an unfair labor practice charge with the state public employment relations board. The board upheld the charge based on a state statute that required public employers to grant unions access to their "means of communication." After an initial appeal, the board found the state statutory requirement for right of access fell within the "letters of the carrier" and the "private hands" exceptions to the Private Express Statute.

Holding: [5/1x2] A public employer's delivery of a union's un-stamped letter to employees through its inter-building mail service violates the federal Private Express Statutes.

Basis: The Court rejected the applicability of the letters-of-the-carrier exception, which allows the internal delivery of mail that relates to the carrier's "current business." An organizing campaign is the union's, not the employer's, current business. The language, legislative history, and single previous Supreme Court interpretation of this exception support this narrow view. Similarly, the Court rejected the applicability of the private-hands exemption, which is limited to delivery "without compensation." Based on legislative history and previous judicial interpretation, the Court construed compensation to include the service the employer would be performing for the employees that would otherwise be paid for by them or the union.

Martin v. Wilkes, 490 U.S. 755 (1989)

Facts: Black plaintiffs and the NAACP sued a city and its county, alleging that its officials had engaged in racially discriminatory hiring and promotion practices in violation of Title VII. The trial court issued consent orders that included goals for hiring and promoting black firefighters. White firefighters sued, claiming that they were being denied promotions based on their race, in favor of less qualified blacks.

Holding: [5x4] White public employees are not precluded from challenging the allegedly reverse-discrimination employment actions taken pursuant to judicial consent decrees.

Basis: Based on civil procedure, the Court observed that one is not bound by a judgment to which he has not been a party or to which he has not been made a party by service of process. Under ordinary applications of the Federal Rules of Civil Procedure, a party seeking a judgment binding on another cannot obligate that person to intervene; he must be joined. The Court therefore rejected the "impermissible collateral attack" doctrine that immunizes parties to a consent decree from discrimination charges by non-parties for actions taken pursuant to the decree.

Fort Stewart Schools v. Federal Labor Relations Authority, 495 U.S. 641 (1990)

Facts: Schools owned and operated by the Army and housed on a military facility refused to negotiate with the teachers union in matters relating to salary and fringe benefits. The Federal Labor Relations Authority ruled that the Federal Service Labor Management Relations Statute required school officials to engage in collective bargaining with respect to these matters.

Holding: [8/1x0] Under the relevant federal statute, Department of Defense Dependent Schools (DoDDS) have a duty to collectively bargain salary and fringe benefits.

Basis: The statute defines "conditions of employment" as matters "affecting working conditions," excluding political activities. Deferring to the expertise of the enforcing agency and its reasoning that wages are a central prerequisite to accepting employment, the Court found no merit to the DoDDS claim that they are not a condition of employment.

Milkovich v. Lorain Journal Company, 497 U.S. 1 (1990)

Facts: A high school wrestling coach's team got into a fight at a match with another team. After a hearing before the state interscholastic athletic association, at which both he and the school superintendent testified, the association placed the team on probation. They again testified when several parents filed suit, resulting in a county court overturning the association's ruling. The day after the court's decision, the local newspaper published a column that implied that the coach lied under oath in court. He then sued the newspaper and its reporter for defamation, alleging that the column accused him of committing the crime of perjury, damaging him in his profession as teacher and coach.

Holding: [7x2] The First Amendment does not prohibit applying state defamation laws to a newspaper article containing an opinion.

Basis: While the First Amendment does limit the application of state defamation laws under *New York Times* v. *Sullivan* (376 U.S. 254, 1964) for public officials, the breathing space that the freedom of expression requires to survive is adequately secured by existing constitutional law. For a media defendant, a statement on matters of public concern must be provable as false before there is liability. Statements that cannot be reasonably interpreted as stating actual facts about an individual are protected. There is no wholesale defamation exemption for opinion. This decision balances the First Amendment's guarantee of free discussion of public issues with the important social values that underlie defamation law and society's pervasive and strong interest in protecting and redressing attacks on reputation.

Board of County Commissioners v. Umbehr, 518 U.S. 668 (1996)

Facts: An independent contractor was an outspoken critic of the county commissioners with whom he had an at-will contract. They voted to terminate or, at least, prevent the automatic renewal of his contract. Alleging that they did so because of his criticism, he filed a civil rights suit based on First Amendment freedom of expression.

Holding: [6/1x2] Independent contractors are entitled to First Amendment protection — as measured by the *Pickering* balancing test adjusted to weigh the government's interests as contractor, rather than employer — against governmental retaliation for their exercise of the freedom of speech.

Basis: The Court found various similarities between government employees and government contractors with respect to this issue and concluded that the pertinent differences can be accommodated by applying the *Pickering-Mt. Healthy-Connick* public employee framework. Moreover, the application of this multi-step, fact-sensitive, and deferential approach is superior to a rule that would give the government carte blanche to terminate independent contractors for exercising their free speech rights. Citing the typical "lowest-responsible bidder" requirements in a wide range of government contracting laws and policies, the majority disagreed with the dissent's assertion of a tradition of allocating such contracts on the basis of political bias. The Court clarified that on remand, 1) the independent contractor must initially show both that his speech was on a matter of public concern and that it was a motivating factor in his termination, and 2) the board will prevail if it demonstrates that its legitimate interests as contractor, viewed deferentially, outweighed the individual's free speech interests or if, in light of their knowledge, perceptions, and policies at the time of termination, the board members would have voted to terminate the contract regardless of his speech. Finally, the Court clarified, if the independent contractor prevails, evidence that board members discovered facts after termination that would have led to termination at a later time, and evidence of mitigation of his loss, would be relevant in assessing the appropriate remedy.

O'Hare Truck Service, Inc. v. City of Northflake, 518 U.S. 712 (1996)

Facts: The city maintained a rotation list of available companies to perform towing services at its request. The policy had been to remove companies from the list only for cause. However, the city removed a particular towing company after its owner refused to contribute to the mayor's election campaign and instead supported his opponent. The towing company filed suit, alleging that the removal was retaliation in violation of First Amendment speech and association.

Holding: [7x2] The established rule that government officials may not discharge public employees for refusing to support a political party or its candidates, unless political affiliation is an appropriate requirement for the job, also applies to independent contractors.

Basis: The Court found unacceptable the proposition that those who perform the government's work outside the formal employment relationship are subject to direct and specific abridgement of First Amendment rights of expression and association at their core area — political activity. Allowing the constitutional claim to turn on a distinction between employees and independent contractors would invite manipulation by government, which could avoid constitutional liability by simply attaching different labels to particular jobs. The government in this case also failed to show that applying the Court's public employee precedents to independent contractors would lead to numerous lawsuits or stifled discretion. Similarly, the Court did not accept the absolute right or compelling need for a pure patronage system.

Chandler v. Miller, 520 U.S. 305 (1997)

Facts: A Georgia statute required candidates for designated state offices to certify that they had taken a urinalysis drug test within 30 days prior to qualifying for nomination or election. The nominee or candidate selected the date of testing.

Libertarian Party nominees for state offices subject to this statute's requirements filed suit, claiming that the drug tests violated their constitutional rights.

Holding: [8x1] A requirement that specified government officials pass a drug test violates the Fourth Amendment where it does not meet the narrow "special needs" exception for "suspicionless" searches, that is, searches conducted without individualized reasonable suspicion.

Basis: Applying the balancing test for search cases, the Court found that although the government's testing method is relatively noninvasive, the government failed to show a substantial or sufficiently vital special need to override the Fourth Amendment's normal requirement of individualized suspicion. Unlawful drug use is incompatible with the discharge of public functions, but the government presented no evidence of such a problem among these public officials. Even though such evidence is helpful but not essential, the testing regime here — unlike in *Vernonia* and other Court decisions* that upheld the exception — was not well designed to identify violators or deter violations. Moreover, the officials did not perform high-risk and safety-sensitive tasks, and they are subject to day-to-day public scrutiny.

Gilbert v. Homar, 520 U.S. 594 (1997)

Facts: The state police arrested a campus policeman at a public university, charging him with a drug felony. Administrators at the university suspended him without pay, effective immediately, pending their own investigation. One week later, the criminal charges were dismissed, but his suspension remained in effect. After an additional two weeks, the administrators provided him with the opportunity to tell his side of the story to them. They then demoted him to

---

Customs Service Employees v. *Von Raab*, 489 U.S. 656 (1989), and *Skinner* v. *Railway Labor Executives Association*, 489 U.S. 602 (1989).

groundskeeper. He filed suit, claiming that their failure to provide him with notice and a hearing before the suspension without pay violated the Fourteenth Amendment due process clause.

Holding: [9x0] Fourteenth Amendment due process does not require notice and a hearing prior to suspension of a tenured public employee without pay for serious wrongdoing, provided that these procedural safeguards are provided at a reasonably prompt time after the suspension.

Basis: Reasoning that Fourteenth Amendment procedural due process is a flexible concept, the Court refused to apply the limited notice and hearing requirements for termination, under *Cleveland Board of Education* v. *Loudermill (supra)* to the lesser property or liberty denial of a suspension. Precedent dictates the balancing of three factors. First, the individual's loss of income is limited provided the post-termination hearing is sufficiently prompt. Second, the public employer has a substantial interest in immediately suspending public employees charged with felonies, at least when they occupy positions of trust and visibility. Finally, ensuring that the suspension without pay has reasonable grounds is covered by the arrest and filing of charges.

Christensen v. Harris County, 529 U.S. 576 (2000)

Facts: The Fair Labor Standards Act (FLSA) permits states and their political subdivisions to compensate their employees for overtime work by granting them compensatory time; but when the employees do not use their compensatory time, the employer must pay cash compensation under certain circumstances. A related proviso requires permitting an employee, on request, to use compensatory time unless doing so would unduly disrupt the employer's operations. Fearing the consequences of having to pay for accrued compensatory time, the local government employer in this case adopted a policy requiring employees to schedule time off in order to reduce the accumulated amount. The employees sued, claiming that the FLSA does not permit such a compulsion.

Holding: [5/1x4] Nothing in the FLSA or its regulations prohibits a public employer from compelling the use of compensatory time.

Basis: The guideline of interpretation that "expression of one thing is the exclusion of another" does not imply a prohibition against compelling employees to use compensatory time. Rather, the negative inference to be drawn from the FLSA's proviso is only that an employer may not deny a request for a reason other than undue disruption, thus ensuring their liquidation of compensatory time. Moreover, related provisions of the FLSA support this interpretation. A contrary Department of Labor opinion letter is not entitled to deference, inasmuch it is not in the form of a regulation, it is not persuasive, and the relevant regulations are not ambiguous.

CHAPTER FIVE

Discrimination: Disability, National Origin, Race, and Sex

Plessy v. Ferguson, 163 U.S. 537 (1896)*

Facts: A man who was a citizen of the United States and a resi dent of Louisiana challenged a Louisiana law that required railway companies to provide separate-but-equal facilities for whites and blacks and that provided criminal penalties for passengers who insisted on being seated in a car not reserved for their own race.

Holding: [7x1] A law requiring segregation of the races in railway cars and providing for separate-but-equal facilities for both whites and blacks is constitutional.

Basis: 1) The Thirteenth Amendment abolished slavery but is not a bar to actions, short of involuntary servitude, that neverthcless may burden the black race. 2) The Fourteenth Amendment prohibits the state from making any law that impairs the life, liberty, or property interest of any person under the jurisdiction of the United States. Although this Amendment requires equality between the races before the law, it does not require the social commingling of the races or the abolition of social distinctions based on skin color.

Cumming v. Richmond County Board of Education, 175 U.S. 528 (1899)

Facts: A state law required the provision of separate-but-equal public education facilities to children of both races. How-

---

*Reversed by *Brown* v. *Board of Education* (*"Brown I"*) *infra.*

ever, the local school board ceased operation of the high school that served 60 black students while continuing to support a high school for white girls and to aid a high school for white boys. The school board claimed its action was caused not by hostility toward blacks but by a lack of funds, which obliged a choice between an elementary school for blacks or a high school for blacks.

Holding: [9x0] It is constitutionally permissible for a school district to provide a high school education for white children but not for black children where the reason is lack of funds, rather than hostility toward the black race.

Basis: Absent the state's clear and unmistakable disregard of rights secured by the Constitution, federal interference with a state program of public education cannot be justified. The board's action in closing the black high school for lack of funds was not an arbitrary denial of equal treatment under the law such as is prohibited by the equal protection clause of the Fourteenth Amendment.

Farrington v. Tokushige, 273 U.S. 284 (1927)

Facts: Numerous private Japanese language schools challenged as unconstitutional a Hawaiian statute that required schools conducted in languages other than English or Hawaiian to obtain a written permit and to pay an annual fee of $1.00 per pupil to the department of public instruction. Other sections of the statute limited the hours of instruction, the subjects taught, and the texts used. The statute also required that students reach a certain age and level of academic achievement before being permitted to attend a foreign language school.

Holding: [9x0] A state law that gives affirmative directions concerning the intimate and essential details of private schools and that entrusts their control to public officers and denies both owners and patrons reasonable choice and discretion with respect to teachers, curriculum, and texts is unconstitutional.

Basis: The Fifth Amendment, which provides that no person shall be deprived of life, liberty, or property without due process of law, applies to the federal government and to the governments of federal territories. 1) The pervasive regulation of private schools mandated by the statute in question infringes on the property interests of the foreign language schools since it would probably result in most of them going out of business. 2) The statute infringes on the liberty interests of parents who wish their children to be instructed in a foreign language since it severely burdens and limits such instruction. 3) The statute cannot be justified by an overriding public interest and is therefore an unreasonable infringement on property and liberty interests in violation of the Fifth Amendment.

Gong Lum v. Rice, 275 U.S. 78 (1927)*

Facts: The superintendent of education of Mississippi excluded a Chinese student from attending a white school because she was not a member of the white race. The superintendent was acting pursuant to the state constitutional provision that stated: "[s]eparate schools shall be maintained for children of the white and colored races."

Holding: [9x0] No right of a Chinese citizen is infringed by classifying him or her with black children for purposes of education and by denying him or her the right to attend schools established for the white race.

Basis: A state may regulate the method of providing for the education of its youth at public expense. The establishment of separate schools for white and black students is permitted. The separation between white and yellow students is not treated differently. The decision to place Chinese students in the black schools is within the state's authority to regulate its

---

*This decision was overruled at least in part by *Brown* v. *Board of Education* (*infra*).

public schools and does not conflict with the Fourteenth Amendment.

Brown v. Board of Education, 347 U.S. 483 (1954) ("Brown I")*

Facts: Four separate cases from the states of Kansas, South Carolina, Virginia, and Delaware were consolidated and decided in this case. In each of the cases, black students sought admission to the public schools of their community on a nonsegregated basis. Kansas, by state law, permitted but did not require segregated schools. South Carolina, Virginia, and Delaware had state constitutional and statutory provisions that required the segregation of blacks and whites in public schools. State residents and taxpayers who were challenging these laws were denied relief, except in the Delaware case. The courts denying relief relied on the "separate-but-equal" doctrine announced by the Court in *Plessy* v. *Ferguson (supra)*. That case stated that constitutionally required equality of treatment is attained when the races are provided substantially equal, although separate, facilities. The Delaware court granted relief only because the schools that black children attended in that area were substantially inferior.

Holding: [9x0] Students cannot be discriminated against in their admittance to public schools on the basis of race.

Basis: The Fourteenth Amendment guarantees that students receive equal protection of the laws. The states' segregation of children in public schools solely on the basis of race deprives minority children of equal educational opportunities, even though the physical facilities and other tangible factors may be equal. Therefore, these school systems violate the equal protection clause of the Fourteenth Amendment.

---

*For predecessor decisions in higher education, see *Sweatt* v. *Painter*, 339 U.S. 629 (1950) and *McLaurin* v. *Oklahoma State Regents for Higher Education*, 339 U.S. 637 (1950).

Bolling v. Sharpe, 347 U.S. 497 (1954)

Facts: Black children in Washington, D.C. were refused admission to public schools attended by white children solely on the basis of race. They challenged the constitutionality of the segregation of the public schools of the District of Columbia.

Holding: [9x0] The federal government may not discriminate against school children on the basis of race.

Basis: The Fifth Amendment prohibits the federal government's denial of due process of law to the people. Since racial segregation serves no acceptable governmental purpose, the denial of liberty to black school children in order to achieve separation of the races is unconstitutional. The Fourteenth Amendment prohibits the states from maintaining racially segregated public schools. It is unthinkable that the same Constitution would impose a lesser duty on the federal government.

Brown v. Board of Education, 349 U.S. 294 (1955) ("Brown II")

Facts: Brown I (supra) declared the fundamental principle that racial discrimination in public education is unconstitutional. All provisions of federal, state, or local law requiring or permitting such discrimination must yield to this principle. Because of the complexities involved in moving from a dual, segregated system to a unitary system of public education, the Court here considered the suggestions of the parties involved and of state and federal attorneys general. The Court then returned the cases to the local federal courts, from which they had come, for action in accord with the guidelines below and with the *Brown I* decision.

Holding: [9x0] 1) Local school authorities have the primary responsibility for implementing the *Brown I* decision. The function of the federal courts is to decide whether a school board is complying in good faith and to reconcile the public interest in orderly and effective transition to constitutional school systems with the constitutional requirements themselves. 2) However, the principle of equal educational opportunity cannot yield simply because of public disagreement. A "prompt and reasonable start" toward full compliance must be made, and compliance must proceed "with all deliberate speed."

Basis: The Fourteenth Amendment, as interpreted in *Brown I*, guarantees students equal protection of the laws and requires that racially segregated public schools be declared unconstitutional.

Cooper v. Aaron, 358 U.S. 1 (1958)

Facts: In compliance with the *Brown* decisions *(supra)*, a school board developed a plan for the gradual desegregation of the public schools. The plan called for the admission of nine blacks to a previously all-white high school. The state legislature passed laws intended to thwart implementation of the plan, and the governor dispatched troops to keep the black students from entering the high school. The public violently opposed the desegregation of the high school, and the black students were able to attend the school only under the protection of federal troops and at serious risk to their safety. In this case, the school board sought to postpone implementation of the desegregation plan because of the severity of the negative reaction to it.

Holding: [8/1x0] Public hostility, especially when encouraged by the acts of the state legislature and other state officials, can not justify the postponement of implementation of school desegregation plans.

Basis: The Fourteenth Amendment, as interpreted by the *Brown* decisions, is the supreme law of the land; and Article VI of the U.S. Constitution makes it binding on the states. The Fourteenth Amendment prohibits state action that denies people equal protection of the law. Thus, state support of segregated public schools is prohibited by the Fourteenth Amendment.

Goss v. Board of Education, 373 U.S. 683 (1963)

Facts: Two Tennessee school boards proposed desegregation plans that provided for the rezoning of school districts without reference to race. Each plan also contained a transfer provision under which any student would be permitted, solely on the basis of the student's own race and the racial composition of the school to which the student was assigned by virtue of rezoning, to transfer from a school where the student would be in the racial minority back to the student's former segregated school. The transfer provisions clearly worked to move students in one direction, across racially neutral zoning lines and back into segregated schools. Black students challenged the validity of these desegregation plans.

Holding: [9x0] An official transfer plan that works to produce racially segregated schools and that is based on racial factors is unconstitutional.

Basis: The Fourteenth Amendment prohibits state action that denies equal protection of the law. State action creating or maintaining segregated public schools is prohibited under this Amendment.

Griffin v. County School Board, 377 U.S. 218 (1964)

Facts: In 1954, *Brown I (supra)* held that Virginia school segregation laws were unconstitutional and ordered that black students in Prince Edward County be admitted to the public schools on a racially nondiscriminatory basis "with all deliberate speed." Faced with an order to desegregate, in 1959 the county school board refused to appropriate funds for the operation of public schools. However, tax credits were given for contributions to private white schools. The students in these private schools became eligible for county and state tuition grants in 1960. Public schools continued to operate elsewhere in Virginia. The local federal court ordered the reopening of the public schools. The validity of this court order was in question here.

Holding: [7/2x0] A school board's action in closing county public schools while at the same time giving state financial assistance to white, private school students is unconstitutional. The time for "all deliberate speed" had run out.

Basis: The equal protection clause of the Fourteenth Amendment requires that the states provide equal educational opportunity to both black and white students. The closing of public schools while state financial aid is given to white, private school students in the same county denies black children equal educational opportunity and is therefore unconstitutional.

Bradley v. School Board of Richmond, 382 U.S. 103 (1965) ("Bradley I")

Facts: Plans for desegregating two school systems were approved by the local district court, although they did not contain provisions for the nonracial assignment of school teachers within the districts.

Holding: [9x0] The assignment of faculty on a nonracial basis is an important factor and must be considered in a desegregation plan.

Basis: The Fourteenth Amendment, as interpreted in the *Brown* decisions *(supra)*, requires desegregation of the public schools previously segregated by law or by state action. Racially neutral assignment of teachers, when proposed by those seeking to desegregate schools, is a factor that merits serious consideration. The Court was unable to decide on the merits of the case because the district court had not held a full evidentiary hearing on the issue. The Court remanded the case to the district court for this purpose.

Rogers v. Paul, 382 U.S. 198 (1965)

Facts: The desegregation plan adopted by the school system was a "grade-a-year" plan. This plan, which started at the lower grades, left some high school students still attending segregated classes. The black students attended a high school that did not have the range of courses offered at the white high school. Those students challenged this situation and also the allocation of faculty on a racial basis at all grade levels.

Holding: [5/4x0] 1) Where equal course offerings are not available to black students in grades that have not yet been desegregated under a "grade-a-year" plan, the black students must be admitted immediately to the white school that has a superior curriculum. 2) The racial allocation of teachers denies students an equal educational opportunity and is unconstitutional. Students seeking desegregation of the school system are entitled to a hearing at which the basis of teacher allocation can be established.

Basis: The Fourteenth Amendment as interpreted in the *Brown* decisions *(supra)* required, at this date, immediate establishment of unitary school systems in those districts previously segregated by law or by state action. The time for "all deliberate speed" had passed.

Green v. County School Board, 391 U.S. 430 (1968)

Facts: A school system in Virginia was serving about 1,300 students, approximately half of whom were black. There was no residential segregation in the county; persons of both races resided throughout. The school system had only two schools, one for whites and one for blacks. Each school served the whole county, and 21 buses traveled overlapping routes in order to transport students to segregated classes. In 1965 the school board, in order to remain eligible for federal financial aid, adopted a "freedom-of-choice" plan for desegregating the schools. The plan permitted students, except those entering the first and eighth grades, to choose annually between schools. Those not choosing were assigned to the school they had previously attended. First- and eighth-graders had to affirmatively choose a school. During the plan's three years of operation, no white student had chosen to attend the all-black school; and although 115 blacks had enrolled in the formerly all-white school, 85% of the black students in the system still attended the all-black school. The adequacy of this desegregation plan was challenged in this case.

Holding: [9x0] A "freedom-of-choice" plan, when established in a district with a long history of segregated schooling, offers little real promise that the required nonsegregated school system will be established. A desegregation plan that is ineffective must be discontinued, and an effective plan must be established.

Basis: The Fourteenth Amendment, as interpreted in the *Brown* decisions *(supra)*, requires desegregated school systems. Thirteen years after the Brown decisions, ineffective plans cause intolerable delay. Effective plans must be adopted immediately so that the Fourteenth Amendment requirement of equal protection under the law for black students can be met.

Raney v. Board of Education, 391 U.S. 443 (1968)

Facts: A school district serving approximately 880 students, of whom 580 were black and 300 were white, consisted of two combination elementary and high schools, one primarily white and one all black. The district's students and staffs were totally segregated. In order to remain eligible for federal financial aid, the school board adopted a "freedom-of-choice" plan that permitted students to choose annually between the two schools. Those not choosing were assigned to the school they had previously attended. After the plan was in use for three years, not a single white child had tried to enroll in the all-black school, and more than 85% of the black students were still attending the all-black school. During the plan's first year of operation, the number of students applying for enrollment in the fifth, tenth, and eleventh grades at the white school exceeded the number of places available; the applications of 28 black students were denied. This situation prompted a suit on behalf of the excluded students. Their complaint sought injunctive relief against 1) their being required to attend the all-black school, 2) the provision of inferior school facilities in the all-black school, and 3) the district's operation of a racially segregated school system.

Holding: [9x0] A "freedom-of-choice" plan, when established in a district with a long history of segregation, is inadequate to convert it to a unitary, nonracial school system.

Basis: The Fourteenth Amendment requires desegregated school systems. The district courts should retain jurisdiction in school segregation cases to ensure that 1) a constitutionally acceptable plan is adopted, and 2) it is operated in a constitutionally permissible fashion so that the goal of a desegregated, nonracially operated school system is rapidly and finally achieved.

Monroe v. Board of Commissioners, 391 U.S. 450 (1968)

Facts: In an effort to desegregate its elementary and junior high school systems, a city instituted a "free-transfer" plan, which permitted children, after registering in their assigned school in their attendance zone, to transfer freely to another school of their choice if space was available. After three years of operation of the plan, the one black junior high school in the system still was completely black, one of the two white junior high schools still was almost all white, and three of the eight elementary schools still were attended by only blacks. The black children challenged the adequacy of this plan and of the school board's efforts to meet its responsibility to effect a transition to a unitary school system.

Holding: [9x0] A free-transfer plan that does not result in effective desegregation is inadequate and does not constitute compliance with the order requiring the school board to carry out its affirmative duty to convert to a unitary school system.

Basis: No official transfer plan or provision that has the inevitable consequence of racial segregation may stand under the Fourteenth Amendment. If it cannot be shown that a transfer plan will further, rather than delay, conversion to a unitary, nonracial, nondiscriminatory school system, the transfer plan is unacceptable.

United States v. Montgomery County Board of Education, 395 U.S. 225 (1969)

Facts: From 1964 to 1969, the local district court worked to push the desegregation of the county's schools. The general pattern was one of tokenism and delay on the part of the school board and patience and persistence on the part of the court. The nonracial allocation of faculty was a facet of the program that especially was lagging. The trial court finally ordered the nonracial allocation of faculty and required school board compliance with definite mathematical ratios. The school board challenged the reliance on mathematical ratios.

Holding: [9x0] In view of the pattern of lagging compliance by the school board and the judge's record of fairness and patience, the need for specific goals is evident and the numerical ratios are proper guidelines for desegregation.

Basis: The Fourteenth Amendment prohibits state action denying people equal protection of the law and, as interpreted by the *Brown* decision *(supra)*, requires the establishment of nonracial school systems in those districts previously segregated by law or by state action. The effective nonracial assignment of faculty is part of this requirement.

Alexander v. Holmes County Board of Education, 369 U.S. 19 (1969)

Facts: The Fifth Circuit Court of Appeals granted a motion for additional time and delayed implementation of an earlier order mandating desegregation in some Mississippi school districts educating thousands of children. The delay was challenged in this case.

Holding: [9x0] Stating that delay can no longer be tolerated, the Supreme Court instructed the lower court to order immediate desegregation of the school districts. Modifications of and objections to the order could be considered while the order was implemented, but the implementation could not be delayed any longer.

Basis: The equality of educational opportunity required by the Fourteenth Amendment and by the *Brown* decisions *(supra)* can not be delayed. The rights of black students must be supported by the courts; delays should not be granted. Amendments to desegregation plans must be reviewed by the courts and permitted only if they will work to further the goal of desegregation.

Dowell v. Board of Education, 396 U.S. 269 (1969)

Facts: The trial court approved the school board's desegregation proposal for immediate alteration of school attendance zones and ordered the school board to submit comprehensive plans for the desegregation of the entire school system. Upon being challenged, the order approving the attendance zone changes was vacated by the court of appeals, which stated that action should await the adoption of the comprehensive plan. Black students challenged the court of appeals' decision.

Holding: [9x0] The immediate change of attendance zones to promote desegregation is permissible, pending formulation of a comprehensive desegregation plan.

Basis: The Fourteenth Amendment requires, at this late date, immediate desegregation of school systems segregated by state action. Desegregation orders are to be implemented pending appeal, as further delay can no longer be tolerated.

Carter v. West Feliciana Parish School Board, 396 U.S. 290 (1970)

Facts: Soon after the Court in *Alexander* v. *Holmes County Board of Education (supra)* vacated a lower court order granting a three-month delay in desegregation and mandated immediate action, the Fifth Circuit Court of Appeals decided *Singleton* v. *Jackson Municipal Separate School District* (419 F.2d 1211, 5th Cir. 1969). This case was a consolidation of 16 major school cases and involved hundreds of thousands of school children. The Fifth Circuit required desegregation of faculties, facilities, activities, staff, and transportation no later than 1 February 1970, but was reluctant to require relocation of these children in the middle of an ongoing school year. Therefore, it delayed integration of the student bodies until the beginning of the next school year. An order was sought to reverse the order to delay student integration.

Holding: [1/8x0] Immediate desegregation of the student bodies was required; a maximum period of eight weeks was allowed for implementation of this order.

Basis: The Fourteenth Amendment's equal protection clause requires desegregation of public school systems where such segregation is caused or supported by state action. The time for "all deliberate speed" is past. Compliance with constitutional requirements must be immediate and complete.

Northcross v. Board of Education, 397 U.S. 232 (1970)

Facts: In 1960 the federal district court approved a desegregation plan for the Memphis school system that permitted unrestricted free transfers. The plaintiff parents moved for a court order for a new plan that would eliminate such transfers and that would add complete faculty desegregation. The court dismissed the motion but ordered the defendant board of education to file a revised plan containing a modified transfer provision, a faculty desegregation provision, and a director of desegregation. After the *Alexander* decision *(supra)*, the parents moved to require a plan for a unitary system in the current school year.

Holding: [6/1x0] *De jure* segregated school districts must move at once to become "unitary" systems, that is, one in which no person is effectively excluded from any school because of race or color.

Basis: Inasmuch as substantial evidence supported the district court's finding that the school board's present and proposed plans were not effective in eliminating the state-imposed dual system, the Court ruled that it was in error for the lower appellate court to find that the district was operating a unitary system. Relying on *Alexander*, the Court ordered prompt proceedings to reach a unitary result.

Griggs v. Duke Power Co., 401 U.S. 424 (1971)

Facts: Prior to 2 July 1965, when the 1964 Civil Rights Act took effect, a power company had openly discriminated on the basis of race in the hiring and assignment of employees in one of its plants. In 1955 the company began to require that employees have a high school diploma for initial assignment to any but the lowest paid, traditionally black department and for transfer to the higher paying white departments. In 1965 the company also began to require that transferees to higher paid, white departments obtain satisfactory scores on professionally prepared general aptitude tests. It was shown that whites who met neither of these criteria had been adequately performing jobs in the higher paid departments for years. Black employees challenged these diploma and testing requirements, which tended to render a disproportionate number of blacks ineligible for employment and transfer.

Holding: [8x0] Diploma or degree requirements and generalized aptitude tests may not be used when they work to disqualify a disproportionate number of minority group members, unless the employer can show a direct correlation between the skills tested and adequate on-the-job performance.

Basis: Title VII of the Civil Rights Act of 1964 prohibits employers from using tests and diploma requirements that work to disqualify a disproportionate number of minority group members, unless such tests are shown to be directly indicative of the ability to perform adequately on the job. The requirements here in question were not shown to be directly related to job performance and were therefore invalid.

Williams v. McNair, 316 F. Supp. 134 (D.S.C. 1970), aff'd, 401 U.S. 951 (1971)*

Lower Court Holding: Where a limited number of state-supported schools, which are part of a general coeducational system, are restricted to one sex in order to further a program of education of generally greater interest to one sex, there is no constitutional violation.

Swann v. Charlotte-Mecklenburg Board of Education, 402 U.S. 1 (1971)**

Facts: A school system with a student body that was 71% white and 29% black remained largely segregated in 1969, despite a 1965 desegregation plan based on geographic zoning with a free-transfer provision. After the school board failed to produce a new plan, the district court imposed one. This plan grouped several outlying elementary schools with each black inner-city school and required extensive busing. The plan also required that as many schools as practicable reflect the 71/29 white/black ratio then existing in the district as a whole. The new plan was challenged as too burdensome.

Holding: [9x0] When school authorities fail to devise effective remedies for state-imposed segregation, the district courts have broad discretion to fashion a remedy that will ensure transition to a unitary school system. 1) District courts may constitutionally order that teachers be assigned to achieve

---

*For subsequent decisions relevant to this ruling, see, *Vorcheimer (infra)*; *Mississippi University for Women* v. *Hogan*, 458 U.S. 718 (1982), which held that a single-sex admissions policy at a state-supported university's nursing program violated the equal protection clause; and *United States* v. *Virginia (infra)*.

**For a follow-up decision, see *North Carolina State Board of Education* v. *Swann (infra)*.

faculty desegregation. 2) District courts may forbid patterns of school construction and abandonment that serve to perpetuate or re-establish a dual system. 3) Racial quotas, when used not as inflexible requirements but as a starting point for the shaping of a desegregation plan, may be imposed by the courts. Once desegregation is achieved, school boards will not be required to make yearly adjustments in the racial composition of student bodies. 4) District courts may alter school attendance zones, may group and pair noncontiguous zones, and may require busing to a school not closest to the students' homes in order to achieve desegregation. Only when the travel time is excessive will objections to busing for integration be sustained.

Basis: The equal protection clause of the Fourteenth Amendment, as interpreted in *Brown I (supra)*, forbids state segregation of public schools on the basis of race. When school authorities default in their obligation to provide acceptable remedies, the district courts have broad power to fashion a remedy that will ensure a unitary school system.

Davis v. Board of School Commissioners, 402 U.S. 33 (1971)

Facts: The metropolitan area of Mobile, Alabama, is divided by a major north-south highway. About 94% of the black students in the metropolitan area lie east of the highway. The schools in the western section were relatively easy to desegregate. However, the plan formulated by the Department of Justice and approved by the court of appeals resulted in nine nearly all-black schools in the eastern section (serving 64% of all of the black elementary school students in the metropolitan area). In addition, more than half of the black junior and senior high school students in metropolitan Mobile were attending all- or nearly all-black schools. The plan that resulted in this number of black schools dealt separately with the eastern and western sections and did not provide for the movement of students across the highway as a means for effective desegregation. The adequacy of the plan was challenged.

Holding: [9x0] Plans to create constitutionally mandated unitary school systems are not limited by the neighborhood school concept. The transition from a segregated to a unitary school system should include every effort to achieve actual desegregation. Bus transportation and split zoning must be given adequate consideration by courts in formulating effective plans and must be used when other measures are ineffective.

Basis: The equal protection clause of the Fourteenth Amendment creates a *present* right in black school children to public education free of state-created or state-supported segregation. A school system that has operated under state segregative policies has an immediate duty to make an effective transition to unitary schools. The time for delay has passed; effective action is required now.

North Carolina State Board of Education v. Swann, 402 U.S. 43 (1971)

Facts: This case is ancillary to *Swann* v. *Charlotte-Mecklenburg Board of Education (supra)*, in which the Supreme Court held that district courts have broad discretion to fashion a remedy that will ensure desegregation. Subsequently, the district court specifically directed the school board to consider specific alternatives that would effectuate a racially unitary system. While the board of education was engaged in submitting various proposals to the district court for approval, the North Carolina Legislature enacted the Anti-Busing Law, which forbade assignment of any student on account of race or for the purpose of creating a racial balance in the schools.

Holding: [9x0] An absolute prohibition against transportation of students assigned on the basis of race or for the purpose of creating a racial balance or ratio is an unconstitutional impairment of desegregation remedies.

Basis: State policy must give way when it hinders or violates federal constitutional guarantees. If a state-imposed limitation on a school authority's discretion inhibits or obstructs the operation of a unitary school or impedes the disestablishing of a dual school system, it must fall. The statute's absolute prohibition would inescapably operate to obstruct the court-awarded desegregation remedies. Further, its apparently neutral form of correction would, against the background of segregation, render illusory the intent of *Brown*.

McDaniel v. Barresi, 402 U.S. 39 (1971)

Facts: The Board of Education of Clarke County, Georgia, which had a white-black ratio of elementary school pupils of approximately two-to-one, devised a student assignment plan for desegregating elementary schools. The plan relied primarily on geographic attendance zones drawn to achieve greater racial balance. Additionally, the pupils in five heavily black attendance zones either walked or were transported by bus to schools located in other attendance zones. The resulting black elementary enrollment ranged from 20% to 40% in all but two schools, where it was 50%. Parents of the white students sued to enjoin the plan's operation, alleging that it violated the equal protection clause "by treating students differently because of their race and that transporting pupils in order to achieve racial balance is prohibited by Title IV of the Civil Rights Act."

Holding: [9x0] School boards that operate dual school systems are charged with the affirmative duty to take whatever steps might be necessary, including transporting students based on race, to convert to a unitary system in which racial discrimination would be eliminated.

Basis: 1) The transition from a dual to a unitary school system will almost invariably require that students be assigned differently on the basis of race, and the equal protection clause of the Fourteenth Amendment requires, rather than prohibits, this.

2) The plan was not barred by Title IV of the Civil Rights Act, because the act was directed only at federal officials and did not restrict state officials in assigning students within their systems.

Spencer v. Kugler, 326 F. Supp. 1235 (D. N.J. 1971), *aff'd*, 423 U.S. 1027 (1972)

Lower Court Holding: A state law establishing a reasonable system of school districting that is not segregative in intent is constitutional, even though subsequent population shifts result in *de facto* school segregation under that system.

Wright v. Council of Emporia, 407 U.S. 451 (1972)

Facts: Until the 1969-70 school year, the public schools in a county in Virginia were run on a segregated basis. All of the white students in the county attended schools located in the city of Emporia. Black students attended schools located largely outside of Emporia; there was one school for blacks in Emporia. In 1967 Emporia changed its status from a "town" to a "city," which, under state law, could maintain a separate school system. However, Emporia chose to remain part of the county school system. But after the court ordered adoption of a plan by which all children enrolled in a particular grade level would attend the same school, Emporia withdrew from the county system and proposed a plan for an Emporia-only desegregated school district. Emporia's proposal would have resulted in the perpetuation of the segregation between the better-equipped white schools in Emporia and the black county schools. Its validity was challenged here.

Holding: [5/4x0] Where *de jure* segregation has been county-wide, the withdrawal of a locality that is the site of better-equipped, traditionally white schools from the county school system is unconstitutional.

Basis: Because Emporia's withdrawal from the county system would impede the establishment of a desegregated school system and perpetuate a dual school pattern, the Fourteenth Amendment forbade the establishment of a separate Emporia school district while the transition from a segregated system to a unitary system was under way.

United States v. Scotland Neck City Board of Education, 407 U.S. 484 (1972)

Facts: The schools of a county in North Carolina were completely segregated until 1965. In that year, the school board adopted a "freedom-of-choice" plan that resulted in little actual desegregation. In 1968 the Department of Justice and the school board agreed to a plan to create a unitary system for the county in the 1969-70 school year. In 1969 the state legislature passed a bill enabling a city that was part of the county school district to create, by majority vote, its own separate school district. The newly created district would be 57% white and 43% black. The schools in the rest of the county would be about 90% black. The effect of this plan would be to nullify the 1968 desegregation plan and to maintain a system in which the city's schools were largely white and the outlying schools were largely black. Its validity was challenged in this case.

Holding: [5/4x0] The dismantling of a segregated school system may not be impeded by the legislative creation of two new districts, one white and one black.

Basis: The Fourteenth Amendment, as interpreted in the *Brown* decision *(supra)*, forbids state action creating, supporting, or perpetuating segregated public schools. That the state action involved here was by the legislature, rather than by the school board, does not change its segregative effect or make it valid.

Keyes v. School District No. 1, Denver, Colorado, 413 U.S. 189 (1973)

Facts: Although the Denver, Colorado, school system had never been operated under a state constitutional provision or law that mandated or permitted school segregation, many of the city's schools were segregated. In 1969 the school board adopted a voluntary plan for the desegregation of the predominantly black Park Hill section of the city. A new school board election resulted in a majority of the members opposed to the plan. Subsequently the court, finding that the segregation in Park Hill had resulted from prior school board actions, ordered the desegregation of the Park Hill section. In this case, those favoring integration sought desegregation orders for the remaining schools in the district and the counting of Hispanic, as well as of black children, as minority students.

Holding: [5/1½x1½] 1) Absent a showing that a school district is divided into clearly unrelated units, proof of a state action, for example, school board action causing segregation in a substantial portion of that district, supports a finding that the entire district is segregated. Therefore, the court may order a districtwide remedy if, in fact, the segregation in one part of the district results in segregation in the rest of the district, unless the district proves a lack of "segregative intent" with respect to the other schools. 2) For purposes of defining a segregated school, blacks and Hispanics shall be considered together as minority students, since both groups suffer the same educational inequities when compared to the education offered Anglo students.

Basis: 1) The Fourteenth Amendment prohibits state action that results in segregated public schools and that denies minority students equal protection of the law by denying them equal educational opportunity. 2) Although Hispanics have been recognized as an identifiable class for Fourteenth Amendment purposes, the Court found that blacks and Hispanics shared the disadvantages of economic and cultural deprivation and discrimination. Since blacks and Hispanics suffered identical discrimination in Denver, they were entitled to have predominantly Hispanic and black schools included in the category of segregated schools.

Norwood v. Harrison, 413 U.S. 455 (1973)

Facts: Since 1940 Mississippi had been buying textbooks and lending them free to students in both public and private schools without reference to whether any participating private school had racially discriminatory policies. The number of private, nonsectarian schools had increased from 17 in 1963-64 (enrolling 2,170 white students) to 155 in 1970-71 (enrolling about 42,000 white students). The creation and enlargement of these private schools was in direct response to the desegregation of the public schools. Thousands of students who were attending private, all-white schools received free textbooks. While 90% of the state's school children still attended public schools, some school districts had lost all of their white students to private, segregated schools. There was no proof that, absent the free texts, any children would withdraw from segregated, private schools and enroll in unitary, public schools. The provision of texts to segregated, private schools at state expense was challenged here.

Holding: [7/2x0] The state may not, at least in the absence of a unitary system, grant tangible, specific financial aid — for example, free books or tuition grants — to private, segregated schools.

Basis: Racial discrimination in state-operated schools is barred by the equal protection clause of the Fourteenth Amendment. The state may not induce, encourage, or promote private persons to accomplish what it may not constitutionally accomplish itself. The state provision of free texts may not be essential to the continued operation of private, segregated schools; but it does constitute substantial state support of discrimination and therefore is prohibited by the Fourteenth Amendment.

Lau v. Nichols, 414 U.S. 563 (1974)

Facts: The San Francisco school system, which according to state statute has, as a major goal, the acquisition of English proficiency for all students, failed to offer remedial English language instruction or any other special compensatory program to about 1,800 Chinese-speaking pupils. This class of pupils claimed that the school board was in violation of the equal protection clause of the Fourteenth Amendment and of Title VI of the Civil Rights Act of 1964, which prohibits recipients of federal aid from discriminating against students on the basis of race, color, or national origin. H.E.W. had authority under the Act to promulgate implementing regulations. A pertinent H.E.W. guideline stated: "where inability to speak and understand the English language excludes national-origin minority group children from effective participation in the educational program offered by a school district, the district must take affirmative steps to rectify the language deficiency in order to open its instructional program to these students."

Holding: [5/4x0] A school district receiving federal aid must provide special instruction for non-English-speaking students whose education is severely hampered by the language barrier, at least when there are substantial numbers of such students within the district.

Basis: The failure to provide 1,800 non-English-speaking students with special instruction denied them a meaningful opportunity to participate in the public education program and thus violated Title VI and the H.E.W. regulations and guidelines implementing the Act. The Court did not decide whether the failure to provide such a program violated the equal protection clause of the Fourteenth Amendment. Nor did it decide whether the remedy was bilingual education, leaving this matter to the trial court.

Cleveland Board of Education v. Lafleur; Cohen v. Chesterfield County School Board, 414 U.S. 632 (1974)

Facts: Public school teachers who became pregnant challenged the constitutionality of the mandatory maternity leave rule that required them to leave work before they desired to do so. One school district's rule required every pregnant teacher to take a maternity leave without pay beginning five months before the expected birth. Application for such leave was required to be made no later than two weeks prior to the date of departure. A teacher on maternity leave was not allowed to return to work until the beginning of the next regular school semester following the date when her child reached three months of age. A doctor's certificate of health was required.

Another school district's rule required pregnant teachers to leave work at least four months prior to the expected birth. Notice was required to be given six months prior to the expected birth. Return to work was guaranteed no later than the first day of the school year following the date when the teacher presented a doctor's certificate and could assure the board that care of the child would cause only minimal interference with her job.

Holding: [5/2x2] Mandatory maternity leave rules that have an absolute, early exit date and an absolute, belated return date are unconstitutional.

Basis: The mandatory termination provisions and the mandatory waiting period before return to work violate the due process clause of the Fourteenth Amendment. Freedom of personal choice in matters of family life is a liberty protected by the Fourteenth Amendment; state rules affecting this liberty must not needlessly, arbitrarily, or capriciously impinge on it. Since the ability of any particular pregnant teacher to continue or return to work is an individual matter, the rules creating absolute presumptions of inability to work violate due process. The notice provisions are rationally related to school board needs for planning and do not impair the teachers' right or offend the Constitution.

Mayor of Philadelphia v. Educational Equality League, 415 U.S. 605 (1974)

Facts: Under the city charter, the mayor appointed both the school board nominating panel and the nine members of the school board, who are nominated by the above-mentioned panel. The nominating panel consists of 13 members, four of whom are chosen from the citizenry at large and nine of whom must each be the highest ranking officer of a governmental, community, or educational organization. There was some evidence that the mayor was unaware of some of the black civic groups, whose officers could have been eligible for consideration. A newspaper reported a statement by the mayor that he would appoint no more blacks to the school board in 1969.

A citizen's group charged that the mayor unconstitutionally discriminated against blacks in making his appointments to the 1971 panel and sought an order barring that panel from nominating prospective school board members. It also sought an order mandating that the mayor correct the racial imbalance of the present panel and appoint racially balanced panels in the future, but it did not seek imposition of strict numerical quotas on the mayor's appointment power. By the time the mayor was succeeded in office, no evidence as to his successor's policies had been introduced.

Holding: [5x4] Where there is no clear evidence of racial discrimination in the appointment of the school board nominating panel, no action will be taken by the courts to alter the method of selection of appointees. The fact of numerical racial imbalance alone is not proof of unconstitutional discrimination in this case.

Basis: Absent clear evidence of a violation of the Fourteenth Amendment, the Court declines to interfere with the appointment power of governmental officials.

Bradley v. School Board, 416 U.S. 696 (1974) ("Bradley II")

Facts: Following a long court battle for a more effective school desegregation plan that reached the Supreme Court (see *Bradley I, supra*), the federal district court awarded the parents and guardians of black students their expenses and attorneys' fees incurred during the litigation. The federal district court found that the actions taken and the defenses made by the school board had caused unreasonable delay in desegregation of the schools and had caused the parents to spend large sums in order to protect the children's constitutional rights. The court of appeals voided the award of fees because there was no federal statute authorizing such payment either at the time that the legal services were rendered or while the desegregation case was pending. Before the court of appeals reached its decision as to the propriety of the fee award, Congress passed a law authorizing such payments to deserving prevailing parties.

Holding: [7x0] A law authorizing fee awards that became effective while a case concerning the propriety of such awards was pending may be applied to that case and may authorize payment for legal services rendered prior to the law's enactment.

Basis: An appellate court must apply the law in effect at the time of the decision unless to do so would be unjust. The nature of the parties and rights involved and the law's effect on those rights determine the justice of its application to cases arising before its effective date. The law is properly applied to compensate parents who bore a heavy financial burden in order to vindicate a public right, and its application works no injustice on the school board whose duty to provide a unitary school system is unchanged by the law.

Geduldig v. Aiello, 417 U.S. 484 (1974)*

Facts: California had a disability insurance plan for private employees temporarily disabled by an injury or illness that was not covered by workmen's compensation. Employees contributed 1% of their salary up to an annual maximum amount, and the program was compulsory unless suitable

---

*For subsequent developments concerning pregnancy benefits, see *Cleveland Board of Educ. v. LaFleur (supra)*, *California Federal Savings (infra)*, and *Nashville (infra)*.

private insurance was substituted. The plan's coverage was not comprehensive and certain disabilities were excluded. Among the conditions that were not compensated was disability resulting from a normal pregnancy. This exclusion was challenged here.

Holding: [6x3] The exclusion of disability arising in a normal pregnancy from eligibility for benefits under a state-run insurance program is constitutional.

Basis: Since the exclusion of disability arising in normal pregnancy is not sex-based discrimination, it is not barred by the equal protection clause of the Fourteenth Amendment. Also, the equal protection clause does not require the state to compensate all disabilities or none. The legislature may attempt to ameliorate part of a problem without attacking the whole; and absent intentional discrimination, its action will pass the constitutional test. The state's insurance plan was designed to provide minimally adequate coverage affordable by even low-income groups. The inclusion of benefits for normal pregnancy would force a major alteration of this reasonable program and was not required.

Gilmore v. Montgomery, 417 U.S. 556 (1974)

Facts: In 1959 the district court ordered the city of Montgomery, Alabama, to desegregate its public parks. Thereafter, the city coordinated a program with the racially segregated Y.M.C.A. and managed to continue to run segregated recreational programs. This case was begun in 1971. The complaint was that the city permitted racially segregated private schools and other segregated private groups to use city recreational facilities.

Holding: [5/3½ x½] 1) A city may not permit segregated private schools and school groups to have exclusive access* to pub-

---

*The term "exclusive access" does not include the situation where only part of a facility may be allocated to or used by a group. For example, the use of two of a total of 10 tennis courts by a private school group would not constitute an exclusive use; the use of all 10 courts would.

lic recreational facilities. 2) If non-exclusive use by private school groups directly impairs an existing school desegregation order or constitutes a vestige of the type of state-sponsored segregation of the city's recreational facilities that was prohibited by the district court, it should be enjoined. 3) However, unless it is shown that the city is actively participating in the discrimination practiced by segregated, non-school groups, it should not be enjoined from permitting such groups to use park facilities on an equal basis with other members of the public.

Basis: 1) The city was under an order to desegregate its schools in accord with requirements of the Fourteenth Amendment. The allocation of exclusive use of recreational facilities to private, segregated schools worked to support those schools and constituted state interference with the desegregation order, which was unconstitutional. 2) The First Amendment's freedom of association prohibits the state from refusing access to private, nonschool groups merely because they are segregated. However, the Fourteenth Amendment prohibits state support of segregation.

Milliken v. Bradley, 418 U.S. 717 (1974) ("Milliken I")

Facts: This case arose after a district court ordered a desegregation plan for Detroit's schools that encompassed a number of outlying school districts, as well as the city of Detroit proper. Detroit did not have a history of segregation ordered or permitted by law. However, there was a long history of public and private discrimination that had helped to produce residential segregation. Detroit school children and their parents claimed that the school board's imposition of school attendance zones over the existing segregated residential pattern had produced an unconstitutional dual school system in Detroit. They cited the school board's policy in school construction and its approval of optional attendance zones in fringe areas. That unconstitutional segregation existed in

Detroit was not questioned here. What was in question was the constitutionality of the court-ordered desegregation plan extending to outlying districts with no history of segregative action on the part of their school boards or local governments.

Holding: [5x4] Absent a showing that outlying districts have failed to operate unitary school systems or have committed acts that fostered segregation in other school districts, a court-ordered school desegregation plan cannot cross school district lines in order to include them in the plan.

Basis: The Fourteenth Amendment prohibits state action that denies minority group school children equal protection of the law by maintaining a segregated school system. The Court rejected the argument that the outlying districts are subdivisions of the state, that the state contributed to segregation in Detroit, and therefore that the outlying districts are subject to a multi-district school desegregation plan. In order for a multi-district remedy to be ordered by a court, the local governments of outlying districts must have committed segregative acts.

Evans v. Buchanan, 393 F. Supp. 428 (D. Del. 1975), aff'd, 423 U.S. 963 (1975)

Lower Court Holding: Where a statute explicitly or effectively makes goals of racial minorities more difficult to achieve, such a statute is unconstitutional.

Washington v. Davis, 426 U.S. 229 (1976)*

Facts: As part of its selection procedure for police academy recruits, Washington, D.C., officials administered "Test 21," which also was used generally in the federal civil service to test verbal ability. A passing score on the test was positively

---

*For a subsequent Supreme Court decision that was vacated in light of *Washington* v. *Davis*, see *Austin Independent School District* v. *United States*, 443 U.S. 915 (1979).

correlated with successful completion of the course of study at the police academy. However, a positive correlation between a passing score on the test and the quality of an applicant's on-the-job performance was not shown. The police department actively sought black recruits and raised the percentage of black recruits so that it was roughly equal to the percentage of 20- to 29-year-old blacks in the area from which personnel were drawn. While there was no showing of discriminatory intent or action in administration of the test, four times more blacks than whites had failed the test. In this case, black applicants claimed that the test had a racially disproportionate impact and therefore was unconstitutional.

Holding: [4/3x2] A test that is racially neutral on its face, that is administered without racially discriminatory action or intent, and that is reasonably related to a legitimate state purpose, for example, that of ensuring a minimum level of verbal ability in police recruits, is constitutional.

Basis: 1) The due process clause of the Fifth Amendment prohibits the federal government from acting with racially discriminatory purpose. However, a law or other official act is not necessarily unconstitutional solely because it has a racially disproportionate impact. Here, the test was racially neutral on its face and was administered to serve a legitimate purpose. There was no official intent to discriminate and there was, therefore, no constitutional basis for invalidating the testing procedure. 2) Title VII of the Civil Rights Act of 1964 requires that applicant screening tests with disproportionate racial impact be abandoned unless the employer can show a direct correlation between skills tested and job performance. However, Title VII was not a basis for this decision since it was, at the time of this case, not applicable to federal employees. It has since been extended to cover such employees.

Runyon v. McCrary, 427 U.S. 160 (1976)

Facts: Two black children applied for admission to private, nonsectarian schools that advertised in the yellow pages and through bulk mailings in order to attract students. Both children were denied admission solely on the basis of race. In this case, the children challenged the private schools' acts of racial discrimination.

Holding: [5/2x2] Private, nonsectarian schools that offer enrollment to qualified applicants from the public at large may not limit their offering only to whites and refuse admission to others solely on the basis of race.

Basis: 1) The Thirteenth Amendment to the Constitution prohibits slavery and the badges and incidents of that condition. The Thirteenth Amendment also provides that the federal government shall enforce these prohibitions by appropriate legislation. Sec. 1981, which provides, in part, that all persons shall have the same right in every state to make and enforce contracts, is appropriate federal legislation under the Thirteenth Amendment. It prohibits private acts of racial discrimination in the offering of contracts to the public, for example, contracts for employment or education. 2) The Court did not conclude that promotion of the concept of racial segregation is barred by Sec. 1981; the Court only prohibited implementation of such a policy. 3) The Court did not decide whether sectarian, private schools that practice racial discrimination for religious reasons are prohibited from doing so by Sec. 1981.

Pasadena City Board of Education v. Spangler, 427 U.S. 424 (1976)

Facts: As a result of a lawsuit brought by parents, students, and the U.S. government, the City of Pasadena was ordered to desegregate its public schools. The court order required that, beginning with the 1970-71 school year, there would be no school "with a majority of any minority students." The board of education assigned students in a racially neutral manner, and in 1970-71 the "no majority" requirement was met.

In the years following 1970-71, the school system had an increasing number of schools that were not in compliance with the requirement. This change in student population was not caused by segregative school board action but by random population shifts in the district. The board of education sought to have the "no majority of minority students" requirement dropped.

Holding: [6x2] 1) Although the students who originally brought the desegregation suit had graduated from the school system, the court orders still could be litigated since the United States remained an interested party. 2) Once desegregation of student populations is achieved to eliminate school system discrimination brought about by official action, school officials may not be required to make yearly alterations of student assignment plans in order to maintain a strict numerical ratio of majority to minority students. Such ratios may be used only as guidelines or starting points for the initial transition from segregated to unitary schools.

Basis: 1) Because the students already graduated and no longer had a legal interest in Pasadena's public schools and because their court action was not properly certified as a class action, the case would be moot under Article III of the Constitution, and the desegregation orders would be void but for the continued interest of the United States, as authorized in Title VI of the Civil Rights Act of 1964. 2) The Fourteenth Amendment requires the desegregation of school systems segregated by public officials. Once desegregation is achieved, there is no constitutional requirement of any particular racial ratio in the public schools.

Arlington Heights v. Metropolitan Housing Development Corporation, 429 U.S. 252 (1977)*

Facts: A nonprofit builder contracted to purchase land with boundaries on a neighboring village in order to build racially

---

*For subsequent Supreme Court decisions that were vacated in light of *Arlington Heights*, see *Metropolitan School District* v. *Buckley*, 429 U.S. 1068 (1977) and *School District of Omaha* v. *United States*, 433 U.S. 667 (1977).

integrated low- and moderate-income housing. The builder applied for the necessary rezoning from a single-family to a multiple-family classification. The village denied the builder's request. The builder and individual minority persons filed suit to compel acceptance of their application, alleging that the denial was racially discriminatory and violated the equal protection clause of the Fourteenth Amendment and the Fair Housing Act of 1968.

Holding: [5/1x2] An official action that results in a racially disproportionate impact is not unconstitutional unless proof of a racially discriminatory intent or purpose is shown.

Basis: Disproportionate impact is not irrelevant to the equal protection clause of the Fourteenth Amendment, but it is not the sole touchstone of an invidious racial discrimination. Because legislators and administrators are properly concerned with balancing numerous competitive considerations, courts refrain from reviewing the merits of their decisions, absent a showing of arbitrariness or irrationality. However, racial discrimination is not just another competing factor. When there is proof that a discriminatory purpose has been a motivating factor in the decision, this judicial deference is no longer justified.

Vorcheimer v. School District of Philadelphia, 532 F.2d 880 (3d Cir. 1976), *aff'd by an equally divided court,* 430 U.S. 703 (1977)*

Lower Court Holding: If attendance at single-sex high schools is voluntary, if coeducational alternatives are available, and if the educational opportunities offered at the schools for males and for females are comparable, then the maintenance of such schools is constitutional.

---

*This case has negligible, if any, precedential value.

International Brotherhood of Teamsters v. United States, 431 U.S. 324 (1977)

Facts: The federal government brought this action under Title VII of the Civil Rights Act of 1964, which prohibits discrimination in employment. The government claimed that a large carrier of motor freight had discriminated against minority group members by hiring them only as local city drivers while reserving the higher paying, long-distance line driver jobs for whites. The government further claimed that the seniority system agreed on by the union and the employer perpetuated the effects of this past discrimination, since under that system a city driver transferring to a long-distance line driver job had to forfeit all his city-driver seniority and start at the bottom of line drivers' "board." The government sought a court order permitting city drivers to transfer to line driver status with full seniority.

Holding: [7/1x1] Employees who, after the effective date of Title VII, either were denied jobs because of racial or ethnic discrimination or were deterred from applying for such jobs because of the company's known discrimination policy, are entitled to retroactive seniority dating back to no later than the effective date of the Act. Employees who suffered only pre-Act discrimination are not entitled to relief.

Basis: Seniority systems in a bargaining agreement may perpetuate the effects of past racial and ethnic discrimination. Lower-paid employees, if made to forfeit their seniority in order to transfer to a higher-paid job, may show that the company is engaged in a practice that violates Title VII.

Milliken v. Bradley, 433 U.S. 267 (1977) ("Milliken II")

Facts: In *Milliken I (supra)* the Supreme Court decided that the district court's interdistrict remedy for segregation in the Detroit school system was not constitutionally mandated, and the case was sent back to that court for the formulation of a Detroit-only remedy. The district court's new order consisted of a Detroit-only pupil assignment plan and of four remedial education programs designed to combat the effects of prior segregation. These programs, which had been proposed by the Detroit School Board, were remedial reading, inservice teacher training, student testing, and counseling. The district court ordered that one-half the cost of these programs would be borne by the school district and that the other one-half would be borne by the state. In this case, the state challenged the district court's authority to order remedial programs and its power to allocate one-half the financial burden for such programs to the state.

Holding: [6/2x0] 1) As part of a desegregation decree, a district court can order remedial educational and supportive programs for children who have been subjected to segregation in the past, especially when such programs are supported by evidence and proposed by the local school board. 2) The court may constitutionally require that the state pay one-half of the cost of such remedial programs.

Basis: 1) The Fourteenth Amendment prohibits segregation in public schools and requires that segregated schools be converted to unitary ones. The federal courts, giving consideration to the scope of the constitutional violation, the interests of local governments in managing school affairs, and the remedial nature of a desegregation order, may require remedial education programs, as well as pupil assignment plans, in order to implement the transition to a unitary school system. 2) The Eleventh Amendment, which protects the states from financial liability for past acts of state officials, does not bar courts from ordering a state to participate in or to financially support compliance with the constitutionally mandated desegregation of public schools. The Tenth Amendment protects the states from federal interference with their governmental form and functioning but does not preclude a federal court from ordering that state funds be expended in the implementation of Fourteenth Amendment guarantees.

Hazelwood School District v. United States, 433 U.S. 299 (1977)

Facts: In the Hazelwood School District, which is located in St. Louis County, the percentage of black teachers was 1.4% in 1972-73 and 1.8% in 1973-74. In St. Louis County as a whole, the percentage of black teachers was 15.4% during those years. The city of St. Louis was, during that time, attempting to maintain a 50% black teaching staff. Excluding the city, the percentage of black teachers in the county was 5.7%. Title VII of the Civil Rights Act of 1964, which prohibits racial discrimination in hiring and employment, became applicable to school districts in March 1972. Hazelwood School District hired 3.7% black teachers in 1972-74. In this case, Hazelwood School District challenged a lower court ruling based on a comparison of the racial composition of the school district's teaching force with that of St. Louis County. That ruling stated that the district engaged in discriminatory employment practices in violation of Title VII.

Holding: [6/2x1] In determining whether an employer's hiring practices are in violation of Title VII of the 1964 Civil Rights Act, a court should compare the number of qualified minority group members available for employment in the relevant labor pool with the number of minority group members hired by the employer in question. 1) This comparison should be concerned only with the number of minority group members hired since the effective date of the Act; employers are not liable for pre-Act discrimination. 2) There was disagreement between the lower courts concerning which statistics should be used to determine whether the school district engaged in discriminatory employment practices. In determining which figures provided the most accurate basis for comparison, the Supreme Court identified numerous other considerations that had to be evaluated by the trial court.

Basis: Title VII of the Civil Rights Act of 1964 prohibits discrimination in hiring and employment but will not require that remedial measures be taken when a low percentage of minority group employees in the work force is caused only by pre-Act patterns of discrimination.

Dayton Board of Education v. Brinkman, 433 U.S. 406 (1977) ("Dayton I")

Facts: Students in an Ohio school system alleged that the local and state boards of education were operating a racially segregated school system in violation of the equal protection clause of the Fourteenth Amendment.

The district court found that *de jure* segregation existed in the Ohio school district based on the following three factors: 1) substantial racial imbalance in student bodies throughout the system, 2) the school board's use of optional attendance zones for high schools that had a segregative effect (the district court found that the use of such zones was racially neutral at the elementary school level and also that no students in the optional zone were denied their choice of school because of race), and 3) the school board's rescinding of a prior board's resolution acknowledging its role in racial segregation and calling for remedial measures. The district court, at the insistence of the court of appeals, ordered a systemwide remedy for the schools, the propriety of which was challenged here.

Holding: [7/2x0] Where segregative acts of a school board are not shown to have systemwide effect, a systemwide remedy cannot properly be imposed. The case was remanded so that the district court could establish whether other segregative acts of the school board could be established so as to warrant a systemwide remedy, or whether a more limited order had to be formulated. Pending the new determination, the district court's present plan was to take effect.

Basis: The Fourteenth Amendment forbids the states to engage in acts that establish or further segregate public schools. The power of the courts to order remedial measures to combat segregation is dependent on the scope of the Fourteenth Amendment's prohibition. Therefore, courts can order desegregation only of schools in which segregation is the product of governmental action. The rescinding of the prior board's resolution calling for desegregation action was not a segregative act unless evidence established the existence of prior *de jure* segregation.

Nashville Gas Co. v. Satty, 434 U.S. 136 (1977)*

Facts: Pursuant to the employer's mandatory maternity leave policies, employees who were disabled by pregnancy did not receive sick pay, while those who were disabled by reason of nonoccupational sickness or injury did. Also, on return from pregnancy leave, employees lost all accumulated job seniority; thus they would be re-employed in permanent jobs only if no other employees applied for the positions. A female employee took maternity leave, gave birth a month thereafter, and sought re-employment after three more months. She obtained only a temporary position, which had a lower rate of pay than she had received previously. The three permanent positions for which she applied were awarded to employees who had started work while she was on maternity leave.

Holding: [6½/2½x0] 1) A policy denying their accumulated seniority to employees returning from pregnancy leave violates Title VII of the Civil Rights Act of 1964. 2) A policy of not awarding sick leave pay to pregnant employees is not a violation of Title VII, unless it can be shown to be a mere pretext designed to effect an invidious discrimination against members of one sex.

Basis: On its face the seniority policy is neutral in its treatment of male and female employees. However, it is apparent that the

---

*For a case vacated and remanded in light of this decision, see *Richmond Unified School District v. Berg*, 434 U.S. 158 (1977).

policy had a discriminatory effect, imposing on women a substantial burden that men need not suffer. There was no proof of any business necessity to justify this disparate burden.*

United States v. South Carolina, 445 F. Supp. 1094 (D.S.C. 1977), *aff'd,* 434 U.S. 1026 (1978)

Lower Court Holding: Despite its racial impact, the governmental use of minimum score requirements on the National Teacher Examinations for both certification purposes and as a factor in determining teacher salaries is not a violation of the equal protection clause of the Fourteenth Amendment nor of Title VII.

Los Angeles v. Manhart, 435 U.S. 702 (1978)

Facts: Based on a study of mortality tables and its own experience, a public employer determined that its female employees would, as a class, outlive its male employees. As a result, it required female employees to make significantly larger pension fund contributions than their male counterparts, thus causing a differential in take-home pay. A class action suit was brought to seek an injunction and restitution. While the action was pending, California enacted a law prohibiting certain municipal agencies from requiring higher pension fund contributions from female employees. The employer amended his plan accordingly.

Holding: [4/2½x1½] A pension plan that requires larger contributions from female employees than from male employees is a violation of Title VII. Retroactive relief in such cases is available only under certain circumstances

Basis: Citing the language and purpose of Title VII, the Court reasoned that the existence or nonexistence of sex discrimi-

*The Court upheld a similar policy in *General Electric Co.* v. *Gilbert,* 429 U.S. 125 (1976), but it recognized there and in *Geduldig (supra)* that on its face the neutrality of such a policy would not suffice if it can be shown to be a pretext for sex discrimination.

nation is to be determined by comparison of individual, not class, characteristics. The Court also concluded that one senator's isolated comment on the Senate floor cannot change the effect of the plain language of the Bennett Amendment,* which allowed compensation differentials based on sex that had been authorized by the four specific exceptions in the Equal Pay Act of 1963. The meshing of the decision with *General Electric Co. v. Gilbert*, 429 U.S. 125 (1976), and *Geduldig (supra)* was achieved by the Court only with great difficulty, as reflected in the split votes.

Regents of the University of California v. Bakke, 438 U.S. 265 (1978)**

Facts: A white male applied to the medical school of a public university in two consecutive years and was rejected both times. The medical school had two admissions programs for each year's entering class of 100 students, the regular admissions program and the special admissions program. Sixteen of the 100 openings were allocated to the special program, which had somewhat relaxed requirements for minority group candidates. During the three-year period until his second rejection, 63 minority students were admitted under the special program and 44 under the regular program. No disadvantaged whites were admitted under the special program, although many applied. In both years in which Bakke was rejected, based on his applications under the regular program, special applicants were admitted with lower scores than his. After his second rejection, he filed suit in state court to compel his admission to Davis' medical school, alleging that the special admissions program operated to exclude him on the basis of race in violation of the Fourteenth Amend-

---

*For a subsequent case concerning the Bennett Amendment, see *County of Washington (infra)*.

**For a more recent related but limited ruling, see *Texas v. Lesage*, 528 U.S. 18 (1999).

ment's equal protection clause, a provision in the California constitution, and Title VI of the Civil Rights Act of 1964, which provides, among other things, that no person shall on the ground of race or color be excluded from participating in any program receiving federal financial assistance.

Holding: [1/4x4] Race may be used as a factor, but not *the* factor, in governmental actions unless there is compelling justification.

Basis: In view of its legislative history, Title VI must be held to proscribe only those racial classifications that would violate the equal protection clause. Whether the special admissions program's allocation is described as a quota or as a goal, it is a line drawn on the basis of race and ethnic status. Racial and ethnic distinctions of any sort are inherently suspect and thus call for strict judicial scrutiny. The medical school's purposes of helping victims of societal discrimination, promoting better health-care delivery to deprived citizens, and attaining a diverse student body were not shown to be sufficiently compelling in this case to justify foreclosing consideration to persons like the plaintiff.

Board of Trustees v. Sweeney, 439 U.S. 24 (1978)

Facts: A teacher who was first appointed to a state college faculty in 1969 and granted tenure in 1972 sought promotion to the rank of full professor. Although her department head recommended in favor of the promotion, the faculty's Evaluation Advisory Committee voted not to grant the promotion, and its decision was upheld by the Faculty Appeals Committee. She applied again, and was turned down. After the faculty appeals process produced no findings of erroneous or biased treatment, the college president initiated his own inquiry into the matter. He found no evidence of sex discrimination. The following year she was elevated to the rank of full professor. She had sought relief from the Equal Employment Opportunity Commission (EEOC) after her second unsuccessful attempt. Inasmuch as this case involved disparate treatment rather than disparate impact, the district court properly identified the burden-shifting analysis of the *Furnco* and *McDonnell Douglas* decisions (see "Basis" below) as the appropriate framework. Expressly refusing to follow the doctrine of judicial deference for the academic process, the court of appeals held that the defendant institution had failed to rebut the prima facie case because it failed to prove the absence of a discriminatory motive.

Holding: [5x4] In Title VII employment discrimination cases, the employer need only articulate some legitimate, nondiscriminatory reason for the employee's rejection; it need not prove absence of discriminatory motive.

Basis: As outlined in *McDonnell Douglas Corp. v. Green*, 411 U.S. 792 (1973), and refined in *Furnco Construction Corp. v. Waters*, 438 U.S. 567 (1978), the Court developed a three-step process for Title VII trials: 1) plaintiff bears the initial burden of establishing a prima facie case of employment discrimination; 2) the burden shifts to the defendant to rebut the prima facie case by showing that a legitimate, nondiscriminatory reason accounted for its actions; and 3) if the rebuttal is successful, the burden shifts back to the plaintiff to show that the stated reason was a mere pretext for discrimination. The court of appeals used two contradictory standards for the second step, implying that they were interchangeable. The latter standard — proving the absence of a discriminatory motive — would make superfluous the third step in the *Furnco* and *McDonnell Douglas* analysis.

Southeastern Community College v. Davis, 442 U.S. 397 (1979)*

Facts: A student suffering from a serious hearing disability enrolled in a state community college that received federal

---

*For an application of this decision to Medicaid recipients, see *Alexander v. Choate*, 469 U.S. 287 (1985).

funds. She was denied admission to the college's associate degree nursing program based on the assessment of the executive director of the state board of nursing, who stated that it would be unsafe for the student to participate in the regular clinical training program and to practice as a nurse. The executive director concluded that those modifications needed to enable her to participate safely would prevent her from fully realizing the benefits of the program. Upon her request for reconsideration, the college's nursing staff deliberated and again voted to deny her admission. Plaintiff then filed suit in federal court alleging a denial of her Fourteenth Amendment rights and of Sec. 504 of the Rehabilitation Act of 1973. Sec. 504 prohibits discrimination against an "otherwise qualified handicapped individual" in federally funded programs "solely by reason of his handicap."

Holding: [9x0] The refusal of an educational institution to admit an individual with a severe hearing disability to a nursing or similar program does not violate Sec. 504 of the Rehabilitation Act.

Basis: Sec. 504 by its language does not compel educational institutions to disregard the disabilities of individuals or to make substantial modifications in their programs to allow disabled persons to participate. The H.E.W. regulations reinforce, rather than contradict, the conclusion that an "otherwise qualified" person is one who is able to meet all of a program's requirements in spite of his or her handicap.

Given the present record, it appears likely that the student could not benefit from any affirmative action that the regulations could reasonably be interpreted as requiring. If the regulations were to require more substantial adjustments, they would constitute an unauthorized extension of the statute.

United Steelworkers v. Weber, 443 U.S. 193 (1979)

Facts: A collective bargaining agreement entered into between a union and a corporation contained an affirmative action plan to eliminate conspicuous racial imbalances in the corporation's almost exclusively white craft work force. At one plant where the craft work force was less than 2% black, even though the local work force was 39% black, the corporation established a training program and selected trainees on the basis of seniority, with the provision that at least 50% of the new trainees were to be black until the aforementioned percentages reached an approximate balance. During the first year of the plan, the most junior black trainee selected had less seniority than several white production workers who had been rejected from the program. One such white worker instituted a class action suit in federal court, alleging that the plan's selection system violated Title VII of the Civil Rights Act of 1964.

Holding: [5x2] A private corporation's voluntary affirmative action plan, which is established through an agreement with the union and grants preference to black employees over more senior white employees for admission to training programs for traditionally segregated job categories, does not violate Title VII.

Basis: Emphasizing the narrowness of its inquiry to voluntary and private-sector affirmative action plans, the Court reasoned that a literal interpretation of Title VII would result in practices completely at variance with the purpose of the statute. It cited legislative history in support of the broad purposes of the statute.

Columbus Board of Education v. Penick, 443 U.S. 449 (1979)

Facts: A group of students brought a class action claiming that cumulative actions of the board of education had the purpose and effect of causing and perpetuating racial segregation in violation of the Fourteenth Amendment. The district court found: 1) at the time of *Brown* v. *Board of Education (supra)*, the board had not been operating a racially neutral unitary school system, since separate, black schools were operating in one area of the city as a direct result of intentional acts of the board and its administrators; 2) the board had failed to discharge its constitutional obligation to disestablish the dual school system in the interim since 1954; and 3) since 1954 the board's actions and practices had aggravated, rather than alleviated, racially identifiable schools through decisions involving such matters as teacher assignment, attendance zoning, and school site selection. Concluding that at the time of trial the board's intentional segregative acts and omissions violated the Fourteenth Amendment, the district court enjoined continuing discrimination on the basis of race and ordered submission of a systematic desegregation plan.

Holding: [5/2x2] Such local board actions as teacher assignment, attendance zoning, and school site selection can constitute sufficient proof of discriminatory intent and impact to establish an equal protection violation and to warrant a systematic remedy.

Basis: Proof of purposeful and effective maintenance of separate black schools in a substantial part of a school system is itself prima facie proof of a dual school system and, absent sufficient contrary proof, supports a systematic remedy.

Dayton Board of Education v. Brinkman, 433 U.S. 526 (1979) ("Dayton II")

Facts: After the Court had vacated the lower courts' order of a systemwide remedy in *Dayton I (supra)*, the district court held a supplementary evidentiary hearing. Based on a review of the entire record, the district court found that, although there had been various instances of purposeful segregation in the past, the plaintiffs had failed to prove that these acts had any current incremental segregative effects. The court of appeals reversed the district court's dismissal, holding that the consequences of Dayton's dual system in combination with the intentionally segregative impact of its various past practices constituted an appropriate basis for a systemwide remedy.

Holding: [5x4] In order to establish sufficient proof of current systemwide segregation and thus the appropriateness of a systemwide remedy, students need to show only the school board's failure to fulfill its affirmative duty to disestablish its dual system; they do not need to prove the individual effect on current patterns of segregation of each subsequent act of discrimination.

Basis: The Court cited *Wright*, *Davis*, and *Keyes (supra)* in reasoning that the measure of the post-*Brown I (supra)* conduct of a school board that had operated a systemwide dual program in 1954 is the effectiveness, not the purpose, of its actions in decreasing or increasing the segregation caused by the dual system. The Court cited *Keyes* and *Columbus (supra)* to support 1) the heavy burden on a school board found to be in violation of *Brown*, and 2) the inferential connection between substantial and systemwide discrimination.

Board of Education v. Harris, 444 U.S. 130 (1979)

Facts: The New York City Board of Education sued to enjoin H.E.W. to fund its 3.5 million dollar Emergency School Aid Act (ESAA) application, which had been given a favorable ranking but was denied funding based on the Act's eligibility requirements. The 1972 ESAA provided funds to encourage the voluntary elimination, reduction, or prevention of minority group isolation in elementary public schools. The Act declared an education agency ineligible if, after the date of the Act, 1) "it had in effect any practice which results in the disproportionate demotion or dismissal of instructional or other personnel from minority groups" or 2) "otherwise engages in discrimination . . . in the hiring, promotion, or assignment of employees." H.E.W. found the board ineligible based on statistical evidence showing a pattern of racially disproportionate assignments of minority teachers in relation to the number of minority students at the respective schools. The board claimed that the racially disproportionate teacher assignments resulted from compliance with state law, provisions of collective bargaining agreements, licensing requirements for particular teaching positions, demographic changes in student population, and the *Aspira* bilingual education consent decree.

Holding: [5x4] The H.E.W. regulations, which, pursuant to the ESAA, call for the withholding of funds based on evidence of disparate impact (without evidence of intentional discrimination) for both standards of the Act's ineligibility provision, are consistent with the Act.

Basis: The overall structure of the Act, Congress' statements of purpose and policy, the legislative history, and the text of the Act's ineligibility provision all point in the direction of the impact test. Although the language of the ineligibility provision is ambiguous, the underlying philosophy of the Act is to reach *de facto* as well as *de jure* segregation by means of an enticement approach. If there is a distinction between the two standards of the ineligibility provision, there is an irrebuttable presumption of a disparate impact standard for the first standard and a less strict, rebuttable disparate impact standard for the second standard. In the latter situation, herein at issue, the burden is on the party against whom the statistical case has been made. That burden could perhaps be carried by proof of "educational necessity," analogous to the "business necessity" defense under Title VII.

A ruling of ineligibility does not make the children who attend New York City schools any worse off. The funds for which the schools competed are not wasted because they are used to benefit other similarly disadvantaged children. Thus, the Court concluded, "It is a matter of benefits, not of deprivation, and it is a matter of selectivity."

Armour v. Nix, No. 16708 (N.D. Ga. Sept. 24, 1979), aff'd, 446 U.S. 930 (1980)

Lower Court Holding: Where the vestiges of racial segregation are *de minimus* or only intradistrict, an interdistrict remedy will not be ordered.

Texas Department of Community Affairs v. Burdine, 450 U.S. 248 (1981)

Facts: An accounting clerk was promoted to the position of field services coordinator. When her division director resigned, she was assigned additional duties. She applied for the director's position, but it remained vacant for six months. After being pressured by its federal funding agency to fill the position, the department hired a male from another division in the agency. In reducing staff to improve efficiency, he fired the coordinator and two other employees, retaining one male as the only remaining professional employee in the division. The coordinator was soon rehired by the department and assigned to another division, where she received salary and promotions commensurate with what she would have received had she been appointed to the director's position in her former division. She filed suit in federal court, alleging that the failure to promote and the subsequent decision to terminate her had been predicated on sex discrimination in violation of Title VII.

Holding: [9x0] When an individual in a Title VII case has proven a prima facie case of employment discrimination, the employer bears the burden of explaining clearly the nondiscriminatory reasons for its actions.

Basis: The fear that the employer could compose fictitious legitimate reasons for it actions is unwarranted because: 1) the defendant's explanation of its legitimate reasons must be clear and reasonably specific, 2) the defendant retains an incentive to persuade the trial court that the employment decision was valid, and 3) the liberal discovery rules in federal court are supplemented in a Title VII suit by the plaintiff's access to EEOC investigatory files concerning her complaint (see *EEOC* v. *Associated Dry Goods, infra*). The Court clarified that in the second step of this type of Title VII case (see *Sweeney, supra*), the employer has the burden of production, not the burden of persuasion. To rule otherwise would require an employer to give preferential treatment to minorities or women, whereas Title VII demands neutrality, leaving the discretion to the employer to choose among equally qualified candidates according to lawful criteria.

Northwest Airlines v. Transport Workers Union, 451 U.S. 77 (1981)

Facts: Continuously from 1947 to 1974, Northwest Airlines paid higher wages to its male cabin attendants, who were classified as pursers, than to its female cabin attendants, who were classified as stewardesses. During that period both the male and female cabin attendants were represented by first one union and then another; and their wages were fixed by collective bargaining agreements. In 1970 one of the female cabin attendants filed a class action against the company, contending that the wage differential violated the Equal Pay Act of 1963 and Title VII of the Civil Rights Act of 1964. Finding the two classifications of positions to require equal skill, effort, and responsibility, the district court entered judgment of 20 million dollars to the plaintiff class. The defendant company then brought this action asserting claims of contribution and indemnification against the two unions.

Holding: [8x1] An employer held liable to its female employees for back pay because collectively bargained wage differentials were found to violate the Equal Pay Act and Title VII does not have a federal statutory or common law right to contribution from unions that allegedly bear at least partial responsibility for the statutory violations.

Basis: The *Cort* factors (see *Cannon, infra*) do not favor an implied cause of action for contribution under either statute. The power of federal courts to fashion appropriate remedies for unlawful conduct is very limited and does not extend to comprehensive legislative schemes, such as these two statutes.

County of Washington v. Gunther, 452 U.S. 161 (1981)

Facts: Four women employed to guard female prisoners were paid substantially lower wages than the male guards were paid to guard male prisoners. When the county eliminated the female section of the jail, it transferred the female prisoners to the jail of a nearby county and discharged the four women guards. They filed suit in federal court seeking back pay and other relief under Title VII.

Holding: [5x4] The Bennett Amendment* does not restrict Title VII's prohibition of sex-based wage discrimination to claims of equal pay for equal work.

Basis: The language of the Bennett Amendment suggests, and its legislative history supports, an intention to incorporate only the affirmative defenses of the Equal Pay Act into Title VII. Additional support is found in the remedial purposes of Title VII and the Equal Pay Act.

The women did not base their claim, and thus the Court did not decide, on the controversial issue of "comparable worth," under which the intrinsic worth or difficulty of a job is compared with that of other jobs in the same organization or community.

Board of Education v. Rowley, 458 U.S. 176 (1982)

Facts: Parents of a deaf student attending regular elementary classes in a public school requested a sign-language interpreter in all her academic classes. The school had provided an FM hearing aid, specialized tutoring for one hour each day, and speech therapy for three hours each week. The

---

*The Bennett Amendment provides: "It shall not be an unlawful employment practice under [Title VII] for any employer to differentiate upon the basis of sex in determining the amount of wages. . . to be paid to employees. . . if such differentiation is authorized by [the Equal Pay Act]."

school district also had provided an interpreter for a two-week experimental period, until the interpreter reported that his services were not needed. When their request for an interpreter was denied, the parents requested a hearing before an independent examiner. The hearing examiner determined that an interpreter was not necessary, and this decision was affirmed on appeal by the New York Commissioner of Education. The parents then filed suit, claiming that this decision constituted a denial of the free appropriate public education guaranteed by the Education for All Handicapped Children Act (now the Individuals with Disabilities Education Act).

Holding: [5/1x3] The "appropriate" education provision of the Act requires personalized instruction with sufficient support services to permit the child to benefit educationally from that instruction. If the child is being educated in regular classrooms of the public school system, the individualized education program (IEP) should be reasonably calculated to enable the child to achieve passing grades and to advance from grade to grade.

The standard for judicial review is: 1) whether the State has complied with the procedures set forth in the Act, and 2) whether the IEP is reasonably calculated to enable the child to receive educational benefits.

Basis: Based on the language and legislative history of the Act, the Court concluded that the primary purpose was to open the door to, rather than provide a floor for, publicly provided education of disabled children. Thus the Act is designed with an emphasis on procedural compliance more than a substantive standard.

Washington v. Seattle School District No. 1, 458 U.S. 457 (1982)

Facts: In 1978 Seattle adopted a desegregation plan that made extensive use of mandatory busing. Two months after the plan went into effect, the voters of Washington voted to adopt an initiative to terminate mandatory busing for the purpose of achieving racial integration. This initiative prohibited school boards from assigning a student to any school other than the one geographically nearest or next nearest his home. Racial balance was not one of the seven permissible exceptions in the initiative. Seattle and two other school districts joined in a suit against the state, contending that the initiative violated the equal protection clause of the Fourteenth Amendment.

Holding: [5x4] A state initiative precluding school boards from requiring attendance at other than neighborhood schools violates the equal protection clause of the Fourteenth Amendment.

Basis: Emphasizing that the core of the Fourteenth Amendment is the prevention of meaningful and unjustified official distinctions based on race, the Court concluded that the state initiative was drawn specifically for racial purposes, and its effect was to reallocate power from local school boards to the state in such a way as to burden minority interests.

Crawford v. Board of Education, 458 U.S. 527 (1982)

Facts: In California desegregation litigation, the state court found *de jure* segregation in the Los Angeles Unified School District in violation of both the state and federal constitutions; and it ordered the district to prepare a desegregation plan. Ultimately, the trial court approved a desegregation plan that included substantial mandatory student reassignment and busing. Meanwhile, the voters of California ratified Proposition I, an amendment to the state constitution that forbade state courts to order mandatory pupil assignment or busing unless a federal court would do so to remedy a violation of the Fourteenth Amendment's equal protection clause. In light of this constitutional amendment, the school district asked the court to halt all mandatory reassignment and busing.

Holding: [7½/1½x0] A state constitutional amendment precluding state court-ordered busing in the absence of a Fourteenth Amendment violation does not violate the equal protection clause.

Basis: Proposition I does not inhibit enforcement of any federal law or constitutional requirement. Quite the contrary, by its plain language the Proposition seeks to embrace only the requirements of the federal Constitution with respect to mandatory school assignments and transportation. The Court rejected the allegation that this constitutional amendment employs an explicit racial classification and imposes a race-specific burden on minorities who seek to vindicate state-created rights. The Court found the purposes of Proposition I to be legitimate and nondiscriminatory, emphasizing that even when a neutral law has a disproportionately adverse effect on a racial minority, the Fourteenth Amendment is violated only if a discriminatory purpose is shown.

Grove City College v. Bell, 465 U.S. 555 (1984)*

Facts: As part of the Education Amendments of 1972, Congress enacted Title IX to proscribe gender discrimination in education programs or activities receiving federal funding. Grove City College, a private, coeducational liberal arts college, deliberately sought to preserve its autonomy by consistently declining state and federal financial assistance. However, several of the college's students received Basic Educational Opportunity Grants (BEOGs) from the government. Therefore, the U.S. Department of Education concluded that the college was a recipient of federal financial assistance and would have to comply with the regulations of Title IX. When the college refused to execute the assurance of compliance required by the regulations, the Department of Education initiated proceedings to declare the college and

---

*This decision was legislatively reversed by the Civil Rights Restoration Act of 1988.

its students ineligible for the BEOGs. The college and four students filed suit to preserve the grants.

Holding: [6/2x1] 1) Title IX applies to a college that receives no direct aid, but enrolls students who receive federal grants. 2) Title IX regulates only the specific programs that receive the federal assistance, not the entire institution. 3) The U.S. Department of Education may properly condition federal financial assistance on execution of the Title IX Assurance of Compliance. 4) Application of Title IX's regulations does not infringe on the First Amendment rights of a college or its students.

Basis: 1) The legislative history and the statutory language draw no distinction between indirect financial aid and direct financial aid; both trigger the application of Title IX regula tions. With the benefit of clear statutory language, powerful evidence of Congress' intent, and a long-standing and coherent administrative construction of the phrase, "receiving Federal financial assistance," the Court concluded that Title IX coverage is not foreclosed because federal funds are granted to Grove City's students, rather than directly to one of the college's education programs.

2) Citing *North Haven v. Bell (infra)*, the Court concluded that education grants do not trigger institutionwide coverage under Title IX. Both the purpose and the effect of the BEOGs are to provide relief to the college's own financial aid department. The Court found the ripple effect and other expansive theories not to correspond with Congress' program-specific intent.

3) The Assurance of Compliance corresponded with the program-specific requirement of Title IX and its regulations. Its status as a precondition to funding was established in Title VI regulations and cases prior to the enactment of Title IX.

4) Congress is free to attach reasonable and unambiguous conditions to federal financial assistance that education

institutions are not obligated to accept. Grove City College can avoid Title IX regulations by terminating its participation in the BEOG grants. Students could either use their BEOGs in another college or attend Grove City without federal financial assistance. The Court stated that "Requiring Grove City to comply with Title IX's prohibition of discrimination as a condition for its continued eligibility to participate in the BEOG program infringes no First Amendment rights of the College or its students."

Irving Independent School District v. Tatro, 468 U.S. 883 (1984)

Facts: A special education student, born with spina bifida, suffered from orthopedic and speech impairments and a neurogenic bladder. Due to her condition, the student needed clean intermittent catheterization (CIC) every three to four hours to avoid injury to her kidneys. CIC is a simple procedure that can be performed in a few minutes by a lay person with less than one hour of training. Pursuant to the Education for All Handicapped Children Act (now the Individuals with Disabilities Education Act), the school district developed an individualized education program (IEP) for the child that did not include provisions for school personnel to administer CIC. The parents filed suit, invoking the Act and also Section 504 of the Rehabilitation Act.

Holding: [6/½x1½] Under the Act, CIC is a "related service" and, therefore, the school district is required to provide that service to a disabled child needing it during the school day.

Basis: The Act's "free appropriate public education" requirement includes "related services," which in turn are defined as "supportive services" including medical services for diagnosis and evaluation as may be required to assist a disabled child to benefit from special education. Without CIC during the school day, the child could not attend school and thus could not benefit from education. In interpreting the medical exclusion, the Court accorded deference to the Act's regulation that excluded services provided by a licensed physician, not those provided by a school nurse. Comparing CIC to oral medication and emergency injections, the Court treated it as within the school nurse's authorized role.

Smith v. Robinson, 468 U.S. 992 (1984)*

Facts: A child suffering from a variety of physical and emotional disabilities was denied funding by his school district to attend a private, hospitalized program. The district contended that Rhode Island law placed the responsibility for educating an emotionally disturbed child on the state's Division of Mental Health, Retardation and Hospitals. The student's parents appealed this decision to the school board and subsequently pursued relief through the state administrative process and the federal laws, including the Education for All Handicapped Children Act (now the Individuals with Disabilities Education Act), Sec. 504 of the Rehabilitation Act, and Sec. 1983. The district court determined that under state law the school board, rather than the state mental health agency, is primarily responsible for financing the child's special education. The parents demanded attorneys' fees under Sec. 505 (which is tied to Sec. 504) and Sec. 1988 (which is tied to Sec. 1983).

Holding: [6x3] Where relief is clearly available under the Act, parents of disabled children may not resort to the remedies under Sec. 504 and, through Sec. 1983, under the Constitution. Inasmuch as the Act does not provide for attorneys' fees, the parents are not entitled to such an award in an action that may be resolved under the Act.

Basis: Parents were not entitled to attorneys' fees under Sec. 1988 for the following reasons: 1) the due process claim and the

---

*The decision was legislatively overruled by the Handicapped Children's Protection Act of 1986, an amendment to the EAHCA (now the IDEA).

parents' ultimate grounds for prevailing were not sufficiently related to support an award of attorneys' fees; 2) Congress intended the Act to be the exclusive avenue for pursuing an equal protection claim on behalf of a disabled child; 3) where, as here, the parents have presented distinctly different claims for different relief, based on different facts and legal theories, and have prevailed only on a nonfee claim, they are not entitled to a fee award simply because the other claim was a constitutional claim that could be asserted through Sec. 1983.

Parents were not entitled to relief under Sec. 505 because, here again, the Act provides a more comprehensive scheme for protecting the rights of handicapped children. Where, as here, whatever remedy might be provided under Sec. 504 is provided with more clarity and precision under the Education for All Handicapped Children Act, a plaintiff may not circumvent or enlarge on the remedies available under the Act by resort to Sec. 504.

Anderson v. City of Bessemer City, 470 U.S. 564 (1985)*

Facts: A city's selection committee, which had one female member, interviewed several applicants, including one female, for the position of recreation director. The male members of the committee voted for one of the male applicants; the female member voted for the female applicant. The committee offered the position to the male. Believing that she was more qualified than the successful male candidate, the female applicant filed charges with the Equal Employment Opportunity Commission (EEOC). Finding reasonable cause to believe her charges were accurate, the EEOC gave her a right-to-sue letter after conciliation proceedings were unsuccessful. She then brought suit under Title VII. The trial court determined that she was the most qualified candidate for the position, that the male committee members were biased against hiring her because she was a woman, and that the

---

*For a subsequent elaboration of the holding of this decision in a Title VII case, see *Bazemore* v. *Friday*, 478 U.S. 385 (1986).

reasons they offered for their choice of the other candidate were pretextual. The court of appeals reversed, holding that the trial court's findings were clearly erroneous.

Holding: [7/2x0] If the district court's account of the evidence is plausible in light of the record viewed in its entirety, the court of appeals may not reverse it. Where there are two permissible views of the evidence, the trial court's choice between them cannot be clearly erroneous.

Basis: Federal Rule of Civil Procedure 52(a) enunciates the standard governing appellate review of a district court's findings: "Findings of fact shall not be set aside unless clearly erroneous, and due regard shall be given to the opportunity of the trial court judge of the credibility of the witnesses." The Court interpreted this "clearly erroneous" standard with due regard to the position and experience of the trial court in terms of fact finding.

Board of Education v. National Gay Task Force, 729 F.2d 1270 (10th Cir. 1984), *aff'd,* 470 U.S. 903 (1985)

Lower Court Holding: 1) A statute permitting a teacher to be fired for engaging in public homosexual activity does not violate the Fourteenth Amendment's equal protection clause; 2) the statute's definition of public homosexual activity, that is, "the commission of an act defined in [the criminal code] that is committed with a person of the same sex and is indiscreet and not practiced in private," is not unconstitutionally vague; 3) the portion of such a statute that provides punishment for mere advocacy of homosexual activities is unconstitutionally overbroad.

Burlington School Committee v. Department of Education, 471 U.S. 359 (1985)

Facts: The school district's proposed individualized education program (IEP) for a disabled student, when he completed third grade, was a self-contained special education class in one of its public schools. The parent rejected the proposed

IEP and sought review by the state's education agency. The hearing, originally scheduled for the intervening summer, was postponed in favor of mediation, which was unsuccessful. Based on the recommendation of experts, the parents unilaterally placed the student at their own expense in a private school for children with hearing handicaps. There then ensued several administrative hearings and protracted litigation. The school district pointed to the stay-put, or status quo, provision of the Education for All Handicapped Children Act (now the Individuals with Disabilities Education Act), which calls for the child to remain in his "then current educational placement" during any proceedings under the Act.

Holding: [9x0] Parents who unilaterally place their child in a private special education school while proceedings are pending under the Act are entitled to reimbursement for tuition and related expenses where courts ultimately determine that the placement chosen by the parents is appropriate and the placement formulated by the school district is inappropriate.

Basis: The Court based its holding on the language and purpose of the Act. The language of "appropriate" relief was viewed as conferring broad discretion on the courts, including retroactive reimbursement, to ensure the child a "free appropriate public education" under the Act. Moreover, if the "status quo" provision of the Act were interpreted to cut off the reimbursement, the principal purpose of the Act would be defeated. This approach is supported by the regulations for the Act.

Wygant v. Jackson Board of Education, 476 U.S. 267 (1986)*

Facts: The collective bargaining agreement between the board of education and the teachers' union contained a clause that

---

*For more recent decisions where the Court clarified that the "trustworthy" standard applies to government-funded race-conscious programs, see *Adarand Constructors* v. *Pena*, 515 U.S. 200 (1995); *Richmond* v. *J.A. Croson Co.,* 488 U.S. 469 (1989).

provided preferential protection against layoffs to members of certain minority groups. After the layoff provision was upheld in litigation arising from the board's noncompliance with the provision, the board adhered to it, resulting in layoffs of nonminority teachers and in retention of minority teachers with less seniority. Displaced nonminority teachers filed suit, alleging violations of the equal protection clause and of certain federal and state statutes.

Holding: [3½/1½x4] A board policy or provision that provides preferential protection against layoffs based on racial or ethnic criteria violates the equal protection clause where there is no clear evidence that the board engaged in discrimination and also no evidence that the retained minority employees had been the victims of such discrimination.

Basis: The Court's plurality cited precedent for the principle that 1) direct or reverse racial discrimination must be justified by a compelling state purpose, and 2) the means chosen to achieve that purpose must be narrowly tailored. The board of education maintained that their interest was to provide minority role models for students in an attempt to alleviate the effects of societal discrimination. Societal discrimination in general, as contrasted with strong evidence of prior discrimination by the government unit involved, is not a compelling justification for imposing remedies that work against innocent people. Other, less intrusive means of accomplishing such purposes, such as hiring goals that to a considerable extent diffuse the burden among society generally, are available. The swing vote of Justice White added the view that none of the rehired minority teachers had been shown to be a victim of any racial discrimination.

Meritor Savings Bank v. Vinson, 477 U.S. 57 (1986)

Facts: A female bank employee filed an action against the bank and her supervisor, alleging that during her employment she had been subjected to sexual harassment by her supervisor in violation of Title VII. The supervisor's defense was that the sexual relationship was voluntary and had nothing to do with her continuous employment. The bank claimed it had no knowledge or notice of such an allegation and therefore could not be held liable.

Holding: [5/4x0] 1) Unwelcome sexual advances that create an offensive or hostile working environment violate Title VII. 2) Employers are not automatically liable for sexual harassment committed by their supervisors; however, absence of notice does not necessarily insulate the employer from liability in such cases.

Basis: 1) The language of Title VII's proscription against discriminatory employment practices is not limited to economic or tangible injuries. Furthermore, EEOC's guidelines, which, while not controlling, do merit due deference, support the view that harassment leading to noneconomic injury can violate Title VII. The "hostile environment" (as compared to "quid pro quo") theory is supported by a substantial body of EEOC and lower court decisions. The Court considered the allegation that the sexual activity was "voluntary" to be an invalid defense in a sexual harassment suit under Title VII; "the test of a sexual harassment claim is whether the alleged sexual advances were unwelcome."

2) While declining the parties' invitation to issue a definitive ruling on employer liability, the Court viewed Congress' decision to define "employer" in Title VII to include any agent of the employer as evidence of an intent to follow common law principles of agency in this area. EEOC guidelines that required automatic liability were not followed.

Local 28 of the Sheet Metal Workers' International Association v. Equal Employment Opportunity Commission, 478 U.S. 421 (1986)

Facts: In 1975 the district court found the union guilty of violating Title VII by discriminating against nonwhite workers in recruitment, selection, training, and admission to the union.

The court-appointed administrator proposed, and the court adopted, an affirmative action program. Based on the proportion of nonwhites in the relevant labor pool, the court established a 29% nonwhite membership goal. In 1982 and 1983, the district court found the union guilty of civil contempt for disobeying the court's affirmative action orders. The court levied a fine against the union for purposes of establishing a fund to increase nonwhite membership in the union and in its apprenticeship program. The union then challenged the district court's contempt finding and also the remedies the court had ordered both for the Title VII violation and for contempt.

Holding: [4/1½x3½] A district court may, in appropriate circumstances, order race conscious, affirmative relief benefiting individuals who are not the actual victims of discrimination as a remedy for violations of Title VII.

Basis: The plurality interpreted the language and legislative history of Title VII as allowing race-conscious affirmative relief to further the broad purposes of the Act. Similarly, the plurality interpreted its precedents as not precluding such a remedy. Warning that such relief is not always proper, the plurality found in this case that the membership goal and fund order were necessary to remedy the defendant's pervasive and egregious discrimination. Moreover, these measures were regarded as temporary and not unnecessarily trammeling the interests of white employees. Justice Powell's concurring swing vote emphasized that there was a compelling need for the membership goal and for the fund order in this particular case, that the violations of Title VII were egregious, that the remedy was narrowly tailored, and that no other effective remedy was available.

Local No. 93, International Association of Firefighters v. Cleveland, 478 U.S. 501 (1986)

Facts: An organization of black and Hispanic firefighters who were employed by the city filed a suit charging the city with discrimination on the basis of race and national origin in hiring, assigning, and promoting firefighters in violation of Title VII and on other grounds. The labor union representing a majority of the city's firefighters was allowed to intervene. Over the union's objection, the court adopted a consent decree that provided for the use of race-conscious relief and other affirmative action in promoting firefighters.

Holding: [5/1x3] Courts may, in appropriate cases, enter consent decrees under Title VII that benefit individuals who were not the actual victims of an employer's discriminatory practices.

Basis: Congress intended that voluntary compliance be the preferred means of achieving Title VII's objectives. Therefore, Title VII enforcement provisions preclude a court from entering an "order" that requires an employer to give relief to an employee. However, a consent decree is not an "order" within the meaning of the enforcement provision of Title VII; therefore, the court may adopt a consent decree. Furthermore, the union's consent was not required to obtain court approval of a consent decree.

United States v. Paradise, 480 U.S. 149 (1987)

Facts: In 1972 a federal district court held that the Alabama Department of Public Safety had systematically excluded blacks from employment as state troopers in violation of the Fourteenth Amendment, and the court imposed a hiring quota. Eleven years later, after two interim consent decrees and the continued failure of the department to develop promotion procedures that did not have an adverse impact on blacks, the district court ordered the promotion of one black trooper for each white trooper elevated in rank, as long as qualified black candidates were available, until the department implemented an acceptable promotion procedure.

Holding: [4/1x4] A court-ordered decree that makes use of a mathematical ratio, such as a one-for-one promotion requirement, is permissible under the equal protection clause where the defendant agency or institution has engaged in pervasive, systematic, and obstinate discriminatory exclusion of blacks.

Basis: The plurality viewed the government as having a compelling interest in correcting past and present discrimination by a government agency. Several factors are considered in determining whether race-conscious remedies are appropriate, including the necessity for the relief and the efficacy of alternative remedies; the flexibility and duration of the relief, including the availability of waiver provisions; the relationship of the numerical goals to the relevant labor market; and the impact of the relief on the rights of third parties. After weighing all these factors, the plurality concluded that the relief was narrowly tailored to serve its many purposes, being an effective, temporary, and flexible measure. Justice Stevens' concurring vote saw such situations as not differing fundamentally from the courts' broad equitable powers to remedy blatant equal protection violations in desegregation cases.

School Board v. Arline, 480 U.S. 273 (1987)

Facts: A teacher suffered three relapses of tuberculosis within a two-year period after a 20-year period of remission. The school district suspended her with pay for the remainder of the school year and at the end of the year discharged her, after a hearing, because of the continued recurrence of tuberculosis. She brought suit in federal district court, alleging a violation of Sec. 504 of the Rehabilitation Act.

Holding: [7x2] 1) A person afflicted with the contagious disease of tuberculosis may be a "handicapped individual" within the meaning of Sec. 504. 2) Whether such a person is "otherwise qualified" requires findings of fact about the nature, duration, severity, and the risk of transmissibility, and whether, in light of these medical findings, the employer could reasonably accommodate the employee.

Basis: The Court relied on 1) the broad definition of "handicapped individual" in Sec. 504, including a record of a physical or mental impairment that substantially limits one or more of a person's major life activities, and 2) the regulations promulgated by the Department of Health and Human Services that define "physical impairment" to include a physiological disorder or condition affecting one's respiratory system and that define "major life activities" to exclude walking and working. In this case, the teacher's original hospitalization sufficed to show a record of impairment. Citing legislative history and the amended definition, the Court rejected an exemption for contagious diseases per se as being inconsistent with the basis of Sec. 504.

The Court also relied on the general principles enumerated in *Southeastern Community College (supra)* and the specific factors recommended by the American Medical Association for the two-step "otherwise qualified" inquiry.

Johnson v. Transportation Agency, 480 U.S. 616 (1987)*

Facts: The county transportation agency voluntarily adopted an affirmative action plan for hiring and promoting females and minorities. The plan provided, among other things, that in making promotions to positions within a traditionally segregated job classification in which women have been significantly underrepresented, the agency is authorized to consider as one factor the sex of the applicant. When a vacancy for a road dispatcher arose, none of the more than 200 positions in the pertinent skilled workers classification was held by a woman. After interviews, the agency promoted a well-qualified female employee, passing over a male employee who was as well qualified and perhaps slightly better qualified. After receiving a right-to-sue letter from the EEOC, the male employee filed suit in federal court alleging a violation of Title VII.

---

*For public sector cases vacated in light of *Johnson*, see *Corporate City of South Bend* v. *Janowiak*, 750 F.2d 557 (7th Cir. 1985), and *Tisch* v. *Shidaker*, 782 F.2d 746 (7th Cir. 1986).

Holding: [5/1x3] A voluntary affirmative action plan that uses sex as one factor for hiring or promotion to traditionally segregated job categories in which women are conspicuously underrepresented is not a violation of Title VII.

Basis: Guided by *United Steelworkers* v. *Weber (supra)*, the Court viewed affirmative action plans as not restricted to prior discriminatory practices. Where the job requires special training, the comparison for determining whether an imbalance exists should be between the employer's work force and those in the area labor force who possess the relevant qualifications. The standard here was not blind hiring by numerical quotas, but by taking numerous factors, including qualifications, into account. Given the temporary, moderate, and gradual approach, the rights of male employees were not infringed unnecessarily.

Honig v. Doe, 484 U.S. 305 (1988)

Facts: The school district suspended two emotionally disturbed students for less than 10 days. One student was suspended for physically assaulting a fellow student; and the other student was suspended for continuing to make sexual comments to female classmates after being warned not to do so. In both cases, the school district scheduled an expulsion hearing and extended the suspension indefinitely pending the outcome of the hearing.

Holding: [5½/½x2] School authorities may not exclude disabled students from school for more than 10 days without the due process procedures of the Education for All Handicapped Children Act (now the Individuals with Disabilities Education Act) or, in special cases where the school district shows that exhausting those procedures would be futile or inadequate and that the disabled child is dangerous, without a court order.

Basis: The Court viewed the language of the "stay-put" provision in the Education for All Handicapped Children Act as unequivocal, and it viewed the legislative history as evidence of an intent not to provide an exception for "dangerousness." The Court denied that its interpretation left educators "hamstrung," because it did not affect their resort to such "normal procedures" as timeouts, detention, restriction of privileges, and — deferring to the U.S. Department of Education policy — suspensions for up to 10 days. Finally, the Court interpreted the Act as allowing, in special circumstances, judicial review and relief to temporarily enjoin dangerous disabled children from attending school without having to exhaust the administrative process under the Act.

Dellmuth v. Muth, 491 U.S. 223 (1989)

Facts: A parent unilaterally placed his son, who is a child with a disability as defined by the Education for All Handicapped Children Act (EAHCA, now the IDEA), in an approved private school. While the administrative proceedings were ongoing, Muth sued the school district seeking reimbursement for the private school tuition. The state, which was responsible under state law for part of the tuition at approved private schools, claimed that it was immune from such suits under the Eleventh Amendment.

Holding: [5/1x4] The Act does not abrogate the Eleventh Amendment immunity from suit; thus state governments, as compared to local governments, may not be held liable in suits under the Act.*

Basis: Congress may abrogate a state's immunity only when it makes its intention unmistakably clear in the statute. Inasmuch as the EAHCA does not have clear language in the statute abrogating a state's immunity, the state cannot be sued for tuition reimbursement under this law.

---

*This holding was effectively reversed by the 1990 amendments to the Act, in which Congress unmistakably waived states' Eleventh Amendment immunity in EAHCA (now IDEA) litigation.

Missouri v. Jenkins, 495 U.S. 33 (1990) ("Missouri II")*

Facts: Ruling that a school district and the state had operated a segregated school district, a federal trial court issued an order detailing a desegregation remedy and the financing necessary to implement it. It allocated the costs of the remedy between the district and state. After determining that several state-law provisions would prevent the district from being able to pay its share and that the district had exhausted all means of raising revenue, the trial court ordered the district to increase its property tax levy.

Holding: [8/1x0] A federal trial court abuses its discretion when it imposes a tax increase to pay for desegregation without first giving local officials the opportunity to devise their own solutions.

Basis: Citing *Brown* and *Milliken (supra)*, the Court noted that local authorities have the primary responsibility for solving the problems of desegregation. This is especially true for financing desegregation remedies. Local officials should at least have the opportunity to devise their own solutions. If local officials fail to devise new solutions, the trial court can enjoin the operation of state tax laws that hinder the district from collecting more revenues to fund the desegregation remedy.

Board of Education v. Dowell, 498 U.S. 237 (1991)

Facts: In 1972, finding that previous efforts to desegregate the city's schools had not been successful, the courts imposed a desegregation order on the school district. In 1977, the district court found that the district had achieved "unitary status" and entered an order terminating the case. Black students and their parents did not appeal. In 1984, the district adopted a Student Reassignment Plan (SRP) in which several previously desegregated schools were returned to primarily one-

---

*This case is known as *Missouri* v. *Jenkins II*. In *Missouri* v. *Jenkins I*, 491 U.S. 274 (1989), attorneys' fees were awarded to the plaintiffs for winning a desegregation remedy.

race status for the purpose of alleviating busing burdens on black children. The federal trial court denied respondent black children's motion to reopen the case, holding that its 1977 order was a final resolution of the case. The federal court of appeals reversed, ruling that the order could be challenged because the district was still subject to the desegregation decree. On remand, the trial court ruled that the original plan was no longer workable, that the district had in good faith complied with the order for more than a decade, and that the SRP was not designed with discriminatory intent. The court of appeals reversed, holding that a desegregation order remained in effect until a school district can show "grievous wrong evoked by new and unforeseen conditions" and that circumstances had not changed enough to justify modification of the 1972 order.

Holding: [5x3] School desegregation decrees are not intended to remain in effect in perpetuity. In deciding whether the board made a sufficient showing of constitutional compliance, the district court should decide whether the district had complied in good faith with the desegregation decree and whether the vestiges of past *de jure* desegregation had been eliminated to the extent practicable.

Basis: A finding by the trial court that the school district was in compliance with the equal protection clause of the Fourteenth Amendment — and that it is unlikely that the school district would return to its former ways — is a finding that the purposes of desegregation litigation had been achieved.

Franklin v. Gwinnett County Public Schools, 503 U.S. 60 (1992)

Facts: Claiming that she had been subjected to *quid pro quo**
sexual harassment by a teacher, a female high school student

---

*This transactional type of sexual harassment is the other judicially recognized form, in addition to the offensive-atmosphere breach of *Meritor (supra).*

sued her school district for monetary damages under Title IX of the Education Amendments of 1972. After she filed suit, the teacher resigned on condition that all claims pending against him be dropped. The school closed its investigation of the matter.

Holding: [7/2x0] A damages remedy is available for a lawsuit brought under Title IX.

Basis: Under *Cannon (infra)*, Title IX is enforceable through an implied right of action. The general rule is that federal courts have the authority to award any appropriate relief in a suit brought under a federal statute, unless Congress clearly states otherwise. To limit the permissible remedies under Title IX to back pay and prospective relief would contravene the general rule. Because she was a student, the back pay remedy would give her no relief. Similarly, because she is no longer a student and the teacher is no longer employed by the school district, prospective relief would be inadequate

Freeman v. Pitts, 503 U.S. 467 (1992)

Facts: In 1969, the respondents, black school students and their parents, asked the district court to dismantle the *de jure* segregated system in their school district. The trial court entered a consent order approving a plan and retaining jurisdiction to oversee the plan's implementation. In 1986, the school officials asked the court to declare that the system had achieved "unitary status" and no longer needed judicial supervision. The court found that the district had been successful in its dedication to equal education for all and declared that the district had achieved unitary status in four of the six factors set forth in *Green (supra)*: student assignments, transportation, physical facilities, and extracurricular activities.

Holding: [5/3x0] While supervising a desegregation plan, a district court has authority to relinquish supervision in incremental stages, before full compliance has been achieved in every area of school operations.

Basis: Acknowledging that *Green* requires a *de jure* segregated district to take all necessary steps to convert to a unitary system until discrimination is ended, the Court interpreted "unitary" as not having a fixed meaning and as not confining a supervising trial court's discretion. Such a court, applying its equitable authority, has the ability to develop feasible and practical remedies to correct a constitutional violation. The factors that must inform the court's discretion to order incremental withdrawal of its supervision are: whether there has been satisfactory compliance with the decree in those aspects of the system where supervision is to be withdrawn, whether retention of control is necessary or practicable to achieve compliance in other areas, and whether the school district has demonstrated to the public and to the parents and students of the once-disfavored race its compliance with the decree and to those legal provisions that were the basis of its decision in the first place.

Florence County School District Four v. Carter, 510 U.S. 7 (1993)

Facts: In 1985, when she was a ninth-grader, Shannon Carter was classified as learning disabled. School district officials proposed an IEP for a child classified as having a specific learning disability under the Individuals with Disabilities Education Act. The IEP provided that she would remain in regular education with three periods of resource-room instruction per week. It also provided specific goals for reading and mathematics of four months' progress for the entire school year. Her parents requested a hearing to challenge the appropriateness of the IEP. In the meantime, they unilaterally enrolled her in a private school for children with disabilities that was not approved by the state. The school district's IEP was determined by a court to be inappropriate. The parents sought tuition reimbursement under *Burlington (supra).*

Holding: [9x0] A court may order reimbursement for parents who unilaterally place their child in a private special education school that is otherwise proper, even if it does not have state approval.

Basis: In light of the overall purpose of IDEA to provide an appropriate program for each child with disabilities, and in light of the lesser information available to parents, the Court reasoned that holding them to the same procedural requirements as school districts would undermine their rights under *Burlington.*

Missouri v. Jenkins, 515 U.S. 70 (1995) ("Missouri III")

Facts: In this 18-year-old school desegregation case, punctuated previously by *Missouri II (supra)*, the state of Missouri challenged the trial court's orders requiring the state to fund salary increases for virtually all instructional and noninstructional staff within the Kansas City, Missouri, School District and to continue funding remedial "quality education" programs in that district because student achievement levels were still "at or below national norms in many grade levels."

Holding: [5x4] 1) The trial court's order approving salary increases, grounded in improving the "desegregative attractiveness" and thereby mitigating white flight, exceeds the court's discretion; that is, its goal of an interdistrict remedy is beyond the intradistrict violation. 2) Similarly, the order requiring the state to continue funding quality education programs cannot be sustained; the focus should be on the *Freeman* factors, rather than on normed achievement levels.*

Basis: The Court reasoned that although a federal district (that is, general trial level) court necessarily has discretion to fashion a remedy for a school district that was unconstitutionally segregated, such remedial power may not extend to purposes beyond the elimination of racial discrimination in public schools. Citing its precedents, the Court clarified that a dis-

---

*See the three criteria specified in the Basis section of *Freeman (supra)*.

trict court's remedial orders must be a proper means to restore the victims of discriminatory conduct to the position they would have occupied absent that conduct and to return to state and local authorities control of a school system that is operating in compliance with the Constitution. The ultimate inquiry is whether the constitutional violator has complied in good faith with the desegregation decree since it was entered and whether the vestiges of discrimination have been eliminated to the extent practicable.

United States v. Virginia, 518 U.S. 515 (1996)*

Facts: Virginia Military Institute is the sole single-sex school among Virginia's institutions of higher education. Using an "adversative method" of training not available elsewhere in the state, the institution has a distinctive mission to produce "citizen-soldiers," men prepared for leadership in civilian life and military service. Reflecting the high value alumni place on their training, the institution has the largest per-student endowment of all public undergraduate institutions in the nation. The United States sued the state, claiming that VMI's exclusively male policy violated the Fourteenth Amendment's equal protection clause.

Holding: [6/1x1] The categorical exclusion of females from the educational opportunities in an institution violates the Fourteenth Amendment's equal protection clause.

Basis: The Court concluded that the state had not provided the requisite "exceedingly persuasive justification" for government gender-based discrimination. The Court found that the state did not prove VMI's single-sex approach yielded the important governmental objectives of diversity in educational approaches and that purportedly substantially related means — providing citizen-soldier, adversative training — was not

---

*For related previous decisions, see *Williams* v. *McNair (supra)* and its footnoted cases.

suitable for women; its hypothetical and stereotypical generalizations were not exceedingly persuasive. Moreover, the Court rejected the proposed remedy of creating a separate such institution for women, at least where it was not substantially equal, as failing to cure the constitutional violation.

Gebser v. Lago Vista Independent School District, 524 U.S. 274 (1998)

Facts: Alida was a female ninth-grader whose English teacher often made sexually suggestive remarks to his students. He was particularly suggestive to her during the substantial amount of time he and she were alone in his classroom. During the spring semester, he visited her home, ostensibly to give her a book she needed for a school project. Finding her alone, he kissed and fondled her. The two had sexual intercourse on various occasions during the remainder of the school year. Their relationship continued during the summer, when she was the only student to attend his advanced placement course, into the following school year. They often had intercourse during school hours, though never on school property. Confused, Alida did not report the relationship to school officials. When other parents reported his inappropriately suggestive remarks in class, the principal spoke to the teacher, who promised to apologize to the parents and avoid such classroom comments in the future, though he asserted not being aware of their offensiveness. The principal reported the matter to the counselor but not to the superintendent, who was the district's Title IX coordinator. Upon discovering Alida and the teacher having intercourse in a parked car, a police officer arrested the teacher. The district terminated his employment, and the state education department subsequently revoked his teaching certificate. Alida's mother filed suit on her behalf, seeking compensatory and punitive damages under Title IX.

Holding: [5x4] A student victim of a school employee's sexual harassment may not recover money damages under Title IX unless an official of the district who has authority to institute corrective measure on the district's behalf has actual notice of, and is deliberately indifferent to, the employee's misconduct.

Basis: Contrasting Title IX with Title VII, the Court rejected constructive notice (that is, having reason to know) and imputed (that is, agency) liability. Reserving the possibility of legislative redirection, the majority prefaced its relatively narrow standard of actual notice and deliberate indifference with the words, "[u]ntil Congress directly speaks on the subject." The dissent referred to the Office for Civil Rights' doctrine of vicarious liability and its approach to constructive notice, finding Title VII analogous.

Bragdon v. Abbott, 524 U.S. 624 (1998)

Facts: A patient infected with HIV but not manifesting its most serious symptoms went to her dentist's office for a checkup. In the course of the examination, she disclosed her HIV infection to the dentist, who discovered a cavity. Informing her of his policy against filling cavities of HIV-infected patients in his office, he offered to perform the work at a local hospital at no extra charge. She declined and filed suit, with the primary basis being the Americans with Disabilities Act, or ADA, which prohibits not only government entities (Title II of the ADA) but also private entities that are places of public accommodation, such as private schools (Title III) from discriminating based on disability. The defendant cited the Title III exception: "Nothing [herein] shall require an entity to permit an individual to participate in or benefit from the . . . accommodation of such entity where such individual poses a direct threat to the health or safety of others."

Holding: [5/2x2] An individual with HIV qualifies as having a "disability" as defined under the ADA even when the infection has not progressed to the so-called symptomatic phase, but whether the individual poses a "direct threat" is determined on the basis of medical or other objective, scientific evidence, not simply the good-faith belief of the entity.

Basis: 1) The ADA definition of "disability," which is "a physical or mental impairment that substantially limits one or more of [an individual's] major life activities," is virtually identical to that in Section 504 of the Rehabilitation Act, which the ADA expressly provides as the lower limit of its interpretation. From the moment of infection, HIV satisfies the element of "physical impairment," as defined by Section 504 regulations. The "major life activity" element — as also clarified by Section 504 regulations — is not limited to public, economic, or daily functions; and in the case of a female, it includes the ability to reproduce and bear children, which are central to the life process itself. Finally, the "substantially limits" element is met by medical evidence in two independent respects. First, if she tries to conceive a child, she imposes on her male partner a statistically significant risk of becoming infected. Second, she risks infecting her child during gestation and childbirth. The Court found further support for its conclusion in the added costs for antiretroviral therapy, supplemental insurance, and long-term health care; laws in some state forbidding HIV-infected persons from having sex, regardless of the other person's consent; the guidance issued by the Department of Justice and other agencies charged with interpreting the ADA; and the uniform body of administrative and judicial precedents under Section 504. 2) Explaining that the ADA's direct-threat provision stems from *School Board* v. *Arline (supra)*, the Court explained that the applicable test is objective reasonableness, rather than subjective good faith, from the point of view of the health care profession. Although doubting that the defendant had advanced evidence sufficient to raise a triable issue of fact on the significance of the risk, the Court remanded the case for more careful reexamination of this issue, cautioning against overreliance on professional guidelines to the extent that they are not based on scientific assessment of the risk of transmission.

Burlington Industries, Inc. v. Ellerth, 524 U.S. 742 (1998)*

Facts: A company's mid-level manager allegedly subjected one of his female subordinates to constant sexual harassment. He had authority to hire and promote employees, subject to higher approval, but not to make policy. Against a background of repeated boorish and offensive remarks and gestures, on three occasions he made specific comments that could be construed as threats to deny her tangible job benefits. She refused all of his advances, yet suffered no tangible retaliation; instead, at one point she received a promotion. Despite knowing that the company had a policy against sexual harassment, she never informed anyone in authority about her supervisor's conduct. After quitting her job, she filed suit, claiming that the company forced her constructive discharge in violation of Title VII, which prohibits employment discrimination based on, among other protected categories, gender.

Holding: [7x2] Under Title VII, an employee who refused the unwelcome and threatening sexual advances of a supervisor, yet suffers no adverse, tangible job consequences, may recover against the employer without showing the employer is at fault for the supervisor's actions. But the employer may raise a defense that it exercised reasonable care to prevent and correct promptly any sexually harassing behavior and that the victimized employee unreasonably failed to take advantage of these preventive or corrective measures or otherwise to avoid harm.

---

*For another relatively recent but narrow ruling concerning Title VII liability, see *Landgraf* v. *USI Film Products*, 511 U.S. 244 (1994) (held that the 1991 amendment to Title VII authorizing money damages does not apply to a Title VII case that was pending on appeal at the time of the amendment's enactment). For a parallel ruling rejecting the retrospective application of a 1991 amendment to Section 1981, see *Rivers* v. *Roadway Express, Inc.*, 511 U.S. 298 (1994).

Basis: Citing *Meritor (supra)*, the Court observed that not only "quid pro quo," but also, like this one, "hostile work environment" claims are cognizable under Title VII. Based on the Title VII definition of "employer" to include "agents," the Court relied on the general common law of agency that a master is liable for the torts, whether intentional or negligent, of its servants committed outside the scope of their employment if the employer is negligent. Inasmuch as sexual harassment by a supervisor is not within the scope of employment, the employer is subject to liability if it knew or should have known about it and failed to stop it. For this purpose, the presence of an antiharassment policy with a grievance procedure is relevant, though not essential or controlling. In contrast, the more stringent standard of vicarious liability applies only when a supervisor subjects a subordinate to a significant, tangible employment action, such as discharge, demotion, or undesirable reassignment.

Farragher v. City of Boca Raton, 524 U.S. 775 (1998)

Facts: After resigning, a female lifeguard alleged that her supervisors had created a sexually hostile work atmosphere by repeatedly subjecting her and other female lifeguards to uninvited and offensive touching, lewd remarks, and sexually offensive comments. She filed suit based on Title VII.

Holding: [7x2] An employer is vicariously liable for actionable sexual harassment by a supervisor but may raise a defense that its conduct was reasonable and that of the victimized employee was not.

Basis: Citing *Meritor (supra)*, the Court cautioned that common-law agency principles might not be transferable en toto. Rejecting misuse of supervisory authority, without more, as irrelevant to scope-of-employment analysis, the Court used the approach in *Burlington Industries (supra)*, which is the companion to this case, that recognition of an affirmative employer defense provides the counter to the automatic liability rejected in *Meritor.*

Cedar Rapids Community School District v. Garret F., 526 U.S. 66 (1999)

Facts: A student in a regular class placement and eligible under the Individuals with Disabilities Education Act (IDEA), Garret is wheelchair-bound and ventilator-dependent. Therefore he requires constant, specialized, nursing care. His parents maintained that this care is a "related service" under the IDEA and, thus, the school district's financial obligation during the school day. Refusing to provide or pay for these nursing services, the district maintained that they fit under the exclusion for medical treatment services under the IDEA definition of "related services." The parents filed for a due process hearing, claiming that the district's refusal was a violation of the IDEA.

Holding: [7x2] Constant, specialized, nursing services, if necessary for an IDEA-eligible child to benefit from special education, is a related, not medical, service; medical services are those that require a physician.

Basis: Adopting this standard for medical services, rather than the cost-based, multi-factor test advocated by the school district, the Court relied on *Tatro (supra)*, which in turn had deferred to the U.S. Department of Education's regulations and policy letters. The cost concerns, according to the majority, are a matter for Congress, not the courts.

Davis v. Monroe County Board of Education, 526 U.S. 629 (1999)

Facts: A male classmate had allegedly sexually harassed Lashonda, a female fifth-grader, for more than five months, including repeated incidents of unwanted touching and vulgar comments. Despite complaints by Lashonda and her mother to classroom teachers and the school principal, the school took no disciplinary action against the harasser. Lashonda's grades dropped, and she contemplated suicide. Her mother filed suit on her behalf, claiming that school officials were liable under Title IX, which prohibits federally funded pro-grams from discrimination based on gender.

Holding: [5x4] A school district may be liable for damages under Title IX for student-to-student sexual harassment only where the district is deliberately indifferent and has actual knowl-edge of harassment that is so severe, pervasive, and objec-tively offensive that it deprives the victim(s) of access to the educational opportunities or benefits provided by the school.

Basis: The majority adopted and adjusted the standard of *Gebser (supra)*, again rejecting agency principles and relying on the language of Title IX. Specifically, the language "subject" and "under the operations of" suggest that the liability of a district, as a recipient of federal funds, is limited to circum-stances where it exercises substantial control over both the harasser and the context of the harassment, which here al-legedly occurred during school hours and on school grounds. Similarly, peer sexual harassment, if sufficiently severe, can likewise rise to the level of "discrimination." Citing a recent precedent in the private sector,* the Court clarified that whether gender-oriented conduct is harassment depends on multiple factors, including the harasser's and victim's ages and the number of persons involved.

Sutton v. United Airlines, 527 U.S. 471 (1999)**

Facts: A commercial airlines company refused employment as pilots to otherwise qualified twin sisters whose severe

---

Oncale v. *Sundowner Offshore Services, Inc.*, 523 U.S. 75 (1998) (held that same-sex sexual harassment is actionable under Title VII).

**This case was one of a trilogy of decisions with the same basic holding. The other two are *Murphy* v. *United Parcel Service*, 527 U.S. 516 (1999) (high blood pressure - medication) and *Albertsons, Inc.* v. *Kirkingburg*, 527 U.S. 555 (1999) (monocular vision - compensatory strategies). For other recent ADA cases, see *Olmstead* v. *L.C.*, 527 U.S. 581 (1999) (held that isolating people with disabili-ties in large state institutions without medical justification violates the ADA); *Cleveland* v. *Policy Management Systems Corporation*, 526 U.S. 795 (1999) (held that an employee is not necessarily barred from pursuing simultaneous claims for both Social Security Disability Insurance and the ADA).

mypoia was correctable to 20/20 vision with eyeglasses. The sole reason was that they did not meet the airlines minimum uncorrected vision requirements. They filed suit, claiming that the refusal violated the Americans with Disabilities Act of 1990. This act, like Section 504,* defines disability as "a physical or mental impairment that substantially limits a major life activity." The sisters relied on Equal Employment Opportunity Commission and Department of Justice interpretations that the measurement of "substantially" should be done without regard to mitigating measures, such as eyeglasses and medication.

Holding: [7x2] Mitigating measures should be considered in determining whether an individual is disabled under the Americans with Disabilities Act.

Basis: The Court based its decision on the plain language of the Act; "substantially limits" is in the present tense, implying that the disability is not hypothetical or conditioned. The Court also pointed to congressional findings that the law was intended to cover a relatively limited number of people, which would be far greater if Congress had meant them to be evaluated in their uncorrected state.

Alexander v. Sandoval, 121 S. Ct. 1511 (2001)

Facts: A recipient of federal financial assistance, Alabama's motor vehicle department, in accordance with its official policy, administers its driver's license examination only in the English language. A driver's license applicant filed a class action (that is, a suit on behalf of similarly situated persons) claiming that this English-only policy violated the federal regulations under Title VI of the civil rights act, which prohibits discrimination in federally funded programs based on,

---

*The basic difference is that Sec. 504 applies only to recipients of federal funds, whereas the ADA also applies to private entities that provide public accommodations, including, for example, private schools, even if they do not receive any federal financial assistance.

among other things, national origin. Specifically, she pointed to the regulation forbidding such programs to use criteria or administrative methods that have a disparate effect on protected persons.

Holding: [5x4] There is no private right of action to enforce the disparate-impact regulations of Title VI.

Basis: The majority concluded that although *Cannon (infra)* allows private individuals to sue to enforce the Title VI legislation, its precedents also make clear that this legislation applies only to intentional discrimination. Following its relatively recent and restrictive view of federal power, the majority refused to infer such a substantive right based on administrative regulations in the absence of clear evidence of congressional intent. Rather, the majority interpreted the text and structure of Title VI as not intending such a private remedy.

Clark County School District v. Breeden, 121 S. Ct. 1508 (2001)

Facts: Breeden, a human resources administrator in a large school district, met with her male supervisor and another male co-worker to review the psychological evaluation reports of four job applicants. The supervisor read out loud the reported comment of one of the applicants, "I hear making love to you is like making love to the Grand Canyon," and, looking at Breeden, stated: "I don't know what that means." The other employee then said, "Well, I'll tell you later," and both men chuckled. Breeden later complained about the matter to central administrators with higher authority than the two men. The district subsequently involuntarily transferred her. She claimed that district officials punished her for complaining about the alleged sexual harassment and also for filing suit against the district based on Title VII, which prohibits sexual harassment and other forms of employment discrimination.

Holding: [9x0] 1) An isolated incident of simple, not egregious, offhand comments does not amount to sexual harassment subject to suit under Title VII. 2) For Title VII retaliation claims, evidence of a causal connection between the protected activity and adverse employment action cannot be based on stretched inferences.

Basis: 1) Citing its various pertinent precedents (for example, *Farragher* and *Burlington Industries*), the Court explained that sexual harassment is actionable under Title VII only if it is so objectively "severe and pervasive" as to alter the conditions of the victim's employment. Here, no reasonable person could have perceived this situation to fit the exception for egregious, or "extremely serious," isolated incidents. 2) Similarly relying on its precedents, the Court clarified that temporal proximity, when used as the sole basis for causality, must be "very close." Here, the district did not receive the notice of suit until one day after its representative indicated any intention of transferring Breeden, and the period between her first filing charges with the EEOC and the initial indication of her transfer amounted to 20 months.

PGA Tour, Inc. v. Martin, 121 S. Ct. 1879 (2001)

Facts: A private organization sponsors professional golf tournaments on three annual tours, for which it leases and operates golf courses. The most common way to gain entry is for a player to compete successfully in a three-stage qualifying tournament known as the "Q-School." Any member of the public may enter the Q-School by submitting two letters of recommendation and paying a $3,000 entry fee. The general Rules of Golf do not prohibit the use of golf carts, but the special rules of the organization prohibit their use at the third stage of the Q-School qualifying tournament and for all the regular tournaments except the open qualifying events and the senior tour. Martin has a degenerative circulatory disorder that prevents him from walking golf courses and that constitutes a disability under the ADA. Fatigue is a factor in the competition, but Martin's fatigue in walking between the cart and his strokes is undeniably greater than the fatigue his ablebodied competitors endure walking the entire course. When Martin turned pro and entered the Q-School, he made a request, supported by detailed medical records, requesting permission to use a golf cart during the third stage. The organization refused, and he filed suit under Title III of the ADA, which requires an entity operating "public accommodations" to make "reasonable modifications" that are necessary unless the entity demonstrates that such modifications constitute a fundamental alteration.*

Holding: [7x2] 1) Title III of the ADA applies to PGA Tour, Inc., as a lessor and operator of golf courses, in relation to competing golfers as well as to its other clients or customers. 2) Failure to waive an athletic eligibility rule violates the ADA where an individualized determination reveals that such waiver not only is reasonable and necessary, but also does not fundamentally alter the nature of the athletic event.

Basis: 1) Citing the legislative history of the ADA's Title III and the case law under the "public accommodations" race-related legislation, the majority concluded that the golf tours and qualifying rounds "fit comfortably" within Title III's coverage and that competing golfers — not just the public spectators — are clients or customers if Title III is implicitly restricted to such a limited category. 2) Inasmuch as the defendant organization did not dispute that a golf cart is a reasonable and necessary modification, the focus was whether it constituted a fundamental alteration. Finding the walking rule not to be an essential, or indispensable, feature of golf generally or tournament golf specifically, the majority ruled that waiving it would be a fundamental alteration if

---

*Title I of the ADA applies to employment, and Title II of the ADA applies to government entities.

only such waiver provided a competitive advantage. Finally, the majority concluded that there would be no such advantage because the evidence was preponderant that pure chance may play a more influential role than fatigue; fatigue is not a significant factor in tournament golf, being more psychological than physical; in the stages and tournaments where carts are allowed, the majority of golfers have opted to walk for strategic reasons; and, most important, Martin endures more fatigue with a cart than his competitors do without a cart. For such determinations, the majority concluded that the ADA requires an individualized inquiry to consider the modification or waiver of such a rule and to weigh the rule's purpose and rationales.

CHAPTER SIX

Civil Rights Cases: Special Rules

McNeese v. Board of Education, 373 U.S. 668 (1962)

Facts: Black students in a public school sued under Sec. 1983, claiming that their Fourteenth Amendment rights had been violated. The school's enrollment was approximately 50% blacks and 50% white. With few exceptions, the black students attended classes in one part of the school, apart from the whites. They were compelled to use entrances and exits separate from the whites.

Holding: [8x1] Citizens may seek to vindicate their rights under Sec. 1983 even though they did not first seek relief under a state law that provided a remedy for them.

Basis: The purpose of Sec. 1983 was to override certain state laws to provide a remedy where state law is inadequate or where the state remedy — though adequate in theory — is not adequate in practice, and to provide a federal remedy in addition to any that state law may provide. Those purposes would be defeated if it were held that assertion of a federal claim in a United States court must await an attempt to vindicate the same claim in state court. In this case it was not clear that, under state law, the suing students had an administrative remedy adequate enough to preclude their seeking vindication from the federal courts.

Wood v. Strickland, 420 U.S. 308 (1975)

Facts: Three high school students were expelled for violating school regulations because they put malt liquor in the punch served at an extracurricular meeting held at the school. The students and their parents brought suit under Sec. 1983, a federal statute that provides that any person who, under the color of state law, deprives anyone within the jurisdiction of the United States of constitutional rights or of rights secured by federal law, shall be liable to the injured party in a lawsuit for money damages or for other relief. The students sought money damages from two school administrators and from the members of the school board.

Holding: [5/2x2] In the context of school discipline, a school official's immunity from liability for money damages sought under Sec. 1983 depends on two elements of good faith: 1) The subjective element requires that to retain immunity, the official acted in the sincere belief that he or she was doing right and without a "malicious intention to cause a deprivation of constitutional rights or other injury to the student."* 2) The objective element causes the school official to lose immunity if "he knew or reasonably should have known that the action he took . . . would violate the constitutional rights of the student affected." The objective part of the good faith requirement is satisfied if the official acts in accordance with the "students' clearly established constitutional rights" and with "settled, indisputable law."

Basis: The Court found that public policy and prior legal decisions require a qualified good faith immunity from damages for officials so that those who act in good faith and within the scope of their duties will not be intimidated in meeting their responsibilities by a fear of being sued.

In light of the importance of civil rights, the Court found that the objective element, requiring the administrator to act in accord with the settled law and with the constitutional

---

*This part of the holding was overruled in *Harlow (infra)*. For subsequent developments regarding the remaining part, see *Owen (infra)* and *Gomez (infra)*.

rights of those affected by official action, was a reasonable condition for their immunity from a lawsuit for damages. On the other hand, if a school official acts out of ignorance or in disregard to settled law, the official may be sued.

Declining to consider questions of interpretation and application of the relevant school regulations, the Court noted that Sec. 1983 provides for federal court correction of only those improper exercises of discretion that result in violation of specific constitutional guarantees. The Court deferred decision as to whether there had been a denial of procedural due process required by the Fourteenth Amendment, sending the case back to the lower court for initial consideration of that issue.

Christianburg Garment Co. v. Equal Employment Opportunity Commission, 434 U.S. 412 (1978)*

Facts: After an employee stopped pursuing a racial discrimination charge under Title VII against her employer, the Equal Employment Opportunity Commission (EEOC) sued the employer. The district court granted summary judgment to the employer on the basis that this case was not pending at the time of the 1972 Amendments to Title VII, which authorized the EEOC to sue in its own name on pending charges. Subsequently, the employer petitioned for the allowance of legal fees against the EEOC pursuant to Title VII.

Holding: [8x0] Although a prevailing plaintiff in a Title VII action is ordinarily entitled to attorneys' fees, a prevailing defendant is to be awarded such fees only when the court finds that the plaintiff's action was frivolous, unreasonable, or without foundation.**

---

*For the Court's endorsement of the American rule that the prevailing party may not, in absence of statutory authorization, recover attorneys' fees, see *Alyeska Pipeline Serv. Co.* v. *Wilderness Society*, 421 U.S. 240 (1975).

**For an extension of this holding to Sec. 1988 cases, see *Hughes* v. *Rowe*, 449 U.S. 5 (1980).

Basis: The Court found two equitable considerations favoring an award of fees to plaintiffs that do not apply to defendants: 1) the plaintiff is Congress' chosen instrument to vindicate a policy that was a national priority; and 2) when a court awards fees to a prevailing plaintiff, it is awarding them against a violator of the law.

Carey v. Piphus, 435 U.S. 247 (1978)*

Facts: Two students were suspended for 20 days, one for smoking marijuana during school hours on school property and the other for wearing an earring in violation of a school rule intended to discourage street gang activities in school. The district court held that both students had been suspended in violation of the Fourteenth Amendment and that school officials were not entitled to qualified immunity from damages under *Wood* v. *Strickland (supra)*, because under *Goss* v. *Lopez (supra)* they should have known that a lengthy suspension without any type of adjudicative hearing violated procedural due process.

Holding: [7/1x0] In the absence of proof of actual injury, students who have been suspended without the requisite procedural due process are entitled to recover only nominal damages.

Basis: The basic purpose of a Sec. 1981 damages award should be to compensate persons for injuries incurred by the denial of constitutional rights. This traditional tort principle hardly could have been foreign to the members of Congress who enacted this post-Civil War legislation. There is no legislative history to indicate an intent to establish a more formidable deterrent. Although the denial of constitutional rights, other than procedural due process, may require more substantial damage awards than the common law tort rules of damages, that is a separate matter not at issue in this case.

---

*For a case vacated and remanded in light of this decision, see *Smalling* v. *Epperson*, 438 U.S. 948 (1978).

Violations of due process do not necessarily cause strong feelings of mental and emotional distress. An award of nominal damages recognizes the absolute right to procedural due process even where there is no proof of actual injury.

Monell v. Department of Social Services, 436 U.S. 658 (1978)*

Facts: Female employees of the Department of Social Services and the Board of Education of New York City brought this class action against the department and its commissioner, the board and its chancellor, and the city and its mayor under Sec. 1983, which provides that every "person" who under color of state law deprives any other person of any federally protected rights, privileges, or immunities shall be civilly liable to the injured party. The individual defendants were sued solely in their official capacities. The essence of the complaint was that the department and the board had, as a matter of official policy, compelled pregnant employees to take unpaid leaves of absence before such leaves were required for medical reasons.

Holding: [6/1x2] Local governing bodies (including school boards) and their officials may be sued in their official capacities under Sec. 1983, except that they cannot be held liable under Sec. 1983 for an injury inflicted solely by their employees or agents.

Basis: Re-examining the language and legislative history of the Civil Rights Act, now codified as 42 U.S.C. Sec. 1983, the Court reversed its prior ruling in *Monroe* v. *Pape*, 365 U.S. 167 (1961) insofar as it had held that local governments are wholly immune from Sec. 1983 suits.

Cannon v. University of Chicago, 441 U.S. 677 (1979)

Facts: A student who sought admission to medical school alleged that her application was denied because she was a woman.

---

*For a case vacated in light of this decision, see *Kornit* v. *Board of Education*, 438 U.S. 902 (1978). For a follow-up decision to *Monell*, see *Pembaur (infra)*.

The medical education program at this private university was receiving federal financial assistance at the time her application for admission was denied. She based her original complaint on several federal statutes; but on appeal, the basis of her allegation was limited to Title IX of the Education Amendments of 1972. Both the district court and the court of appeals held that Title IX does not contain an implied private remedy, that is, an individual right to damages.

Holding: [5/1x3] Title IX contains an implied private cause of action.

Basis: The Court indicated that in cases where the statute is silent or ambiguous about a private remedy, the appropriate test of Congress' intent consists of the four factors identified in *Cort* v. *Ash*, 422 U.S. 66 (1975), which are identified in question form and answered for this case as follows:

1) Was the statute enacted for the benefit of a special class of which plaintiff is a member? Title IX specifically confers a benefit on persons discriminated against on the basis of sex, and plaintiff was clearly a member of that class.

2) Was there any indication of legislative intent to create a private remedy? The legislative history showed that the drafters of Title IX assumed that it would be interpreted in the same manner as Title VI, which already had been constructed by lower federal courts as creating a private remedy.

3) Was implementation of such a remedy consistent with the underlying purposes of the statutory scheme? Such a remedy would assist in achieving one of the two fundamental purposes of the Act, that is, providing individual citizens protection against discriminatory practices.

4) Did the subject matter involve an area not basically of concern to the states? Since the Civil War, the federal government has been the primary forum for protecting citizens against invidious discrimination.

The Court found Title IX to present the atypical situation in which all four factors in *Cort* v. *Ash* are satisfied.

Owen v. City of Independence, Missouri, 445 U.S. 622 (1980)

Facts: In 1967 a chief of police was appointed to an indefinite term by the city manager. In 1972 a new city manager and the chief of police engaged in a dispute over the chief's administration of the police department's property room. The city manager conducted an investigation, which found record-keeping problems but no criminal violations. Subsequently, the manager asked the chief to resign and accept another position in the police department, warning that he would be terminated if he refused. Three days later the city manager issued a public statement reporting the results of the investigation and assuring that steps had been initiated to correct the discrepancies in the administration of the property room. The chief, having consulted with counsel, formally requested written notice of the charges and a public hearing to respond to them. The city council soon thereafter voted that the investigative reports be released to the news media and to the prosecutor, and that the city manager discharge the chief. No reason was given for the dismissal. The chief's earlier demand for a specification of charges and a public hearing was ignored, and a subsequent request for an appeal of the discharge decision was denied. He brought suit under Sec. 1983 for violation of his due process rights.

Holding: [5x4] The qualified immunity of local government officials and agents does not extend to local governing bodies (for example, a municipal corporation) as a defense against liability under Sec. 1983.

Basis: The language of Sec. 1983 and its legislative history are expansive. The Court has found immunities only in contexts where there is a tradition of immunity strongly rooted in the common law and supported by strong policy reasons. There is not a tradition of, nor policy support for, immunity for municipal corporations.

Gomez v. Toledo, 446 U.S. 635 (1980)

Facts: A detective in a police department submitted a sworn statement to his supervisor that two other detectives had offered false evidence in a criminal case under their investigation. As a result, he was transferred to a noninvestigative position. The police department's legal division investigated the matter, concluding that his factual allegations were true. A year later he was subpoenaed to testify as a defense witness in a criminal case arising out of the evidence he had alleged to be false. He was subsequently brought up on criminal charges, based on evidence furnished by the police department, for the alleged unlawful wiretapping of the two other detectives' telephones. The police department suspended him the following month, and two months later discharged him without a hearing. He was subsequently exonerated in the courts. He then sought review of his discharge, which was revoked after a hearing; and the police department was ordered to reinstate him with back pay. He then filed a Sec. 1983 suit in federal court for damages, contending that his discharge violated his procedural due process rights.

Holding: [8/1x0] In a Sec. 1983 action, the good faith element of the qualified immunity is a required part of the public official's defense, not of the plaintiff's claim.

Basis: In *Owen (supra)*, the Court pointed out that as remedial legislation, Sec. 1983 is to be construed generously to further its primary purpose of vindicating constitutional guarantees. In *Wood* v. *Strickland (supra)* and in other cases, the Court accommodated common law tradition and strong public policy reasons by according public officials a qualified immunity from liability for damages for acts done with an objectively reasonable belief that those acts were lawful. As the Court's decisions make clear, the qualified immunity is a defense, based on facts particularly within the knowledge and control of the defendant public official.

Maine v. Thiboutot, 448 U.S. 1 (1980)*

Facts: A married couple with eight children, three by the husband's previous marriage, were notified by the Human Services Department that, in computing welfare benefits, the husband was entitled to benefits for his three children but would no longer be allowed support for the other five children, even though the husband was legally obligated to support them. After exhausting their administrative remedies, the couple brought suit challenging the state's interpretation of the federal Social Security Act and claiming relief under Sec. 1983 for themselves and others similarly situated. Sec. 1983 established liability of any person who under color of state law deprives another person of "any rights, privileges, or immunities secured by the Constitution *and laws*" [emphasis added].

Holding: [6x3] Sec. 1983 and its accompanying attorneys' fees provision, Sec. 1988, apply to violations of federal statutes as well as to violations of the federal Constitution.

Basis: The plain language of Sec. 1983 undoubtedly embraces the couple's claim that the department violated a federal statute. Even if the language were ambiguous, several of the Court's previous decisions (for example, *Monell* and *Owen*, *supra*) have suggested explicitly or implicitly that the Sec. 1983 remedy broadly encompasses violations of federal statutory as well as constitutional law. The legislative history of Sec. 1983 is limited, but it is not inconsistent with this interpretation. The plain language and legislative history of Sec. 1988 (the Civil Rights Attorney's Fees Awards Act) similarly supports its applicability to deprivations of statutory rights, whether brought in state or federal courts.

---

*This decision was applied with further elaboration in *Pennhurst State School and Hospital* v. *Halderman*, 451 U.S. 1 (1981); *Middlesex County Sewerage Auth.* v. *National Sea Clammers Ass'n*, 453 U.S. 1 (1981); and *Wright* v. *Roanoke Redevelopment & Housing Auth.*, 479 U.S. 418 (1987).

Maher v. Gagne, 448 U.S. 122 (1980)

Facts: A recipient of benefits under Connecticut's federally funded Aid to Families with Dependent Children (AFDC) brought a Sec. 1983 action alleging that the state's AFDC regulations denied her credit for portions of her work-related expenses, thus reducing the level of her benefits. The recipient alleged that the regulations violated the Social Security Act and the equal protection and due process clauses of the Fourteenth Amendment. Ultimately the case was settled, but the recipient subsequently filed a claim for attorneys' fees under Sec. 1988, the Civil Rights Attorney's Fees Awards Act.

Holding: [5/3x0] 1) Under Sec. 1988, an award of attorneys' fees is not limited to cases in which Sec. 1983 is invoked as a remedy for a constitutional violation or a violation of a federal statute that provides for the protection of civil rights. Sec. 1988 applies to all types of Sec. 1983 actions, including actions based solely on Social Security Act violations. 2) The fact that the claimant prevailed through a settlement, rather than through litigation, does not preclude her from claiming attorneys' fees within the meaning of Sec. 1988.

Basis: 1) Citing *Maine* v. *Thiboutot* (decided the same day), the Court held that Sec. 1988 applies to all types of Sec. 1983 actions. A statute awarding attorneys' fees in a case where "the plaintiff prevails on a wholly statutory, non-civil-rights claim pendent to a substantial constitutional claim or in one in which both a statutory and a substantial constitutional claim are settled favorably to the plaintiff without adjudication" falls within the category of appropriate legislation. 2) Looking to legislative history, the Court pointed out that the Senate Report expressly provided for the award of counsel fees when an individual's rights were vindicated through a consent judgment or without formally obtaining relief.

Delaware State College v. Ricks, 449 U.S. 250 (1980)*

Facts: A black man from Liberia became a member of the faculty at a state college attended predominantly by black students. Subsequently the college's tenure committee recommended that he not receive a tenured position. The committee agreed to reconsider its position the following year; but when it did so, it confirmed the earlier recommendation. In March 1974 the board of trustees voted to deny him tenure. The teacher immediately filed a grievance alleging national origin discrimination. The board, per its policies, sent him official notice in June 1974 of its decision and offered him a one-year "terminal" contract. Soon after, the grievance committee voted to recommend denial of his grievance. The teacher signed the contract without objection or reservations in September 1974, and a week later the board notified him that it had denied his grievance. In April 1974 he had filed an employment discrimination charge with the Equal Employment Opportunity Commission (EEOC), which it accepted later that month after obtaining a jurisdictional waiver from the state fair employment practices agency. More than two years later, the EEOC issued a "right to sue" letter. The former faculty member filed this lawsuit in September 1977 based on Title VII and Sec. 1981. The college moved to dismiss both claims as untimely, arguing that the applicable time limits (180 days and 4 years, respectively) began to run when the board officially notified him of the decision to deny him tenure and to offer him a one-year terminal contract.

Holding: [5x4] The filing limitation periods of Title VII and Sec. 1981 commence at the time of the alleged discriminatory acts, not when the consequences of the acts culminate. In this case the periods commenced with official notification of the board's decision of denial of tenure, not with the subse-

---

*For a follow-up decision, see *Chardon (infra).*

quent notification of the decision of denial of grievance nor the subsequent expiration of the terminal contract.

Basis: Mere continuity of employment is insufficient to prolong the life of a cause of action for employment discrimination. If the teacher intended to complain of a discriminatory charge, he should have identified the alleged discriminatory acts that continued until, or occurred at the time of, the actual termination of his employment.

Equal Employment Opportunity Commission v. Associated Dry Goods Corporation, 449 U.S. 590 (1981)

Facts: Title VII of the Civil Rights Act of 1964 limits the authority of the Equal Employment Opportunity Commission (EEOC) to make public disclosure of information it has obtained in investigating and attempting to resolve a claim of employment discrimination. Seven employees of a department store chain filed complaints of employment discrimination with the EEOC. The EEOC began its investigation by requesting the company to provide employment records of the complainants and statistics and other information relating to the company's general personnel policies. The company refused to provide the information unless the EEOC agreed beforehand not to disclose any of the requested material to the challenging parties. After the EEOC subpoenaed the material, the company filed suit to enjoin enforcement of the subpoena.

Holding: [5/½x1½] Congress did not include charging parties among those to whom disclosure of confidential information may be denied under Title VII, but charging parties are entitled to the information only in their own files, not in those of other employees.

Basis: The language, logic, scheme, and legislative history of the disclosure provisions support this ruling. Administrative convenience cannot override the prohibitions of the statute.

Parratt v. Taylor, 451 U.S. 527 (1981)*

Facts: A prison inmate filed a Sec. 1983 action against state officials when packages that he ordered were lost when normal procedures for receipt of mail were not followed. He alleged that the officials had negligently caused the loss, thereby depriving him of property without due process under the Fourteenth Amendment.

Holding: [7/1½x½] Where an individual has been deprived of property under color of state law, he has not sufficiently alleged a violation of the Fourteenth Amendment where the deprivation occurred as a result of negligence and where he has an adequate state tort remedy.

Basis: The Court interpreted the language and legislative history of Sec. 1983 as not limiting the statute to intentional deprivation of constitutional rights. However, precedents make clear that post-deprivation remedies made available by a state can satisfy the due process clause. Here, the state's tort claims law provided a sufficient remedy.

City of Newport v. Fact Concerts, 453 U.S. 247 (1981)

Facts: A corporation organized for the purpose of promoting musical concerts sought to obtain a license from a city in Rhode Island to present the city's 1975 jazz festival. The contract gave the corporation control over the choice of performers and type of music to be played, and it granted the city the right to cancel the license without liability if "in the opinion of the City the interests of public safety demand." Shortly before the concert, the corporation hired a replacement for a previously engaged performer who was unable to appear. Members of the city council, including the mayor, attempted to cancel the contract because they felt that the replacement group was a rock band rather than a jazz band,

---

*This decision was extended in *Hudson* v. *Palmer (infra)* and was partially overruled by *Daniels* v. *Williams (infra)*.

and the city had experienced crowd disturbances at previous rock concerts. The corporation obtained a restraining order in state court, and the two-day concert was held as scheduled. However, due to adverse publicity, fewer than half the available tickets were sold. The promoters brought suit against the city, the mayor, and six other council members, alleging that the city's cancellation of the license amounted to a violation of their constitutional rights under color of state law. They sought compensatory and punitive damages under Sec. 1983.

Holding: [6x3] Local governments (including school boards) are immune from punitive damages under Sec. 1983.

Basis: Citing *Owen (supra)*, the Court applied a two-part approach, examining common law history and public policy considerations. When Congress enacted what is now Sec. 1983, the immunity of a municipality from punitive damages at common law was well established. Similarly, public policy considerations in terms of the objectives of punitive damages and their relationship to the goals of Sec. 1983 do not support exposing a municipality to punitive damages for the bad faith actions of the officials.

Chardon v. Fernandez, 454 U.S. 6 (1981)

Facts: Several nontenured administrators were notified prior to 18 June 1977 that they would be terminated on a specific date between June and August 1977. On 19 June 1978, one of the administrators filed suit contending that the terminations violated Sec. 1983. The district court dismissed the case because the applicable one-year statute of limitations had run out.

Holding: [6x3] The statute of limitations for Sec. 1983 suits begins to run from the time the employee has been informed of his termination, not the date when the termination became effective.

Basis: Citing its precedent in *Delaware State College* v. *Ricks* *(supra)* as indistinguishable, the Court considered the question of the tolling of the statute of limitations for Sec. 1983 as having been answered. Both here and in *Ricks*, which involved denial of tenure, the operative decision was made and notice was given in advance of a designated date on which employment terminated. In *Ricks*, the Court held the proper focus is on the time of the discriminatory act, not the point at which the consequences of the act become painful. Further, here, as in *Ricks*, continued employment alone, without alleged unconstitutional acts subsequent to the date on which the termination decisions were made, is insufficient to prolong the life of a Sec. 1983 claim.

North Haven Board of Education v. Bell, 456 U.S. 512 (1982)

Facts: As part of the Education Amendments of 1972, Congress enacted Title IX to proscribe sex discrimination in education programs or activities receiving federal financial assistance. Following the enactment of Title IX, the then Department of Health, Education and Welfare (H.E.W.) promulgated regulations that addressed, among other things, employment practices. Two local boards of education contended that Title IX was not meant to reach the employment practices of school districts. This suit consolidated the districts' challenges to the validity of H.E.W.'s regulations.

Holding: [6x3] 1) Title IX authorizes regulations prohibiting sex discrimination in employment. 2) Such regulations must be program-specific, that is, they may apply only to education programs that receive federal funds.

Basis: 1) The Court reasoned that since Title IX neither expressly nor by implication excludes employees from its reach, it should be interpreted as covering and protecting these persons, as well as students. The Court found support for its conclusion in the legislative history and post-enactment history of Title IX. 2) The Court based its program-specific conclusion on the language and legislative history of Title IX.

Patsy v. Board of Regents of Florida, 457 U.S. 496 (1982)

Facts: An employee at a state university filed a civil rights action under Sec. 1983, alleging that the university had not promoted her and had filled the sought-after positions through intentional discrimination on the basis of race and sex. Prior to filing suit, she did not exhaust the available administrative remedies.

Holding: [5½/1½x2] Exhaustion of state administrative remedies is not required as a prerequisite to bringing a Sec. 1983 action.

Basis: The Court first cited multiple precedents that have categorically established that Sec. 1983 does not require exhaustion of administrative remedies. Then in response to the public employer's argument that the prior decisions should be reconsidered and overruled, the Court examined the legislative history of Sec. 1983 and more recent, related expressions of legislative intent, finding cumulative support for not overruling the precedents. Finally, in response to the public employer's policy justification, the Court pointed out the necessity and appropriateness of congressional deliberations and determinations.

Harlow v. Fitzgerald, 457 U.S. 800 (1982)*

Facts: Two senior White House aides to President Nixon allegedly participated in a conspiracy to violate the constitutional and statutory rights of a government employee who had "blown the whistle" on some military purchasing practices.

---

*By way of partial contrast, see *Bogan* v. *Scott-Harris*, 523 U.S. 44 (1998) (held that local legislatures, like their state and federal counterparts, have absolute immunity under Sec. 1983).

Holding: [7/1x1] Government officials performing discretionary functions generally are shielded from liability for civil damages insofar as their conduct does not violate established statutory or constitutional rights that a reasonable person should have known. Thus the objective standard of *Wood* v. *Strickland (supra)* is reaffirmed, but its subjective standard is overruled.*

Basis: Pointing out that "we do not write on an empty page," the Court pointed to its precedents that executive officials are entitled to a qualified, rather than absolute, immunity in light of the balancing of competing interests. The Court found that the subjective aspect of the *Wood* v. *Strickland* "good faith defense" has proven incompatible with the important governmental interest that insubstantial claims should not proceed to trial. Bare allegations of malice should not suffice to subject government officials to the cost of trial or to the burdens of broad-reaching discovery.

Rendell-Baker v. Kohn, 457 U.S. 830 (1982)**

Facts: Six employees were discharged from a private school that specialized in helping maladjusted high school students who were referred by public school officials or by the state drug rehabilitation agency. Public funds accounted for at least 90% of the school's operating budget. The school was subject to both state and local regulations. The discharged employees filed suit alleging that the discharges violated their First, Fifth, and Fourteenth Amendment rights.

Holding: [6/1x2] Where a private school employee's actions were not compelled or influenced by any state regulation,

---

*For an elaboration of this objective standard, see *Davis* v. *Scherer*, 468 U.S. 183 (1984).

**For a more recent ruling concerning Sec. 1983's under color of law requirement, see *National Collegiate Athletic Association v. Tarkanian*, 488 U.S. 179 (1988).

the school has not acted "under color of state law." Thus, Sec. 1983 does not apply to such actions, even though the school is regulated by public authorities and its income is derived primarily from public sources.

Basis: Seeing the Sec. 1983 "under color of state law" analysis as the same as that for Fourteenth Amendment "state action," the Court examined the public function, symbiotic relationship, and related theories of its relevant precedent decisions. It found the circumstances of this case to not fulfill the alternative theories of state action.

Board of Education v. McCluskey, 458 U.S. 966 (1982)

Facts: A tenth-grade student left school without permission and, with four other students, consumed alcohol and became intoxicated. When he returned to school later that day, he was notified that he was suspended from school. His parents also were informed that he had been suspended pending a hearing before the school board. At the hearing, none of the students denied that they had been drinking; and the board expelled all of them for the rest of the semester. The tenth-grader sought injunctive relief under Sec. 1983 in federal district court. This trial-level court decided that the school board had violated the student's substantive due process rights, finding that it had expelled him based on a written policy requiring such expulsion where the board has determined that the pupil has used, sold, possessed, or been under the influence of "narcotics or other hallucinogenics, drugs, or controlled substances" on school premises or at school activities.

Holding: [6x3] In Sec. 1983 cases, school boards are to be accorded wide latitude in construing their disciplinary regulations. Where a school board's construction of its own rules on mandatory expulsion are at least reasonable, the federal judiciary may not replace its own interpretation for the school board's, even if the court's interpretation is preferable to the board's.

Basis: The Court reiterated its *Wood* v. *Strickland (supra)* position that school authorities are to be given wide latitude in considering school regulations. The Court stated that there may be extreme cases where a school board's interpretation of its own rules would be a violation of substantive due process, but "this is surely not that case." The Court allowed the regulations here in question to be interpreted to include alcohol within the term "drugs."

Hensley v. Eckerhart, 461 U.S. 424 (1983)*

Facts: Involuntarily confined patients filed a class action suit against government officials, challenging the constitutionality of treatment and conditions at the state hospital. The federal district court, after a trial, found constitutional violations in five of the six general areas of treatment. Subsequently, the patients' class filed a request for attorneys' fees under Sec. 1988, which provides that in a federal civil rights action "the court, in its discretion, may allow the prevailing party . . . reasonable attorney's fees." After determining that the patients were prevailing parties, even though they had not succeeded on every claim, the district court refused to eliminate from the fees award the hours spent by their attorneys on the unsuccessful claims.

Holding: [5/2x2] Where a lawsuit consists of related claims, a plaintiff who has won substantial relief should not have his attorneys' fees reduced simply because the district court did not adopt each contention raised. However, where the plaintiff achieved only limited success, the court should award only that amount of fee that is reasonable in relation to the results obtained. Where the plaintiff failed to prevail on a

---

*For application and elaboration of *Hensley* to the calculation of attorneys' fees, see *City of Riverside* v. *Rivera*, 477 U.S. 561 (1986). For an earlier calculation case, see *Blum* v. *Stenson*, 465 U.S. 886 (1984). For a attorneys' fees case in another statutory context, see *Pennsylvania* v. *Delaware Valley Citizens Council for Clean Air*, 483 U.S. 711 (1987).

claim unrelated to the successful claims, the hours spent in the unsuccessful claim should not be included in the fee.

Basis: The congressional intent to limit awards to prevailing parties requires that unrelated claims be treated as if they had been raised in separate lawsuits. Where the legal theories are related, the criterion is the significance of the overall result in relation to the hours reasonably expended.

Migra v. Warren City School District Board of Education, 465 U.S. 75 (1984)

Facts: At a regularly scheduled meeting, the board of education renewed the annual contract of its supervisor of elementary education. She accepted the appointment by letter; but shortly afterward, in a special meeting, the board voted not to renew her contract and so notified her in writing. She sued the board in state court. Following the state litigation, where she prevailed, she initiated a Sec. 1983 suit in federal court. She clamed that the board's actions were intended to punish her for exercising her First Amendment rights and that the board's actions also violated the due process and equal protection clauses.

Holding: [6/3x0] Issues that could have been, but were not, raised in a state court proceeding — like those that were actually litigated in the state court proceeding — have the same preclusive effect in a subsequent Sec. 1983 suit in federal court that they would have in subsequent proceedings in the courts of the same state where the judgment was rendered.

Basis: Citing its precedents, the Court ruled that under the Constitution's full faith and credit clause and Congress' implementing statute, a federal court must give to a state court judgment the same preclusive effect as would be given that judgment under the law of the state in which the judgment was rendered. The Court also pointed to precedent that this principle was not modified by Sec. 1983. Finally, the Court concluded that this principle for actually litigated issues was not different for federal issues that a Sec. 1983 litigant could have raised, but did not raise in the earlier state court proceeding. Without justifying her failure to raise a federal issue in the state court proceedings, the plaintiff is prevented from raising the issue in her subsequent, Sec. 1983 proceeding.

Hudson v. Palmer, 468 U.S. 517 (1984)

Facts: An inmate in a state prison filed a Sec. 1983 action against a corrections officer, alleging that the officer had conducted an unconstitutional search of the prisoner's locker and cell and had intentionally destroyed some of his property during the search.

Holding: [8/1x0] When there is an intentional deprivation of property by a low-level government official and the provision of predeprivation process is impractical or impossible, the existence of an adequate postdeprivation remedy satisfies Fourteenth Amendment due process.

Basis: The ruling and rationale of *Parratt* v. *Taylor (supra)* also applies to intentional deprivation of property. The controlling inquiry is whether the state is in a position to provide predeprivation process, not whether the individual is able to foresee that the process is of any consequence.

Webb v. Board of Education, 471 U.S. 234 (1985)*

Facts: After the board of education terminated a black teacher, he retained counsel to represent him in administrative proceedings before the board. He claimed that his constitutional rights had been violated because the board had not provided him with written charges or a pretermination hearing and because there was reason to believe that the board's action was racially motivated. After unsuccessful hearings before

---

*For an earlier noneducation case concerning the availability of attorneys' fees in state administrative and judicial proceedings that are based on Title VII, see *New York Gaslight Club, Inc.* v. *Carey,* 447 U.S. 54 (1979).

the school board, the teacher filed suit under various civil rights statutes, including Sec. 1983. The case was settled by the entry of a consent order awarding the teacher monetary damages and dismissing the action with prejudice. The teacher also was reinstated. The matter of attorneys' fees was reserved for further resolution by the parties or by the court. After negotiations with the school district, the teacher filed a motion for an award of fees under the Civil Rights Attorney's Fees Awards Act of 1976, Sec. 1988, which provides that "[i]n any action or proceeding to enforce certain statutes, including Sec. 1983, the court, in its discretion, may allow the prevailing party . . . reasonable attorneys' fees as part of the costs." The district court awarded attorneys' fees for services rendered in the formal litigation procedure, but declined to grant fees for services by counsel in the administrative hearings.

Holding: [7x1] Attorneys' fees for work on optional state or local administrative proceedings are not available to a prevailing civil rights litigant under Sec. 1988 where the work is reasonably separable from the work on the litigation.

Basis: First, the Court rejected the applicability of precedent relating to awarding attorneys' fees under Title VII, because that statute requires the claimant to pursue available administrative remedies before commencing proceedings in federal court. In contrast, because Sec. 1983 stands as an independent avenue of relief and the teacher could go straight to court to assert it, the school board proceedings were optional. Inasmuch as Sec. 1988 authorized reasonable attorneys' fees only in an action or proceeding to enforce Sec. 1983, administrative proceedings that are not integral are not covered. Second, the Court rejected the teacher's alternate theory, which was based on a precedent that interpreted Sec. 1988 as allowing attorneys' fees "reasonably expended on the litigation." Where, as here, the judge and the parties had no difficulty separating the time devoted to the administrative proceeding from that devoted to the judicial proceeding, the former work is not expended on the litigation and, thus, is not compensable.

Wilson v. Garcia, 471 U.S. 261 (1985)*

Facts: A citizen alleged that the state police unlawfully arrested and brutally beat him, thus depriving him of his civil rights under the Fourth, Fifth, and Fourteenth Amendments. He filed a Sec. 1983 suit two years and nine months after the claim allegedly arose. The government defendant moved to dismiss on the ground that the action was barred by the two-year statute of limitations contained in the state's tort claims act. Separate state legislation provided a three-year statute of limitations for personal injury claims and a four-year limitation for other actions.

Holding: [7x1] Sec. 1983 claims are best characterized as personal injury actions; hence, the state statute of limitations for personal injuries claims applies.

Basis: Based on the language and rationale of Sec. 1988, federal, rather than state, law governs the characterization of a Sec. 1983 claim for statute of limitations purposes. Only the length of the limitations period, and related questions of tolling and application, are to be governed by state law. The federal interests in uniformity, certainty, and minimization of unnecessary litigation all support the conclusion that simple, broad characterization of all Sec. 1983 claims for statute of limitation purposes is appropriate.

Daniels v. Williams, 474 U.S. 327 (1986)**

Facts: A prison inmate, who was injured when he allegedly slipped on a pillow negligently left on a stairway by a sheriff's deputy,

---

*For an education case that was vacated in light of this decision, see *Springfield Township* v. *Knoll*, 471 U.S. 288 (1985).

**For a companion case to *Daniels,* see *Davidson* v. *Cannon*, 474 U.S. 344 (1986).

filed a Sec. 1983 action alleging that such negligence violated his Fourteenth Amendment due process rights. He contended that the state's sovereign immunity defense to a state tort suit amounted to a lack of due process when he was deprived of his "liberty" interest in freedom from bodily injury.

Holding: [6/3x0] The due process clause is not implicated by a government official's negligent act covering unintended loss of or injury to life, liberty, or property.

Basis: The Court overruled *Parratt* v. *Taylor (supra)* to the extent that *Parratt* stated that mere lack of due care by a state official may "deprive" an individual of life, liberty, or property under the Fourteenth Amendment. To hold otherwise would trivialize the history of the due process clause, which was intended to apply to deliberate decisions of government officials. The Court did not rule out the possibility, however, that other constitutional provisions could be violated by governmental negligence.

Pembaur v. Cincinnati, 475 U.S. 469 (1986)

Facts: A physician who operated a clinic that provided medical services to welfare recipients was indicted for fraud. When the grand jury attempted to subpoena two of his employees, he barred the door to his clinic. When he continued to refuse entrance to deputy sheriffs, the police, at the direction of the county prosecutor, opened the door with axes but failed to find the two employees. The physician was subsequently acquitted of fraud but convicted for obstructing the law. He filed a Sec. 1983 damages action against the county, among other defendants, alleging violation of his rights under the First and Fourteenth Amendments. The lower courts rejected his claim against the county on the ground that the individual officers were not acting according to the kind of "official policy" that is requisite under *Monell (supra)*

Holding: [5/1x3] Municipal liability may be imposed for a single decision by municipal policymakers under certain circumstances.

Basis: Interpreting *Monell* and its related decisions, the Court concluded that the Sec. 1983 underlying principle of "official policy" extends beyond formal rules or understandings to decisions made by the government's authorized decision makers to adopt a particular course of action. The precise level of the decision maker and type of decision, however, was not agreed to by a majority of the Court.

Evans v. Jeff, 475 U.S. 717 (1986)*

Facts: The Civil Rights Attorney's Fees Act (42 U.S.C. Sec. 1988) provides that "the court, in its discretion, may allow the prevailing party . . . a reasonable attorney's fee" in enumerated civil rights actions. In this case a class action was brought on behalf of mentally handicapped children, alleging deficiencies in the educational programs and health care services provided by state officials in violation of federal and state constitutional and statutory provisions. Ultimately, the federal district court approved a settlement granting them the injunctive relief that they sought conditional on their waiver of any claim for attorneys' fees.

Holding: [6x3] It is within the discretion of federal district courts to approve the waiver of attorneys' fees, including where such waiver is in exchange for settlement on the merits of the charges.

Basis: The Court viewed the language and legislative history of Sec. 1988 as adding to the remedies available to combat civil rights violations, a goal not invariably inconsistent with conditioning settlement on the merits of a waiver of statutory attorneys' fees. Settlements were seen as a way of vindicating civil rights in some cases. Thus a general prohibition of waivers would impede vindication of rights in such cases.

---

*For earlier, noneducation cases that deal with the effect of settlements or offers of settlement on attorneys' fees, see *Maher* v. *Gagne (supra)* and *Mareck* v. *Chesney*, 473 U.S. 1 (1985).

Memphis Community School District v. Stachura, 477 U.S. 299 (1986)

Facts: The school board received a number of complaints about a seventh-grade science teacher who had taught a unit on reproduction using pictures and films. The school board summarily suspended the teacher with pay for the remainder of the school year and reinstated him the next fall. The teacher brought a civil rights suit against the school board and others, seeking to recover compensatory and punitive damages for alleged violations of his First and Fourteenth Amendment rights. The district court authorized, and the court of appeals upheld, not only actual compensatory and punitive damages but also damages based on the abstract importance of the constitutional rights violated. The Supreme Court limited its review to the appropriateness of the damages award.

Holding: [5/4x0] Damages based on the abstract value or importance of a constitutional right are not a permissible element of compensatory damages in civil rights cases.

Basis: Citing multiple precedents, the Court reiterated that Sec. 1983, which is the statutory "handle" for recovering damages in civil rights cases, creates a species of tort liability. Thus the level of damages for violations of constitutional rights is ordinarily determined according to traditional principles from the common law of torts. Under these principles, plaintiffs are entitled to compensation for actual injuries, be they out-of-pocket losses, impairment of reputation, or pain and suffering. As *Carey* v. *Piphus (supra)* made clear in the context of Sec. 1983, where no actual injury was present, although an important constitutional right had been violated, no compensatory damages (except a nominal amount) could be awarded. The Court further found that the possible difference between the procedural right at issue in *Carey* and the at least partially substantive right at issue in this case did not constitute a distinction. Finally, the Court concluded that damages for the abstract value or importance of constitutional rights were not legislatively intended nor judicially wieldy.

North Carolina Department of Transportation v. Crest Street Community Council, 479 U.S. 6 (1986)

Facts: Community residents filed an administrative complaint with the U.S. Department of Transportation challenging the North Carolina Department of Transportation's proposed extension of a largely federally funded major expressway through a black neighborhood as violating Title VI. After five years of negotiations, a Final Mitigation Plan was executed that, along with a related consent judgment, resolved the controversy. The residents then filed an action in district court for attorneys' fees under Sec. 1988 for services performed by their counsel in preparing the administrative complaint and in negotiating resolution of the dispute.

Holding: [6x3] Attorneys' fees are not available under Sec. 1988 in a separate federal action that does not attempt to enforce any of the civil rights laws listed therein, but attempts solely to recover attorneys' fees.

Basis: The Civil Rights Attorney's Fees Awards Act of 1976 (Sec. 1988) provides that "in any action or proceeding to enforce" certain enumerated civil rights laws, the court may award attorneys' fees to the prevailing party. The services in this case were rendered during administrative proceedings and negotiations. However, under Sec. 1988's plain language and legislative history, a court may award attorneys' fees only in an action to enforce one of the civil rights. Here, the action for attorneys' fees is not, and never was, an action to enforce any of those laws. The Court did not reach the question of whether negotiations subsequent to the filing of a Title VI administrative complaint are, under Sec. 1988, "proceedings to enforce" Title VI.

Saint Francis College v. Al-Khazraji, 481 U.S. 604 (1987)

Facts: A professor, who was a U.S. citizen born in Iraq, was denied tenure in a private college. He sued, alleging that he had been discriminated against on the basis of his Arabian origin, in violation of Sec. 1981.

Holding: [8/1x0] Sec. 1981 protects identifiable classes of persons who are subjected to intentional discrimination solely because of their ethnic characteristics or ancestry (for example, Arabs).*

Basis: Relying on encyclopedic and dictionary sources, the Court pointed out that the understanding of "race" in the 19th century was different from the current conception of all Caucasians being one race. The legislative history of Sec. 1981, which had its source in the Civil Rights Act of 1866, supports this observation.

Carnegie-Mellon University v. Cohill, 484 U.S. 343 (1988)

Facts: A former employee sued his former supervisor and his employing university for violating the federal Age Discrimination in Employment Act (ADEA) and for various state-law claims, such as breach of contract and defamation. The defendants removed the case from state court to federal court because the ADEA claim and the various state claims arose from the same set of facts. The employee did not contest the removal, but he subsequently moved to amend the complaint to delete, as untenable, the allegation of age discrimination and some of the state claims. At the same time, he filed a motion, contingent upon his amendment of the complaint, to remand the case back to state court. The federal district court granted both motions. The defendants appealed, contending that the district court should have dismissed, rather than remanded, the case.

---

*The same construction was applied to suits under Sec. 1982 in the companion case of *Shaare Tefila Congregation* v. *Cobb*, 481 U.S. 615 (1987), where the suing party was Jewish.

Holding: [5x3] A federal district court has discretion to remand a properly removed case to state court when all federal-law claims in the suit have been eliminated and only pendent state-law claims remain.

Basis: Citing precedent, the Court emphasized that the underlying "doctrine of pendent jurisdiction" gives federal courts not only the power but also the discretion to decide state-law claims arising out of the same cluster of facts as a federal claim. The exercise of this doctrine is flexible, depending on the factors of judicial economy, convenience, fairness, and comity. Extending this principle, the Court reasoned that remanding, rather than dismissing, a case will better accommodate these factors in some cases. For example, the statute of limitations for state-law claims could bar claims that otherwise were filed promptly, thus running counter to the factors of fairness and comity. Even where the statute of limitations has not expired, a remand may save filing costs and time, thus contributing to economy and convenience. On the other hand, in a case where the suing party uses manipulative tactics, the fairness factor would disfavor a remand. Finally, the Court interpreted the language and legislative history of the federal remand statute as supporting its interpretation.

City of Canton v. Harris, 489 U.S. 378 (1989)

Facts: The city police arrested a citizen. She fell down and became incoherent, but she received no medical treatment while in custody. She was diagnosed as suffering emotional ailments that required treatment and hospitalization, but the city subsequently released her. She sued the city, seeking to hold it liable under Sec. 1983 for violating her Fourteenth Amendment due process rights to receive medical treatment while in police custody.

Holding: [8/1x0] A local government may be liable under Sec. 1983 for inadequate training of its employees only where the failure to train in a relevant respect amounts to deliberate indifference to the rights of persons with whom the police come into contact.

Basis: Citing *Monell (supra)*, the Court reasoned that a city is not liable under Sec. 1983 unless a municipal "policy" or "custom" is the moving force behind the constitutional violation. Only when the failure to train reflects a deliberate or conscious choice can a city be held liable. Moreover, the training program's deficiency must be closely related to the ultimate injury a citizen suffers. If these conditions are not met, there is no violation of constitutional rights.

DeShaney v. Winnebago County Department of Social Services, 489 U.S. 189 (1989)

Facts: The county department of social services received complaints that a child was being abused by his father, but it did not remove him from custody. The father finally beat his child so severely that he suffered permanent brain damage resulting in retardation. The child and his mother sued the county under Sec. 1983, alleging that the county had violated his rights under the Fourteenth Amendment's due process clause by failing to protect him.

Holding: [6x3] A social service agency's failure to provide a child with adequate protection against parental abuse does not violate the Fourteenth Amendment due process clause.

Basis: The Court ruled on precedents establishing that the due process clause imposes no duty on the state to provide members of the general public with protective services against private violence. The clause is a limitation on the state's power to act, not a guarantee of certain levels of safety and security. It forbids the state to deprive individuals of life, liberty, or property without due process of law; but it cannot be read to impose an affirmative obligation on the state to ensure that those interests are not harmed by a third party.

Jett v. Dallas Independent School District, 491 U.S. 701 (1989)

Facts: A school district employed a white male as a teacher, athletic director, and football coach at a predominantly black high school. After a number of conflicts relating to school policies and his handling of the football team, the principal recommended that he be dismissed from his positions as athletic director and coach. The superintendent agreed and assigned him to a teaching position without coaching resposibilities in another school. He sued the district under Secs. 1981 and 1983, claiming racial discrimination.

Holding: [5x4] A municipality (or school district) may not be held liable for its employees' violations of Sec. 1981 under a respondeat superior theory. Sec. 1983 provides the exclusive remedy for any rights violated under Sec. 1981 when a claim is brought against a governmental representative.

Basis: Citing *Monell (supra)*, the Court stated that school officials are liable under Sec. 1983 only if they had been delegated policymaking authority or acted pursuant to a well-settled custom that represented official policy.

Patterson v. McLean Credit Union, 491 U.S. 164 (1989)

Facts: A credit union employed a black woman as a teller and file clerk for 10 years. After she was laid off, she sued under Sec. 1981, alleging racial harassment, failure to promote, and firing due to her race. The trial court said that a claim for racial harassment is not available under Sec. 1981 and refused to submit that part of the case to a jury. Instead, it instructed the jury that in order to prevail on her promotion discrimination claim, she had to prove that she was better qualified than the white woman who allegedly received the promotion.

Holding: [5x4] Racial harassment is not actionable under Sec. 1981, which prohibits racial discrimination in the making and enforcement of contracts.

Basis: Refusing to overrule its decision in *Runyon (supra)*, the
Court declared that a lower court must abide by *stare deci-
sis*, that is, the doctrine of precedent, unless there is some
"special justification." No such justification was shown in
this case. Sec. 1981, which provides that all persons shall
have the same right to make and enforce contracts as is
enjoyed by white citizens, does not apply to conduct that
occurs after the formation of a contract and that does not
interfere with the right to enforce established contracts.

Texas State Teachers Association v. Garland Independent School District, 489 U.S. 782 (1989)

Facts: The school district had a policy of prohibiting communications by or with teachers during the school day concerning employee organizations. The teachers association sued
the school district, claiming that this policy violated both
their First and Fourteenth Amendment rights. Upon suc-
ceeding in the litigation of one of their claims, the association sought attorneys' fees under Sec. 1988.

Holding: [9x0] The standard for determining whether the suing
party is a "prevailing party" and thus eligible for an attorneys' fees award under Sec. 1988 is that it "succeed[ed] on
any significant issue in the litigation which achieves some of
the benefit it sought in bringing the suit."

Basis: Based on statutory interpretation, the Court concluded that
the person who brings the suit must be able to point to a resolution of the dispute that materially alters the parties' legal
relationship in a manner that Congress sought to promote in
the attorneys' fee legislation. Where the suing party's success
on a legal issue can be characterized as purely technical or
practically trivial, the court would be justified in concluding
that it is so insignificant as to be insufficient to support "prevailing party" status. In this case, the teachers association
was a prevailing party within the meaning of Sec. 1988
because it prevailed on a significant issue in the lawsuit. Its

success resulted in a significant change in the school district's policy of limiting the rights of the teachers and their organization to communicate with each other.

Howlett v. Rose, 496 U.S. 356 (1990)

Facts: A former high school student filed a Sec. 1983 suit in a state court seeking damages and injunctive relief against a school board. He claimed that the school officials' search of his car violated the Fourth Amendment and that he was suspended in violation of Fourteenth Amendment procedural due process.

Holding: [9x0] When this type of defense is not available if the suit is brought in federal court, a state law sovereign immunity defense is not available to a school board in a Sec. 1983 action brought in a state court that otherwise has jurisdiction.

Basis: The state and its agencies, which traditionally have been immune under the doctrine of sovereign immunity under the Eleventh Amendment, are not subject to suit under Sec. 1983 in either federal or state court. However, under the supremacy clause of the U.S. Constitution, state courts have the concurrent duty to enforce federal law under their regular procedures. Such a court may not deny a federal right in the absence of a "valid excuse." The state court's refusal to hear a Sec. 1983 suit against the state and its entities violates the supremacy clause.

R.A.V. v. City of Saint Paul, Minnesota, 505 U.S. 377 (1992)*

Facts: An individual allegedly burned a cross on a black family's lawn. Local officials charged him with violating the local "bias motivated Crime" ordinance, which prohibits the display of a symbol that one knows or has reason to know "arouses

---

*For a subsequent elaboration allowing such restrictions on conduct as distinct from content, see *Wisconsin* v. *Mitchell*, 508 U.S. 476 (1993).

anger, alarm or resentment of others on the basis of race, color, creed, religion or gender."

Holding: [6/3x0] A criminal ordinance that broadly prohibits or restricts "hate speech" violates the First Amendment.

Basis: The Supreme Court relied on doctrines of overbreadth and viewpoint discrimination. Although a few limited categories of speech — obscenity, defamation, and fighting words — may be regulated because of their constitutionally proscribable content, the ordinance is facially unconstitutional because it imposes special prohibitions on those speakers who express views about race, color, religion, creed, or gender while, at the same time, it permits displays containing abusive invective not addressed to these topics. The practical operation of the ordinance goes beyond mere content to actual viewpoint discrimination. The local government's desire to communicate to minority groups that it does not condone group hatred does not justify selectively silencing speech on the basis of its content.

Farrar v. Hobby, 506 U.S. 103 (1992)

Facts: A state's public officials closed a private school. The co-executors of the owner's estate sought several million dollars in compensatory damages under Sec. 1983 and 1985 for the allegedly illegal closing of the school. The federal trial court awarded only nominal damages and then awarded $280,000 in attorneys' fees pursuant to Sec. 1988.

Holding: [5x4] A person who sues and wins nominal damages is a "prevailing party" under Sec. 1988 but usually is not entitled to an attorneys' fee award.

Basis: Precedents establish that a party prevails when actual relief on the merits of a claim materially alter the legal relationship between the parties by modifying the defendant's behavior in a way that directly benefits the plaintiff. In this case, the suing persons were entitled to nominal damages under *Carey (supra)*, because they were able to establish the state official's liability for due process violations. However, they were not able to prove the actual injury necessary for a compensatory damages award. A judgment for nominal damages modified the governmental defendant's behavior for their benefit by forcing it to pay money it otherwise would not have paid. Although the "prevailing party" issue is not related to the magnitude of the relief obtained, nominal damages do have a bearing on the size of the fee award under Sec. 1988. The critical factor relating to a fee amount's reasonableness is the degree of success obtained. When only nominal damages are obtained, the only reasonable fee is usually no fee at all.

Harris v. Forklift Systems, Inc., 510 U.S. 17 (1993)

Facts: The manager at an equipment rental company sued the company, claiming that the conduct of its president toward her constituted "abusive work environment" harassment based on her gender and in violation of Title VII. The company president insulted her because of her gender and made unwanted sexual innuendoes in the presence of other workers. The trial court, characterizing it as a "close case," ruled that the comments in question did not create an abusive environment because they were not "so severe as to . . . seriously affect [her] well-being or lead her to suffer injury."

Holding: [9x0] To be actionable as "abusive work environment" harassment, conduct need not seriously affect a worker's psychological well-being or lead a complainant to suffer injury.

Basis: Citing *Meritor (supra)*, the Court delineated the Title VII standard as when the workplace is permeated with discriminatory behavior that is sufficiently severe or pervasive to create a discriminatorily hostile or abusive working environment. This requires that a work environment be objectively hostile or abusive — as found by a reasonable person — as well as the victim's subjective view that the environment is abusive. Whether an environment is hostile or abusive can be determined only by looking at all of the circumstances. Psychological harm can be taken into account, but no single factor is required.

Waters v. Churchill, 513 U.S. 804 (1994)

Facts: A public employer terminated a nurse, supposedly because of a statement she made to a co-worker during a work break. The co-worker and a witness claimed that she had made disruptive statements critical of her department and her supervisor. She claimed — and other employees agreed — that her speech was limited to non-disruptive statements critical of a hospital training policy that she thought threatened patient care. She sued under Sec. 1983, claiming that her speech was protected under *Connick (supra)*.

Holding: [5/2x2] The *Connick* two-part test for protected speech should be applied to what the government employer reasonably thought was said, not to what the trier of fact ultimately determines was said.

Basis: The question for deciding when the First Amendment requires a procedural safeguard must be answered on a case by case basis. The relevant factors are 1) the procedure's cost and relative magnitude and 2) the constitutional significance of erroneous punishment or exculpation of protected speech that the procedure entails. When weighing these factors, the key is the governmental employer's interest in achieving its goals as effectively and efficiently as possible. Nevertheless, *Connick* does not apply based on the employer's interpretation without considering the reasonableness of its conclusions. The manager must proceed with the care that a reasonable employer would exercise before making an employment decision, including termination. Here, the employer's actions, taken after an investigation, were entirely reasonable.

McKennon v. Nashville Banner Publishing Company, 513 U.S. 352 (1995)

Facts: After the company fired this employee, she filed suit, alleging that her discharge was in violation of the Age Discrimination in Employment Act (ADEA). Subsequently, during the pretrial proceedings, she admitted that during her final year of employment she had copied confidential company documents.

Holding: [9x0] An employee terminated in violation of the ADEA is not completely barred from all relief when, after her discharge, her employer discovers evidence of wrongdoing that, in any event, would have led to her termination on lawful, legitimate grounds had the employer known of it.

Basis: Partially distinguishing *Mt. Healthy (supra)*, the Court concluded that although evidence of the employee's wrongdoing acquired after the employee's discharge, if proven independently sufficient to warrant discharge, should be taken into con sideration, allowing some recovery vindicates the ADEA's remedial purposes of compensation for and deterrence of age discrimination. The Court clarified that the remedial relief will be determined on a case by case basis; as a general rule, neither front pay nor reinstatement is an appropriate remedy in such cases. The beginning point should be calculation of backpay from the date of the unlawful discharge to the date the new information was discovered.*

O'Connor v. Consolidated Coin Caterers Corporation, 517 U.S. 308 (1996)

Facts: The company fired this employee, aged 56, and replaced him with a 40-year-old worker. He filed suit, alleging that

---

*For a subsequent Supreme Court decision relating to liability under the ADEA, see *Oubre* v. *Entergy Operations, Inc.*, 522 U.S. 422 (1998) (held that discharged employee's receipt and non-return of severance payments under a signed release do not excuse the strict and specific requirements of the amended ADEA for waivers of liability).

his discharge violated the Age Discrimination in Employment Act.

Holding: [9x0] Replacement by an employee under the age of 40 is not an essential element of a suit under the Age Discrimination in Employment Act.

Basis: Although the Age Discrimination in Employment Act limits its protections to persons who are 40 or older, it prohibits discrimination against those protected employees on the basis of age, not class membership. That one member of the protected class lost out to another member is irrelevant, so long as the loss was based on age. It suffices for a prima facie, or threshold, case that the replacement was substantially younger than the discharged employee.

Reno v. Bossier Parish School Board, 520 U.S. 471 (1997) ("Bossier I")

Facts: The Bossier Parish School Board is subject to the preclearance requirements of Sec. 5 of the Voting Rights Act of 1965, thereby needing the approval of either the U.S. Attorney General or the U.S. District Court for the District of Columbia before implementing any changes to a voting "qualification, prerequisite, standard, practice, or procedure." Based on the 1990 census, the board redrew its 12 single-member districts, adopting the redistricting plan that the Attorney General had recently precleared for use in elections of the parish's primary governing body. In doing so, the board rejected an NAACP-proposed plan that would have created two majority-black districts. The Attorney General objected to preclearance, finding that, compared to the NAACP plan, the board's choice unnecessarily diluted the strength of minority voters in violation of Sec. 2 of the Act. The board filed suit, challenging the Attorney General's withholding of preclearance.

Holding: [6/3x1] The Attorney General may not deny preclearance under Sec. 5 of the Voting Rights Act solely on the basis that a covered jurisdiction's new voting "qualification, prerequisite, standard, practice, or procedure" violates Sec. 2 of the Act.*

Basis: Citing its precedents, the Court observed that it has consistently understood Sec. 5 and Sec. 2 to combat different evils and, consequently, to impose very different duties on covered jurisdictions. Sec. 5 is retrogressive and thus uses the jurisdiction's existing plan as the benchmark for comparison, whereas Sec. 2 uses a hypothetical, undiluted plan as the benchmark. Making compliance with Sec. 5 contingent on compliance with Sec. 2 would, for all intents and purposes, replace the standards of Sec. 5 with those of Sec. 2, thus contradicting more than 20 years of Voting Rights Act precedents. Evidence showing that a jurisdiction's redistricting plan dilutes minorities' voting power may be relevant — though not controlling — to establish its intent to retrogress under Sec. 5.

National Collegiate Athletic Association v. Smith, 525 U.S. 459 (1999)**

Facts: Smith played intercollegiate volleyball for two seasons as an undergraduate. She subsequently enrolled in graduate

---

*For Voting Rights Act decisions concerning jurisdictions other than school districts, see, for example, *Lopez* v. *Monterey County*, 525 U.S. 266 (1999); *Abrams* v. *Johnson*, 521 U.S. 74 (1997); *Bush* v. *Vera*, 517 U.S. 952 (1996); *Johnson* v. *De Grandy*, 512 U.S. 997 (1994); *Holder* v. *Hall*, 512 U.S. 874 (1994); *Pleasant Grove* v. *United States*, 479 U.S. 462 (1987); *Beer* v. *United States*, 425 U.S. 130 (1976). For voting cases in such jurisdictions decided on constitutional grounds, see, for example, *Hunt* v. *Cromartie*, 121 S. Ct. 1452 (2001); *Shaw* v. *Hunt*, 517 U.S. 899 (1996); *Miller* v. *Johnson*, 515 U.S. 900 (1995); *United States* v. *Hays*, 515 U.S. 737 (1995); *Mobile* v. *Bolden*, 446 U.S. 55 (1980).

** In a previous decision, the Court held that the NCAA's suspension of a basketball coach of a member university did not suffice to constitute the separable prerequisites of "state action" under the Fourteenth Amendment's due process clause or "action under color of state law" under Section 1983. *National Collegiate Athletic Association* v. *Tarkanian*, 488 U.S. 179 (1988).

school at a different university and sought to play intercollegiate volleyball there. However, the NCAA denied her eligibility on the basis of its postbaccalaureate bylaw, which allows a postgraduate student-athlete to participate in intercollegiate athletics only at the institution that awarded her undergraduate degree. After the NCAA denied the host university's petition for a waiver, the student filed suit, alleging that the NCAA had violated Title IX. The NCAA moved to dismiss the case, contending that it did not meet the Title IX prerequisite of being a recipient of federal funds.

Holding: [9x0] Dues payments from recipients of federal funds do not suffice to subject an athletic association to suit under Title IX.

Basis: The Court relied on the language of Title IX and the message of precedents, including *Grove City College (supra),** to decide this narrow question. It left for another day the student's alternative arguments for the federal funding requirement, inasmuch as the lower courts had not addressed them first.

Kimel v. Florida Board of Regents, 528 U.S. 62 (2000)**

Facts: This case is a consolidation of three separate ADEA suits. In Alabama, two associate professors of business, ages 57 and 58, filed a complaint with the Equal Employment Opportunities Commission alleging that their college employed an evaluation system that had a disparate impact on older faculty members. They subsequently filed suit against their

---

*The Court also cited *Department of Transportation* v. *Paralyzed Veterans of America*, 477 U.S. 597 (1986), which concerned the parallel federal funding requirement of Sec. 504 of the Rehabilitation Act.

**For other recent Eleventh Amendment decisions, which are much less directly relevant to k-12 schools, see *Alden* v. *Maine*, 527 U.S. 706 (1999); *College Savings Bank* v. *Florida Prepaid Postsecondary Education Expense Board*, 527 U.S. 666 (1999); *Regents of the Univ. of California* v. *Doe*, 519 U.S. 425 (1997); *Seminole Tribe of Florida* v. *Florida*, 517 U.S. 44 (1996).

employer, a state university, claiming discrimination and retaliation in violation of the ADEA. They sought various forms of relief, including promotion to full professor, back pay, and money damages. The other two suits arose in Florida, one brought by an employee of that state's department of corrections and the other by a group of current and former faculty and librarians at two state universities. In all of these cases, the defendant state agency moved to dismiss the suit for lack of subject matter jurisdiction based on the Eleventh Amendment, which provides states and their agencies with immunity from private individuals' suits for money damages in federal court.*

Holding: [5/2x2] The ADEA's express and unmistakably clear abrogation of Eleventh Amendment immunity is beyond Congress' authority under Sec. 5 of the Fourteenth Amendment and, thus, is invalid.**

Basis: The majority reasoned that the ADEA was not appropriate legislation under Sec. 5, inasmuch as the substantive requirements it imposes on state and local governments could not be understood to be responsive to, or designed to, prevent unconstitutional behavior. The act, through its broad restriction on age as a discriminating factor, prohibits substantially more state employment practices and decisions than would likely be held unconstitutional under the applicable equal protection, rational basis standard. Moreover, Congress never identified any evidence of age discrimination by the states that rose to the level of constitutional violation. Citing *City of Borne (supra)*, the majority relied on principles of federalism and separation of powers.

---

*See the Appendix for the specific language of this amendment. In a minority of states, school districts are state entities subject to the Eleventh Amendment.

**See the Appendix for this enforcement provision of the Fourteenth Amendment.

Reno v. Bossier Parish School Board, 528 U.S. 320 (2000) ("Bossier II")

Facts: After the Court in *Bossier I* vacated and remanded the case for further proceedings to determine the board's purpose in adopting its plan, the trial court granted preclearance, concluding that there was no evidence of discriminatory but nonretrogressive purpose and leaving open the question of whether Sec. 5 prohibits preclearance of a plan enacted with such a purpose.

Holding: [5/2x2] 1) Inasmuch as the redistricting plan will have probable continuing effect as the benchmark against which the next plan, after the 2000 Census, will be evaluated for preclearance purposes, the case is not moot. 2) Sec. 5 of the Voting Rights Act does not prohibit preclearance of a redistricting plan enacted with a discriminatory but nonretrogressive purpose.

Basis: 1) A case is not moot if it continues to be a controversy, even through a secondary effect. 2) Citing its precedents, the Court rejected a differential standard for purpose, or intent, as compared to effect. As in *Bossier I*, the Court concluded that Sec. 2 and Sec. 5 refer to separate contexts. The more expansive reading would jeopardize the constitutionality of Sec. 5 on grounds of federalism.

Reeves v. Sanderson Plumbing Products, Inc., 530 U.S. 133 (2000)

Facts: Caldwell, aged 45, managed one of the company's departments, where Reeves, aged 57, and Oswalt, in his mid-30s, were supervisory. Caldwell informed the company's director of manufacturing that the department's production was down due to employee attendance problems. The manufacturing director ordered an audit, which, according to him, revealed numerous timekeeping errors and misrepresentations by Caldwell, Oswalt, and Reeves. Based on recommendations of her managers, the company's president fired Caldwell and

Reeves. Reeves filed suit, contending that his discharge violated the Age Discrimination in Employment Act (ADEA). At trial, the company officials maintained that Reeve's inaccurate attendance recordkeeping was the reason for his discharge. Introducing evidence that his attendance records were accurate and that the manufacturing director had directed derogatory age-based comments at him and had singled him out for harsher treatment than younger employees, Reeves maintained that the company's explanation was pretextual. The jury returned a verdict for Reeves, but the appellate court reversed, finding insufficient evidence of causation.

Holding: [8/1x0] A prima facie case of discrimination combined with sufficient evidence for a reasonable factfinder to reject the employer's nondiscriminatory explanation for its decision may suffice to sustain a finding of intentional discrimination under the ADEA.

Basis: Citing a previous decision,* the Court concluded that the factfinding determination of intentional discrimination should not be disturbed by rigid reapplication of the multi-step test once the parties have met their burdens of producing evidence. The exception, where no rational factfinder could conclude that discrimination had occurred, did not apply here.

Brentwood Academy v. Tennessee Secondary School Athletic Association, 531 U.S. 288 (2001)

Facts: The interscholastic athletic association, a not-for-profit organization that regulates sports among the state's public and private high schools, penalized a member private school for violating the association's recruiting rules. The private

---

St. Mary's Honor Center v. *Hicks*, 509 U.S. 502 (1993) (held, in a Title VII case, that the employer's production of evidence of nondiscriminatory reasons satisfied its burden of production, requiring the trier of fact to decide the ultimate question of whether the employee had satisfied the burden of persuasion that the employer had intentionally discriminated against him based on race).

school filed a federal civil rights suit against the association and its executive director, claiming that the rule's enforcement was "state action" that violated the First and Fourteenth Amendments. To support its state-action characterization, the private school pointed to the following features of the association: 84% of the members are public schools, public school officials make up the voting membership of the governing council and control board, and association staff, though not state employees, may join the state retirement system.

Holding: [9x0] The regulatory activity of a nominally private, statewide interscholastic association that is pervasively intertwined with the government is "state action," triggering constitutional limitations.

Basis: Warning that "[n]o one fact is a necessary condition for finding state action, nor is any set of circumstances sufficient, for there may be some countervailing reason against attributing activity to the government," the Court found a close nexus, or pervasive entwinement, between the state and this nominally private entity. The fact-bound analysis that led to this conclusion included the overwhelming composition of the membership, the managerial control of public school officials, and the employees' participation in the state retirement system. This entwinement from the bottom up and top down requires that the association be charged with a public character and judged by constitutional standards, in the absence of a countervailing value at odds with finding public accountability in the circumstances. The specter of a litigation explosion does not provide such a countervailing reason here, because every other federal court of appeals to consider a statewide athletic association like this one has found it to be a state actor, and those jurisdictions have experienced no such explosion.

Board of Trustees v. Garrett, 531 S. Ct. 56 (2001)

Facts: In separate but subsequently consolidated cases, two state employees alleged that their respective employers failed to provide them with reasonable accommodations. One employee was the director of nursing at the hospital of a state university; she had a long period of absence due to treatment for breast cancer. The other employee was a security officer who had chronic asthma. Each of them filed suit for money damages under the ADA's Title I, which prohibits discrimination in public and private employment based on disability. In the ADA, Congress clearly abrogated the states' Eleventh Amendment immunity.

Holding: [5x4] The Eleventh Amendment bars ADA Title I suits in federal court for money damages.

Basis: The majority concluded that the ADA's express abrogation of Eleventh Amendment immunity was not constitutional as applied to Title I. First, in light of precedent, the majority observed that the Fourteenth Amendment requires only a relaxed, "rational-basis" review of state actions toward individuals with disabilities, thus allowing states to "hardheadedly – and perhaps hardheartedly – hold to job-qualification requirements which do not make allowance for the disabled." Then the majority found two fatal problems with the congruence-proportionality requirement: 1) the ADA's legislative record fails to show that Congress identified a history and pattern of irrational employment discrimination by the states against individuals with disabilities, and 2) the rights and remedies created by the ADA against the states do not meet the requirements of *City of Boerne* (*supra*) for Congress' exercise of its enforcement authority under Section 5 of the Fourteenth Amendment: congruence and proportionality between the injury to be prevented or remedies and the means adopted to that end. Narrowly focusing on Title I of the ADA, the majority concluded that its reasonable-accommodation duty "far exceeds what is constitutionally required."

Buckhannon Board and Care Home, Inc. v. West Virginia Department of Health and Human Services, 121 S. Ct. 1835 (2001)

Facts: A company that operates assisted living residences failed an inspection by the West Virginia fire marshal's office because some residents were incapable of "self-preservation," as defined by state law. After receiving orders to close its facilities, the company filed suit in federal court against the state agencies and officials, seeking declaratory and injunctive relief that the "self-preservation" requirement violated the ADA and Fair Housing Amendments Act (FHAA). The defendants agreed to stay their orders pending the case's resolution. The state legislature then eliminated the "self-preservation" requirement, and the federal court granted the defendants' motion to dismiss the case as moot. The company requested attorney's fees as the "prevailing party" under the ADA and the FHAA, basing their entitlement on the "catalyst theory." This theory posits that a plaintiff is a "prevailing party" if it achieves the desired result because the lawsuit brought about a voluntary change in the defendant's conduct.

Holding: [5x4] The "catalyst theory" is not a permissible basis for the award of attorney's fees under the ADA and other federal statutes that authorize attorney's fees to prevailing parties, in the absence of clear congressional intent otherwise.

Basis: Under the "American Rule," parties are ordinarily required to bear their own attorney's fees, absent explicit statutory authority. In various statutes authorizing awards of attorney's fees, Congress has employed the legal term of "prevailing party," typically signifying one who has been awarded some relief by a court. Both judgments on the merits and court-ordered consent decrees create a material alteration of the parties' legal relationship and, thus, permit an award. However, the catalyst theory allows an award where there is no judicially sanctioned change in the parties' legal relationship. A defendant's voluntary change in conduct, though perhaps accomplishing what the plaintiff sought to achieve by the lawsuit, lacks the necessary judicial imprimatur on the change. The majority concluded that the legislative history of the ADA and FHAA is at best ambiguous as to the availability of the catalyst theory, and — in light of the American Rule — is clearly insufficient to alter the clear meaning of "prevailing party" in the fee-shifting statutes. Given this meaning, the majority declined to determine which way the various policy arguments, such as the incentive or disincentive for settlements, cut.

CHAPTER SEVEN

Procedural Parameters

Doremus v. Board of Education, 5 N.J. 435 (1950), *dismissed,* 342 U.S. 429 (1952)

Facts: The parents of a child, who in the interim graduated from the school system, and a resident, who is a taxpayer of the school district, challenged the validity of a New Jersey statute that provided for the reading of five verses from the Old Testament at the beginning of each school day.

Holding: [6x3] The Court cannot decide the constitutional issue raised by these two complainants since 1) the claim of a child who has graduated from the school system is moot, that is, no longer a live controversy; and 2) the taxpayer can not show how the time spent in Bible recitation directly costs sufficient tax dollars to give him a particular financial interest, or standing, in having the statute invalidated.

Basis: The Court is limited by Article III of the Constitution to consideration of concrete cases or controversies. Since neither of the complaining parties has a sufficiently active and direct interest in the issue, the Court lacks jurisdiction over the case.

Ellis v. Dixon, 120 N.Y.S.2d 854 (1953), *dismissed,* 349 U.S. 458 (1955)

Facts: Members of the Yonkers Committee for Peace brought an action claiming that the school board had unconstitutionally denied them the use of a school building for a forum on peace and war. The members did not challenge the school board's right to reasonably regulate nonschool use of school buildings, nor did they challenge the board's regulations as unconstitutionally vague. They asserted that other organizations had been permitted to use school buildings; however, they did not present evidence that they were similar to those other organizations and had therefore been unfairly treated under school board classifications and regulations. Their complaint was dismissed by the state trial court, and their request to be heard on the state appellate level was denied. They challenged the state court action.

Holding: [5x4] The committee did not present a case that must be decided on federal grounds, since it appeared that the state court rulings rested on adequate state grounds.

Basis: 1) The Court cannot decide this case on federal constitutional grounds since insufficient facts were presented in the record of the lower court proceeding to establish the basis for such a claim. 2) Since the Court assumes that the state court's denial of the committee's request to appeal was based on adequate nonfederal grounds, the Court has no jurisdiction to consider the case anew.

Flast v. Cohen, 392 U.S. 83 (1968)

Facts: Titles I and II of the Elementary and Secondary Education Act of 1965 mandated the expenditure of federal funds for educational materials and inschool services to both public and religious school children. Federal taxpayers sought a declaration that the disbursement of public funds to religious schools was unconstitutional. A federal district court dismissed their complaint and ruled that, as taxpayers, they lacked sufficient interest in the matter to maintain the federal action in court.

Holding: [5/3x1] A taxpayer may challenge a statute in federal court if he or she can show that it is: 1) an exercise of Congress' power to tax and to spend (rather than a primarily regulatory act requiring only an incidental expenditure of funds for administration); and 2) in violation of a specific constitutional guarantee, for example, the First Amendment's prohibition of governmental establishment of religion, and therefore beyond Congress' spending power.

Basis: 1) Article III of the U.S. Constitution requires those persons bringing federal suits to have "standing," that is, a personal stake in the outcome of the litigation. Taxpayers have a personal stake in being free of taxing and spending that is in contravention of specific constitutional limitations on Congress' taxing and spending power. 2) The Court does not decide in this case whether the statute in question violates the establishment clause of the First Amendment. The Court decides only that federal taxpayers have standing to seek judicial determination of this question.

Askew v. Hargrave, 401 U.S. 476 (1971)

Facts: In 1968 Florida enacted a law concerned with financing public education through state funding and local *ad valorem* taxes assessed by each school district. The law provided that a school district must limit *ad valorem* taxes to 10 mills of assessed valuation in order to be eligible to receive state funding. The 10-mill limit was challenged as being discriminatory against school children of property-poor districts, since 10 mills would produce less money in those districts. The federal district court invalidated this section of the law on federal constitutional grounds without considering the effect of the entire law on the funding of public education. Before the federal lawsuit was filed, a state court action challenging the 10-mill limit on state constitutional grounds had begun.

Holding: [8/1x0] 1) Federal district courts should not decide federal constitutional questions when the same controversy is challenged in state court on state constitutional grounds. If decided on state constitutional grounds, there would no longer be a need to determine the federal questions involved. 2) Where the effect of an entire funding program on the amount of money available per pupil is crucial to a determination of the federal equal protection issue, a court should not invalidate one section of the legislation without considering the effect of its exclusion on the entire law.

Basis: 1) Where a remedy is available under state law, a federal constitutional claim cannot be decided until the issue of state law has been decided. This policy avoids friction between the states and federal courts and prevents the unnecessary decision of federal constitutional claims, since a complainant who prevails on state grounds will have no need to pursue a federal claim. 2) The equal protection clause of the Fourteenth Amendment requires that persons not be denied equal protection of the laws. The operation of a law in its entirety must be examined to determine whether it results in a violation of this constitutional mandate.

Johnson v. New York State Education Department, 449 F.2d 871 (2d Cir. 1971), *vacated,* 409 U.S. 75 (1972)

Facts: New York enacted a statute providing for state financial assistance ($10 per pupil) for the purchase of textbooks for secondary students. The statute also enabled qualified voters within a school district to vote on a tax for textbooks for elementary students. If the voters failed to approve a proposed property tax to finance school operations, textbooks could be obtained for elementary students only on payment of a rental fee ($7.50 per pupil). Indigent mothers of minor children brought an action claiming the statute to be unconstitutional. The court of appeals upheld the constitutionality of the statute, finding that the legislature's intention to promote education in certain fields by purchasing textbooks to be loaned free to secondary students but not elementary students was based on a constitutionally reasonable classification. While appeal to the Court was pending, voters in the indigent mothers' school district agreed to levy a tax for the purchase of textbooks to be loaned free to elementary students.

Holding: [8/1x0] Since the voters in the school district voted to levy taxes for textbooks to be loaned free to elementary students as permitted by statute, a claim by the indigent mothers that the statute constituted a discriminatory burden might not present a case or controversy. The case was sent back to the district court to determine whether it had become moot.

Basis: Courts will decline to decide arguments based on moot issues, that is, cases no longer presenting live controversies.

DeFunis v. Odegaard, 82 Wash.2d 11 507 (1973), *vacated,* 416 U.S. 312 (1974)

Facts: After being denied admission to a state-operated law school, the rejected student brought suit for himself alone, not for a class of applicants, asking that the school's admission policies be declared racially discriminatory and that he be admitted to the school. The student was admitted under court order, and while appeal of that decision was pending, completed all but the final quarter. The school assured that he would be permitted to complete this final term.

Holding: [7x2] Since the student would be allowed to complete law school regardless of any decision on the merits of the case, there is no present controversy and the case is no longer a proper vehicle for judicial decision making.

Basis: Article III of the U.S. Constitution requires that the courts decide active controversies. Since the issues raised in the case might reach the Court again and since this student's opportunity to complete school is assured, the usual rule in federal cases that an actual controversy must exist at the time of review, as well as at the beginning of the legal action, is followed here.

Mercer v. Michigan State Board of Education, 379 F. Supp. 580 (E.D. Mich. 1974), *aff'd,* 419 U.S. 1081 (1974)*

Lower Court Holding: 1) A physician has no standing to challenge in federal court the constitutionality of legislation pro-

---

*For a more recent ruling relating to standing, here in terms of a "First Amendment over breadth" claim, see *Los Angelos Police Department* v. *United Reporting Publishing Co.,* 528 U.S. 32 (1999).

hibiting birth control instruction or information in health and sex education courses.

2) The teacher has standing to challenge such statutes, but only with regard to how they adversely affect the teacher's interest and not the interest of other persons, for example, students or parents.

3) The state's elimination of birth control instruction from the public school curriculum is constitutional.

Board of School Commissioners v. Jacobs, 490 F.2d 601 (7th Cir. 1973), *vacated,* 420 U.S. 128 (1975)

Facts: Six students who were involved in the publication and distribution of a student newspaper successfully challenged certain actions taken by the school board and other school officials that threatened to impair the students' freedom to publish and distribute the newspaper. However, the students failed to define properly in their pleadings a class of persons adversely affected by the challenged rules. In this case, the school board challenged the court rulings against certain of its rules and actions. The students all had graduated from the school system.

Holding: [8x1] Because the class of students adversely affected by the school board's actions was not properly defined, there was no "class action." Therefore, when the six students graduated, their case ceased to have validity as a controversy. These particular students were no longer adversely affected by school board action and, therefore, had no right to challenge it. The lower court decisions protecting the students had no present validity as to anyone and are void.

Basis: Federal Rules of Civil Procedure 23(c)(1) and 23(c)(3) require that class actions be properly certified and that the class be properly identified, especially when the original complainants are not likely to be actively involved in the controversy by the time the case is appealed.

Citizens for Parental Rights v. San Mateo County Board of Education, 51 Cal. App. 3d (1975), *dismissed*, 425 U.S. 908 (1976)*

Facts: Five California public school districts instituted family life and sex education programs for public school students. The programs did not promote any particular religious viewpoint in their curricula. The programs were operated in compliance with two state statutes that required that parents have both advance notice that such courses would be offered and an opportunity to preview any written or audiovisual materials to be used in them. The statutes provided parents with the right to have their children excused from the programs or from any portion of the programs that were offensive to the parents' religious beliefs. The three-judge federal court on a vote of 2x1 held that family life and sex education courses, which do not promote a particular religious viewpoint and which provide parents objecting to the programs with an opportunity to withdraw their children from them, are constitutional. Appeal was sought here.

Holding: [9x0] Where the Court does not find a "substantial federal question," for example, violation of a federal constitutional provision, it will not further review the case. Thus the Court dismissed the case.

Basis: Under Article III of the Constitution, the judicial power of federal courts includes cases involving "federal questions," that is, those involving federal statutes, treaties, or the Constitution. Furthermore, the federal question must be a substantial one. A case that does not fit into this or any other of the specific categories enumerated in Article III, for example, controversies between citizens of different states, falls beyond the jurisdiction of the federal courts. The Court can not make a final decision in such cases.

---

*For a more recent dismissal on the same grounds, see *Cooper* v. *Eugene School Dist.*, 723 P.2d 298 (Or. 1986), *appeal dismissed*, 480 U.S. 942 (1987).

University of Texas v. Camenisch, 451 U.S. 390 (1981)

Facts: A deaf graduate student filed a complaint alleging that the university had violated Sec. 504 of the Rehabilitation Act of 1973 by discriminatorily refusing to pay for a sign-language interpreter for him. Sec. 504 provides that "no otherwise qualified handicapped individual . . . shall, solely by reason of his handicap, be excluded from participation in, be denied the benefits of, or be subjected to discrimination under any program or activity receiving financial assistance." Finding a possibility that the plaintiff would be irreparably harmed in the absence of an injunction and that he was likely to prevail on the merits, the district court granted a preliminary injunction on condition that he post a security bond pending the outcome of the litigation. The court of appeals affirmed. Meanwhile, the university had obeyed the lower court's injunction by paying for his interpreter, and he graduated.

Holding: [8/1x0] Where the terms of a preliminary injunction have been fully and irrevocably carried out, the question of whether it should have been issued is moot, but the question of damages — as preserved by the injunction bond — should be remanded for a trial on the merits.

Basis: The issues of whether the preliminary injunction should have been granted and whether the university should ultimately bear the cost of the interpreter are significantly different and thus separable matters. Preliminary and permanent injunctions are procedurally and substantively not equivalent, since a decision for a preliminary injunction is not tantamount to a decision on the merits. Thus the first issue is moot; but the second issue requires a trial on the merits.

Schmidt v. Oakland Unified School District, 457 U.S. 594 (1981)

Facts: State legislation requires school districts to award work of more than $12,000 to the "lowest responsible bidder." School district policy required general contractors for projects over $100,000, as a condition of being "responsible," to use minority-owned businesses for at least 25% of the dollar amount of the contract bid. When its low bid for an advertised project was not selected for failing to meet the affirmative action condition, the rejected contractor sued, seeking damages and claiming that the affirmative action policy violated the U.S. Constitution and state law. The trial court upheld the plan on constitutional grounds, and the lower appreals court affirmed.

Holding: [*per curiam*] When a claim is based on state law as well as the federal Constitution, courts should decide the narrower state-law question if its disposition will make unnecessary deciding the constitutional question. The court of appeals abused its discretion in declining to rule on the state law claim that the affirmative action plan was invalid under state law.

Basis: Following a long line of precedents favoring constitutional abstention, the Court regarded the lower courts' failure to rule on the pendent state law claim as an abuse of discretion. If the plan was invalid under state law, the federal constitutional claim does not need to be decided.

Valley Forge Christian College v. Americans United for Separation of Church and State, 454 U.S. 464 (1982)

Facts: Pursuant to its authority under the property clause of the Constitution, Congress enacted the Federal Property and Administrative Services Act of 1949 to provide for disposal of surplus federal government property. Under this Act, the Secretary of Health, Education and Welfare (H.E.W.) conveyed a 77-acre tract that was a former military hospital to a college operated by a religious order. A nonprofit organization of taxpayers for the separation of church and state and several of its employees brought suit alleging that this conveyance of the land violated the establishment clause of the First Amendment.

Holding: [5x4] Neither a pro-religious-neutrality organization nor its employees have standing to challenge the no-cost transfer of surplus federal property to a religious educational institution in the absence of a) an exercise of congressional power under the taxing and spending clause and a showing that the exercise exceeds specific constitutional limits on that power, or b) identification of a personal injury as a direct result of the alleged constitutional error.

Basis: Citing various precedents, including *Flast (supra)*, the Court explained the Article III constitutional requirements and the related precedential principles underlying the threshold prerequisite of standing. Here, the taxpayer organization failed the first prong of the *Flast* test because 1) the target of their complaint was not a congressional action, but a decision by a federal administrative agency; and 2) the property transfer about which they complained was not an exercise of power under the taxing and spending clause, but an exercise under the property clause. They failed to establish standing as employees or citizens because they did not identify any personal injury suffered as a consequence of the alleged constitutional violation.

Hathorn v. Lovorn, 457 U.S. 255 (1982)

Facts: A Mississippi statute provided that boards of trustees of municipal separate school districts in the state shall consist of five members, and that in any county in which a district embraces the entire county "in which Highways 14 and 15 intersect," one trustee shall be elected from each supervisor's district. In the school district for the only county where Highways 14 and 15 intersect, the city's mayor and aldermen appointed three of the district's board of trustees, and the county voters residing outside this city elected the other two members. The county officials never implemented the statute. The county voters filed an action seeking to enforce the statute. The lower state court dismissed the complaint on the basis that the statute violated a state constitutional bar against local legislation. Mississippi's highest court reversed and remanded, making only slight changes in the statute. Then, the defendant county officials raised the argument that the revised statute could not be implemented unless and until the changes had been precleared under the federal Voting Rights Act. The state trial court ordered the county officials to submit the election plan to the U.S. Attorney General for preclearance under the Act, but the state supreme court reversed.

Holding: [7/1x1] A state trial court has the power to decide whether a proposed change in election procedures is subject to preclearance under the Voting Rights Act of 1965. The judgment in this case of the Mississippi Supreme Court is reversed; the disputed change in election procedures may not be implemented until the persons demonstrate compliance with the Act.

Basis: There is a presumption that state courts enjoy concurrent jurisdiction with federal courts to decide federal issues. The language and policies of the Voting Rights Act support the conclusion that state courts may decide whether a proposed change in the election procedure requires preclearance under the Act. Furthermore, granting states this power will help ensure compliance with the preclearance scheme of the Act.

California v. Grace Brethren Church, 457 U.S. 393 (1982)

Facts: The Federal Unemployment Tax Act* established a cooperative federal-state scheme to provide benefits to unemployed workers. The Act exempted from mandatory state coverage employees of "an organization which is operated primarily for religious purposes and which is operated, supervised, controlled, or principally supported by a church

---

*For an earlier decision concerning another part of this statute, see *St. Martin* (*supra*).

or convention or association of churches." Several California churches and religious schools, including religious schools not affiliated with any church, brought suit in federal district court to enjoin the Secretary of Labor from conditioning his approval of the California unemployment insurance program on its coverage of these religious employees and to enjoin the state from collecting both tax information and the state unemployment compensation tax. The district court permanently enjoined the state from collecting unemployment taxes from the religious schools based on the excessive entanglement prong of the tripartite test for the First Amendment establishment clause.

Holding: [7x2] Where there is a plain, speedy, and efficient remedy in state court, including a full opportunity to raise constitutional objections, a federal district court has no jurisdiction to issue declaratory or injunctive relief to religious schools in federal tax disputes.

Basis: Congress' intent in enacting the Tax Injunction Act was to prevent federal court interference with the assessment and collection of state taxes. Since the religious schools could seek a refund through state administrative and judicial practices, and thereby obtain state judicial review of their constitutional claims, their remedy under state law was "plain, speedy, and efficient" within the meaning of the Tax Injunction Act. In such circumstances, the Act deprives the federal court of jurisdiction. The excessive entanglement problem could not be mitigated by carving out an exception for federal judicial relief in such religious school cases.

Ramah Navajo School Board v. Bureau of Revenue of New Mexico, 458 U.S. 832 (1982)

Facts: New Mexico attached a gross receipts tax to businesses. This tax was intended to compensate the state for granting the privilege of doing business. A tribal school board subcontracted with a non-Indian construction company to have a high school built for their Indian children. Based on the New Mexico tax law, the construction company included their tax obligation in the cost structure that was assessed to and paid by the school board. The board challenged the applicability of the statute to tribal members or reservation activities.

Holding: [6x3] Federal law preempts the imposition of a state tax on construction of reservation schools for Indian children.

Basis: Under preemption analysis, the Court found a comprehensive federal regulatory scheme and an express federal policy encouraging tribal self-sufficiency in education. Rather than a strong counterbalancing state interest, the Court found that the only justification for imposing the gross receipts tax was a general desire to increase revenues.

Allen v. Wright, 468 U.S. 737 (1984)

Facts: Parents of black public school children in districts undergoing desegregation alleged in this nationwide class action that the Internal Revenue Service (IRS) had not adopted sufficient standards and procedures to fulfill its obligation to deny tax-exempt status to racially discriminatory private schools. They also claimed that many racially segregated private schools were created or expanded in their communities at the time that the public schools were undergoing desegregation and that these private schools had received tax exemptions despite the IRS policy and guidelines. The parents concluded that they were directly harmed by this government-aided interference with their children's opportunity to receive a desegregated public education, but they did not allege that their children had applied or would ever apply for admission to any private school.

Holding: [5x3] Parents do not have standing as plaintiffs where they do not allege personal injury that is fairly traceable to the defendant's allegedly unlawful conduct (and that is likely to be redressed by the requested relief).

Basis: Citing its precedents based on constitutional and pruden-
tial components, the Court identified three grounds for lack
of standing to sue: injury that is abstract or otherwise inappropriate to be judicially cognizable; attenuated causation
between the illegal conduct and injury; and speculative
prospect of obtaining relief. The Court found that the parents' alleged injuries were defective on one or more of these
grounds. The first alleged injury, that they had been directly
harmed as a result of government financial aid to racially
discriminatory private schools, was regarded as not judicially cognizable in the absence of concrete, personal impact.
The second alleged injury, that federal tax exemptions to
discriminatory private schools in their communities impaired their ability to have their schools desegregated, was
not sufficiently causally linked to the allegedly illegal governmental conduct.

Honig v. Students of the California School for the Blind, 471 U.S. 148 (1985)

Facts: Students of the state school for the blind sued the state
education department, claiming that the school's physical
plant did not meet applicable seismic safety standards. The
complaint alleged violations of both Sec. 504 of the Rehabilitation Act of 1973 and the Education of All Handicapped
Children Act (now IDEA). The court issued a preliminary
injunction requiring the state to conduct tests on the school
grounds relating to safety. Before the case reached the
Supreme Court, the tests ordered by the trial court had been
completed

Holding: [6x3] Where the defendant school officials have complied with the terms of an injunction that is under appeal, the
case becomes moot.*

---

*For mootness rulings in other chapters, see *Reno* v. *Bossier Parish School Board* ("Bossier II") and *Santa Fe Independent School District (supra).*

Basis: Citing *University of Texas (supra)*, the Court ruled that no order it could issue would affect the parties' rights with respect to the injunction because the terms of the injunction were fully and irrevocably carried out.

Bender v. Williamsport Area School District, 474 U.S. 534 (1986)

Facts: A group of high school students formed a nondenominational prayer-group club. The group asked the principal for permission to hold club meetings on the school premises during the student activity periods that were scheduled twice weekly during the regular school day. The matter was referred to the superintendent. On the basis of the school attorney's opinion, the superintendent denied the group's request. The students appealed to the school board, which upheld the superintendent's decision. The students then filed suit in federal district court. The district court ruled in favor of the students. The school district complied with the judgment, allowing the club to conduct meetings. Although the school board did not appeal the judgment, one of its members did.

Holding: [5x4] An individual school board member has no standing to appeal a judgment against the entire board where he participated in the suit only in his official capacity as a member of the board.

Basis: Citing its precedents that have established strict adherence to the standing requirements in constitutional cases, the Court distinguished between the official capacity and the individual capacity of school board members. A board member in his individual capacity has no standing to appeal judgment against him in his official capacity. Nor does he have standing to appeal a judgment against the board that the board has declined to appeal. Finally, he may not bring an appeal as a parent where there is nothing in the record indicating his status as a parent, that he was sued in that role, or that his children have suffered any injury as a result of the trial court's judgment.

Ohio Civil Rights Commission v. Dayton Christian Schools, Inc., 477 U.S. 619 (1986)

Facts: A pregnant teacher was fired by a religious school when she violated the "biblical chain of command" by seeking legal advice when she was denied employment. She filed a complaint with the state civil rights commission, alleging that the nonrenewal decision constituted sex discrimination in violation of state statute. When the commission initiated proceedings against the religious school, the school filed a Sec. 1983 against the commission. The school alleged that the commission's exercise of jurisdiction over the school would violate the free exercise and establishment clauses of the First Amendment.

Holding: [5/4x0] A federal court generally should abstain from enjoining state administrative proceedings where an important state interest is involved and where there will be a full and fair opportunity to litigate the constitutional claims.

Basis: The Court first pointed to its holding in *Younger* v. *Harris*, 401 U.S. 37 (1971), that a federal court should not enjoin a pending state criminal proceeding except in the very unusual situation that an injunction is necessary to prevent great and immediate irreparable injury. The Court then identified precedents where it extended the *Younger* principle to civil proceedings in which important state interests are involved and to administrative proceedings in which important state interests are vindicated so long as the federal plaintiff would have a full and fair opportunity to litigate his constitutional claim. Finding that elimination of prohibited sex discrimination is an important state interest and that the religious school will have an adequate opportunity to raise the constitutional claims, the Court applied the *Younger* abstention doctrine to this case.

Papasan v. Allain, 477 U.S. 619 (1986)

Facts: Federal school land grants to Mississippi in the early 19th century did not apply to lands that were formerly held by the Chickasaw Indian Nation. When the Chickasaws later ceded this area to the United States, Congress gave the land to Mississippi. The state sold these lands and invested the proceeds in loans to railroads that were destroyed during the Civil War. Under current practice, these federal school grant lands constitute property held in trust for the benefit of the public schools. A Mississippi statute provided that all funds derived from these lands shall be credited to the school districts of the township where the land grants are located. With respect to the Chickasaw Cession counties, to which no lands now belong, the state paid interest on the lost principal. This treatment resulted in a disparity in the level of school funds available to the Chickasaw Cession schools as compared to the schools in the rest of the state. Chickasaw Cession school officials filed suit against the state, alleging that the state had abrogated its trust obligation to the school children in perpetuity and that the disparity deprived them of a minimally adequate education and of the equal protection of the laws.

Holding: [2/3½x3½] A claim made against the state government based on breach of trust is barred by the Eleventh Amendment, whereas a claim based on the equal protection clause is not.

Basis: In a widely divided opinion, the Court saw no substantive difference between a not yet extinguished liability for a past breach of trust and the continuing obligation to meet trust responsibilities. Citing precedent, the Court found that in either event the claim on the government trustee is barred by the Eleventh Amendment. Although similarly subject to a clear lack of a majority, the Court ruled that the alleged constitutional violation, the statute's unequal distribution of the benefits of school lands, is the type of continuing violation for which its precedents allow a judicial remedy.

California Federal Savings and Loan Association v. Guerra, 479 U.S. 272 (1987)*

Facts: A state statute required employers to provide unpaid leave and reinstatement to employees disabled by pregnancy. A bank employee took a pregnancy disability leave. When she notified the bank that she was able to return to work, the bank informed her that her job had been filled and there were no other vacancies. The employee filed a complaint with the state administrative agency that was charged with enforcing the statute. Before a hearing was held on this complaint, the bank brought an action in federal court, alleging that said statutory provision is inconsistent with, and preempted by, Title VII.

Holding: [4/2x3] Title VII, as amended by the Pregnancy Discrimination Act, does not preempt a state statute that requires employers to provide leave and reinstatement to employees disabled by pregnancy.

Basis: In any preemption inquiry, congressional intent is the critical issue. The purpose of Title VII, as amended to include pregnancy discrimination, is to achieve equality of employment opportunities and remove barriers that traditionally have operated in the past to favor an identifiable group of employees. California's pregnancy disability leave statute and Title VII share a common goal. Title VII only established a floor of benefits; state legislation is free to embellish or enrich the benefits required under Title VII. The California statute furthers the goal of equal employment opportunity for women.

Karcher v. May, 484 U.S. 72 (1987)

Facts: New Jersey's legislature enacted a permissive moment-of-silence statute for public elementary and secondary schools.

---

*For a case vacated in light of this decision, see *Miller-Wohl Co., Inc.* v. *Montana Commissioner of Labor and Industry*, 692 P.2d 1243 (Mont. 1985), *vacated*, 479 U.S. 1022 (1987).

A teacher, several students, and parents challenged the constitutionality of the statute. When the named defendants — the state education department, the two local boards of education, and the state's attorney general — declined to defend the statute, the speaker of the general assembly and the president of the state senate sought and obtained permission to intervene as defendants on behalf of the legislature. The district court and circuit court of appeals held that the statute violated the establishment clause of the First Amendment. The two legislative heads then lost their leadership posts. They subsequently sought review by the U.S. Supreme Court solely in their official capacities, although their replacements withdrew the legislative appeal.

Holding: [8/1x0] Public officials who have participated as parties in a lawsuit solely in their official capacities do not have standing to appeal an adverse judgment after they have left their particular offices.*

Basis: The Court cited the Federal Rules of Appellate Procedure, which provides that when a public officer is a party to a judicial proceeding in an official capacity and ceases to hold office while the case is pending, the officer's successor automatically is substituted as a party. In response to the argument that they could continue the appeal in their personal or professional capacities, the Court cited *Bender (supra)* to support its conclusion that these defendants may not appeal as individual legislators or as representatives of the expired legislature where the record shows that they did not participate in those capacities in the prior proceedings of the case.

---

*For a similar but more recent ruling showing the overlap of standing and mootness, see *Arizonans for English Language* v. *Arizona*, 520 U.S. 43 (1993) (held that the First Amendment free speech challenge to a state constitutional provision requiring the state to "act in the English language and no other language" was moot when the suing party resigned from his employment with the state).

Texas v. United States, 523 U.S. 296 (1998)

Facts: In 1995, Texas enacted Chapter 39, a comprehensive scheme that holds school boards accountable to the state for student achievement in the public schools. When a school district falls short of Chapter 39's accreditation criteria, the state commissioner of education may select from 10 possible sanctions, including appointment of a master to oversee the district's operations. A covered jurisdiction under Sec. 5 of the Voting Rights Act, Texas submitted Chapter 39 to the U.S. Attorney General for determination of whether any of the sanctions affected voting and thus required preclearance. When the assistant attorney general for civil rights cautioned that under certain circumstances two of the sanctions might result in a Sec. 5 violation, Texas filed suit for a declaratory judgment.

Holding: [9x0] A claim resting upon contingent future events that may not occur as anticipated or at all is not ripe for adjudication.

Basis: Under the Constitution's "case of controversy" requirement and the Court's related precedents, this case is too speculative; its boundaries are not yet crystallized, and the hardship of withholding court consideration until the state chooses to implement one of the two questioned sanctions is insubstantial.

Glossary

Abstention: As used in this book, the doctrine of abstention permits a federal court, in the exercise of its discretion, to relinquish jurisdiction where necessary to avoid needless conflict with the administration by a state of its own affairs.

Ad valorem: "According to the value"; a tax or duty assessed in proportion to the value of the property.

Agency shop: A union security provision whereby, in order to continue employment, any nonunion employee is required to pay a "fair share" fee for the union's collective bargaining and contract compliance expenses.

Appellant: The party, whether plaintiff or defendant at the lower court level, who on losing at the lower level brings the appeal.

Appellee: The party, whether plaintiff or defendant at the lower court level, who is put in the position of defending the decision on its appeal. It should be noted that the same party may become "appellant" and "appellee" at successive stages of the litigation.

Certiorari: "To be made certain of"; a formal request (called a writ) to a higher court to review a lower court's decision. This writ can be refused by the higher court. To be accepted by the Supreme Court, this writ requires an affirmative vote by four Justices.

Class action: A suit brought by one or more persons on behalf of themselves and all other persons similarly situated.

Compensatory damages: A sum of money in a civil case to compensate the suing party for actual injuries and losses.

Comity: Courtesy; respect; a willingness to grant a privilege, not as a matter of right but out of deference and goodwill. In general, the principle of "comity" is that courts of one state or jurisdiction will give effect to laws and judicial decisions of another state or jurisdiction, not as a matter of obligation but out of deference and mutual respect.

Concurrence: An opinion separate from that of the majority filed by one or more Justices who agree with the general result of the majority decision, but who choose to emphasize or differ with the reasoning or grounds for the decision.

Consent decree: A court-approved settlement.

De facto: "In fact"; actually occurring.

De jure: "By law"; occurring as a result of official action.

De minimis: So small as to be legally insignificant.

Dicta: Statements in the court's opinion that are not essential to its decision and, thus, are not part of its holding.

Discovery: Pre-trial procedures, such as depositions and interrogations, that allow each party to ascertain, within limits, the evidence of the opposing side.

Dissent: An opinion that disagrees with the result of the majority and is handed down by one or more members of the Court.

Dismissal: Decision without opinion by the U.S. Supreme Court in the mandatory area of its appellate jurisdiction. This decision summarily disposes of the case because of the procedural status of the parties or issues, for example, mootness, lack of standing, or lack of substantial federal question. Like a summary affirmance, this type of decision is a decision on the merits of the case.*

Hicks v. *Miranda*, 422 U.S. 332 (1975); *Graves* v. *Barnes*, 405 U.S. 1201, 1203 (1972); *Ohio* v. *Price*, 360 U.S. 246 (1959).

Dual: Segregated by law.

Due process: Fundamental fairness in the administration of justice through the rules and forms that have been established for the protection of private rights.

Enjoin: To require a person, by an injunction, to perform or to abstain from performing some act.

Equal protection clause: The provision in the 14th Amendment to the U.S. Constitution that prohibits a state from denying to any person within its jurisdiction the "equal protection of the laws." The courts have interpreted the equal protection clause to prohibit discrimination by governmental units where they do not show certain levels of justification.

Ex post facto: "After the fact"; a law passed after the occurrence of an act that retrospectively changes the legal consequences of the act.

Ex rel.: "Upon information of"; a legal proceeding that is instituted by the Attorney General or other appropriate official in the name of and on behalf of the state, but on the information and the instigation of an individual who has a private interest in the matter.

In loco parentis: "In place of parents"; charged with a parent's rights, duties, and responsibility. In the case of a teacher, this is a condition applying only when the child is under the reasonable control and supervision of the school.

In re: "In the matter of"; designating a judicial proceeding (for example, juvenile cases) in which the customary adversarial posture of the parties is de-emphasized or nonexistent.

Incorporation: Evolving doctrine by which the U.S. Supreme Court has applied a substantial part of the Bill of Rights (for example, the First Amendment) to the states, and thereby to public school officials, by means of the Fourteenth Amendment.

Infra: "Below"; cross-reference to a fuller citation appearing subsequently in the document.

Injunction: A court order to engage in or cease engaging in a specified action.

Injunctive relief: The equitable remedy by a court, typically where damages are inadequate, to enforce a right or redress an injury through prohibiting or requiring performance of a particular act.

Moot: An issue that is not considered by the Court because it no longer contains a live dispute of the sort proper for a judicial decision. A moot case seeks to determine an abstract question that does not arise from facts or rights existing at the time.

Parens patriae: "Parent of the country"; refers to the states having sovereign power of guardianship over persons under a disability, such as minors and insane persons.

Per Curiam: "By the Court"; an opinion in which several or all the members of the Court concurred but that does not disclose the name of any particular Justice as being its author.

Plurality: The prevailing opinion of an appellate court that is subscribed to by less than a majority of the participating judges. Concurring opinions by other judges cause this plurality to prevail.*

Police power of state: The power vested in the legislature to make and establish laws, statutes, and ordinances for the good of the state and its people. This power extends to all areas of health, morals, safety, order, and comfort of the people.

Preemption: The doctrine, adopted by the U.S. Supreme Court, that certain matters are of such a national, as opposed to local, character that applicable federal laws take precedence over state laws. As to these matters, a state may not pass a law inconsistent with federal law.

---

*There is some question about the precedential value of the Supreme Court's plurality decisions. See *Board of Education* v. *Pico*, 457 U.S. 886 n.2 (1982) (Burger, J., dissenting).

Prima facie: "On first appearance" or "on its face"; evidence that is presumed to be sufficient unless rebutted by proof to the contrary.

Punitive damages: Also called "exemplary damages," a sum of money in a civil case beyond compensatory damages to punish the offending party for malicious misconduct.

Remand: "To send back"; action by an appellate court to send the case back to a lower court for further proceedings.

Respondeat Superior: Attaching liability for the acts of an employee, within the scope of employment, to the employer.

Sec. 1983: A federal civil rights statute that allows a person to sue for damages or other relief if a government official (that is, acting "under color of law") violates the person's rights under the U.S. Constitution or federal statutes.

Sovereign immunity: The legal doctrine that prevents a litigant from asserting an otherwise meritorious claim against a sovereign or against a party with sovereign attributes unless that entity consents to the suit. Historically, the federal and state governments, and derivatively cities and towns, were immune from tort liability arising from activities that were governmental in nature. However, most jurisdictions have entirely or partially abandoned this doctrine by legislative or judicial acts.

Standing: Status as a proper party before the Court as determined by the Court; requires an actual injury or immediate interest in the action at hand.

State action: Action by the government, including action by a public school system or its agents.

Statute: A law enacted by the legislative branch of the federal or state government.

Sub nom: "Under the name of"; designation for the change in the name of either or both parties in the course of the litigation, for example, on the death of one of the parties during the appellate process.

Summary affirmance: Decision without an opinion by the U.S. Supreme Court in the mandatory area of its appellate jurisdiction. A summary affirmance gives binding effect to the lower court's decision* but does not have as much precedential value as a full opinion by the Court on the merits.** Thus the Court is less constrained to overrule summary affirmances than full opinions, while it expects lower courts to follow both equally. The jurisdictional statement filed in the parties' briefs to the Court, rather than the lower court opinion, must be the focus of any inquiry regarding the scope and meaning of the summary affirmance.***

Summary judgment: A court decision, prior to a full trial in a civil action, where a party moves and the court agrees that there is no genuine issue of material fact and that the moving party is entitled to prevail as a matter of law.

Supra: "Above"; cross-reference to a fuller citation appearing earlier in the document.

Tolling: A procedure for starting and counting time. For example, there are legal rules about when a statute of limitations begins to take effect and what legal circumstances could interrupt the counting time.

Under color of law: The reference in Sec. 1983 that has been judicially interpreted to include not only acts by government officials within the bounds or limits of their lawful authority, but also certain acts without and beyond the bounds of their lawful authority.

Hicks v. Miranda, 422 U.S. 322, 345 (1975) (summary dismissal). The *Hicks* rule was applied to summary affirmances in *Whitlow v. Hodges*, 539 F.2d 582, 584 (6th Cir. 1976); *Virgin Islands v. 19,623 Acres of Land*, 536 F.2d 566, 571 (3d Cir. 1976); *Brady v. State Bar of California*, 533 F.2d 502, 503 n.1 (9th Cir. 1976); *Bemid v. Stanton*, 528 F.2d 688, 691 (7th Cir. 1976); *Thonen v. Jenkins*, 517 F.2d 3, 7 (4th Cir. 1975); *Doe v. Hodgson*, 500 F.2d 1206, 1207-08 (2d Cir. 1974).

**Hicks v. Miranda*, 422 U.S. 332, 345 n.14 (1975); *McCarthy v. Philadelphia Civil Service Commission (supra)*.

***Edelman v. Jordan*, 415 U.S. 651, 671 (1976).

Unitary: An effectively desegregated school system.

U.S. Reports: Official reports of the U.S. Supreme Court decisions, as contrasted to parallel citations of unofficial reports of the decisions that are available through Shephard's and other such reference volumes.

Vacate: To annul; to set aside; to cancel or rescind. To render an act void, as to vacate an entry of record or a judgment.

Void for vagueness: Constitutional infirmity when a law is so unclear that it does not provide the specificity required by due process, thus making it void.

Appendix

Because they frequently are referred to in the cases, selected federal constitutional provisions are cited below.

Article I, Section 8 (Commerce Clause): "The Congress shall have Power . . . To regulate Commerce with foreign Nations, and among the several States, and with the Indian Tribes;"

Article I, Section 10 (Impairment of Contracts Clause): "No State shall . . . pass any Bill of Attainder, ex post facto Law, or Law impairing the Obligation of Contracts . . ."

Article III, Section 2: "The judicial Power shall extend to all Cases, in Law and Equity, arising under this Constitution, the Laws of the United States, and Treaties [etc.] . . . to Controversies between . . . Citizens of different States; [etc.] . . ."

Amendment I (Establishment and Free Exercise Clauses): "Congress shall make no law respecting an establishment of religion, or prohibiting the free exercise thereof."

Amendment I (Freedom of Expression Clause): "Congress shall make no law . . . abridging the freedom of speech."

Amendment I (Freedom of Assembly Clause): "Congress shall make no law . . . [abridging] the right of the people peaceably to assemble."

Amendment V (Due Process Clause, Congress): "No person shall be . . . deprived of life, liberty, or property without due process of law."

Amendment V (Self-Incrimination Clause): "[No person] shall be compelled in any criminal case to be witness against himself."

Amendment VIII: "[N]or cruel and unusual punishment inflicted."

Amendment X: "The powers not delegated to the United States by the Constitution, nor prohibited by it to the States, are reserved to the States."

Amendment XI: "The Judicial power of the United States shall not . . . extend to any suit in law or equity . . . against one of the United States by Citizens of another State."

Amendment XIII: "Neither slavery nor involuntary servitude, except as a punishment for crime . . . shall exist within the United States."

Amendment XIV (Due Process Clauses, states): "[N]or shall any State deprive any person of life, liberty, or property, without due process of law."

Amendment XIV (Equal Protection Clause): "[Nor shall any State] deny to any person within its jurisdiction the equal protection of the laws.

Amendment XIV (Sec. 5): Congress shall have power to enforce, by appropriate legislation, the provisions of this article.

Table of Cases

The references below are to the page numbers on which the case appears. The page numbers for the principal cases described in this book are in **bold** type. Page numbers for other cases cited are in roman type.

Index

Good News Club, 61-63
Governmental function principle, 107, 115, 118-120

H.E.W.: 275; guidelines, 156; regulations, 156, 176, 179-180, 233
Hawaii, 134
Hearings: academic dismissal, 75-76; corporal punishment, 74; due
    process, 212; employee dismissal, 89-90, 91-92, 93, 98-99, 101-
    107, 110-111, 119-120, 123-124, 239-241; suspension, 72-73,
    131, 149-150, 222-223
Higher education: academic dismissal, 75-76; admissions, 173-174,
    175-176, 206-207, 221-222, 271; discrimination, 173-176, 186-
    188, 206-207, 223-224, 229-230, 246, 260-261, 274; employee
    dismissal, 90-92, 97, 98, 102-104, 229-230, 246-247; junior col-
    lege districts, 10-11, loyalty oaths, 90-91, 95-96, 97; proscribed
    organizations, 90-91, 95-96, 97; religious, 275-276; single-sex
    schools, 148, 206-207; unions, 124-125
Hispano-Americans, 153-154
Homosexuality, 191
Housing, 165-166

IDEA: See Education for All Handicapped Children Act.
Idaho, 74
Illinois, 8, 29, 98
Immunity from suit, 200, 219-223, 225, 226, 231-232, 234-235, 241,
    251, 255, 291, 296
Indiana, 1-2, 5, 88
Interstate commerce, 21, 44-45, 99-100
Interstate travel, 78-79, 104-105
Iowa, 2-3, 85-86

Japanese, 134-135
Jehovah's Witnesses, 67
Jurisdiction of federal courts, 142-143, 246-247, 267-268, 273, 276-
    277. See also Article III.
Jury selection, 9-10
Juvenile courts, 72n

Kansas, 136
Kentucky, 18-19

Land grants: See Public lands.